The Jews on Tin Pan Alley

The Jewish Contribution to American Popular Music, 1830-1940

April 6, 1986

For Keith —
   On your Birthday.
This book is presented
   with great respect
   with great pride
   with great affection
   with great expectations
      and most of all —
with great love.

   Thank you for all you mean to
      others and especially to me.

                    Ken Kanter

The Jews on Tin Pan Alley

The Jewish Contribution to American Popular Music, 1830-1940

Kenneth Aaron Kanter

Ktav Publishing House, Inc. • New York
American Jewish Archives • Cincinnati
1982

Library of Congress Cataloging in Publication Data

Kanter, Kenneth Aaron.
  The Jews on Tin Pan Alley.

  Bibliography: p.
  Includes index.
  1. Music, Popular (Songs, etc.)—United States—
History and criticism. 2. Musical revue, comedy,
etc.—United States—History and criticism.
3. Musicians, Jewish—United States. I. Title.
ML3477.K36   784.5'008992407471   81-18662
ISBN 0-87068-887-1   AACR2

MANUFACTURED IN THE UNITED STATES OF AMERICA

To my parents, family, and friends, who have always brought music to my life;

To Dr. Jacob Rader Marcus, who walked with me every step of the journey that led toward the completion of this book, and who has allowed me the privilege of accompanying him on many walks of his own, this work is proudly dedicated.

Contents

Illustrations

Preface

Both as a business and as an expression of talent and creative artistry, American popular music was in large part shaped and formed by Jews, many of them immigrant newcomers to the American scene. Thanks to the efforts of countless Jewish songwriters and publishers, and of equally countless Jewish performers on Broadway, in vaudeville and burlesque, and in other media, American popular music became what it is today. Without their contributions, it would have been something much different, and to my mind at least, something much less vital and lively—and much less attuned to the psyche and spirit of the American people.

This book tells the story of the Jewish role in the development of American popular music from the 1830's through the year 1940. As it makes abundantly clear, during this period Jews predominated in every area of the music business. Virtually all the great names that come to mind when one considers popular music—Rodgers and Hammerstein, Irving Berlin, Lorenz Hart, Jerome Kern, George and Ira Gershwin, Irving Caesar, and Charles K. Harris, for instance—are Jewish names. Jews wrote the songs, Jews sang the songs, and Jews made sure that the songs were circulated to every corner of the country, for they founded and built America's music publishing industry.

Among the vanguard publishers were M. Witmark, Charles K. Harris, Joseph Stern, Shapiro and Bernstein, Harry Von Tilzer, Leo Feist, T. B. Harms, and Irving Berlin. Collectively their publishing firms came to be known as "Tin Pan Alley." The very name was coined by a Jewish lyricist, Monroe Rosenfeld, and it was the Tin Pan Alley ethos, combining the commercial with the artistic, that gave our popular music its distinctive character.

Before Charles K. Harris, there had never been a "million seller," a song that sold a million copies of sheet music. His "After the Ball" sold 5 million. The most prolific composer on Tin Pan Alley was a Detroit Jew named Harry Gumm, who later became Harry Von Tilzer. He claimed to have written 8,000 songs. Jerome Kern changed the face of the American musical theatre with his emphasis on unity of script and song, paving the way for those who followed, Irving Berlin and the Gershwins. Berlin represents the essence of the Jewish contribution to the song industry. An immigrant, he revolutionized popular music and in the process became as American as the songs he wrote. Berlin's songs called men to serve their country in two World Wars and for many millions of Americans authoritatively signify two "national" holidays, Christmas and Easter. Moreover, he wrote the song that is often considered our second national anthem, "God Bless America." George and Ira Gershwin changed the face of popular music by showing that theatre and popular songs could stand side by side with the more serious music of the concert hall. Lorenz Hart made the popular love song into something more mature and sophisticated than the romantic fluff that prevailed until his time. Rodgers and Hammerstein wrote some of the finest, most beloved songs in the popular repertory and raised the Broadway musical to heights rarely achieved before, or since.

How actively Jewish were the Jews of Tin Pan Alley? It is a difficult question to answer. Some, such as Charles K. Harris, Irving Berlin, and the Gershwins, wrote songs containing Jewish content. Others included in their music or lyrics traditional Jewish themes, such as home, family, immigration, humanism, and "the old country." Oscar Hammerstein II led the fight against anti-Semitism and Nazism in the Hollywood film community; yet he was raised outside his grandparents' Jewish religion. The men and women of Tin Pan Alley were highly assimilated Jews, or tried to be. They belonged to, or were not far from, a generation of immigrants who wanted nothing better than to be "Americanized." Although few, if any, rejected their Jewish heritage, few vociferously espoused it. They were primarily "life-cycle" Jews—Bar Mitzvahs, confirmations, weddings, and funerals provided as much Jewish identity as they desired.

The first part of this book is a history of American popular music as developed by the hundreds of Jews who contributed to it. The events of each period are clearly illustrated by the songs of the day, and in addition there are brief biographies of more than fifty men and women who helped to shape American popular music. The second part of the book is devoted to longer biographies of the twelve men who created popular music as we know it. Each of them represented a specific facet of the industry. Without them, there would not have been a Tin Pan Alley.

There are a number of people without whom there could not have been *The Jews on Tin Pan Alley,* and it is my pleasure to thank them here. First, as was written in the dedication, I must thank Dr. Jacob R. Marcus. Without his encouragement and support, this effort would never have been begun. I am ever grateful for his faith in me. Dr. Marcus's colleague at the American Jewish Archives, Abraham J. Peck, has been my agent, executive editor, counselor, and friend. His efforts allowed this book to be completed. The staff of the American Jewish Archives were always helpful, whether it was searching for an obscure reference or providing the many photographs from the Archives' vast collection used herein.

Mr. Bernard Scharfstein and KTAV Publishing House, Inc., have been marvelous, especially in the choice of editors. Mr. Robert J. Milch has made the first efforts of a neophyte author read very smoothly. I am very appreciative.

There have been many individuals who have shared their expertise with me through the process of preparing this book. First, I am deeply grateful to Richard C. Norton, whose collection of sheet music provided many of the illustrations in the book and whose vast, encyclopedic knowledge of the American theatre has been a constant source of amazement and assistance.

To Jeffrey A. Zeitlin, Eve D. Wahl, Annette R. Levy, and Martin E. Getzendanner, thank you for contributing your special talents. To Rabbi Randall M. Falk, Richard M. Morin, and Congregation Ohabai Sholom in Nashville, my gratitude for the opportunity to "moonlight" and take the time to complete this volume. There are many others who have read the manuscript and provided excellent insights and suggestions. At the risk of omitting one, I thank you all.

The responsibility for the contents of *The Jews on Tin Pan Alley* is mine. I hope the enjoyment is yours!

Part I

Sheet Music of Henry Russell

1

FROM THE BEGINNINGS
TO THE CIVIL WAR

The songs people sing tell their story, perhaps even something of their history. The American popular song is no exception. From colonial times on, the events that shaped the lives of Americans have been immortalized in song.

In the early days of American history, long before the invention of radio, television, the phonograph, and other media of "canned" mass entertainment, singing was one of the most widespread forms of recreation. Songs were sung by rich and poor alike, wherever people gathered, whether the occasion was formal or informal.

The Jewish contribution to American popular music began in the 1830's and 1840's, a time when the Jewish presence in America was quite small, amounting to no more than 15,000 in a population of some 17,000,000.[1] In the earliest days, the Jews were imitators, not explorers, following the prevalent musical styles rather than forging ahead to the originality they were to show in later years.

From its very beginnings, American popular music was dominated by the sentimental ballad. The early masters of sentimental balladry included two Jews, John Howard Payne and Henry Russell. So far as can be determined, however, America's first Jewish songwriter was Jonas B. Phillips, born in Philadelphia in 1805. Despite the early date, Jonas Phillips was by no means of immigrant stock. An eighth-generation American, he was the son of Benjamin J. Phillips and Abigail Seixas, both of whom were members of distinguished families with roots of long

standing in this country. A playwright and lawyer by occupa-
tion, Phillips had written several plays by the mid-1830's. During this period and into the 1840's he also wrote several popular
songs,[2] among them "Light May the Boat Row" (1836), "The
Hunter's Horn," "My Old Wife" (1840), and "The New Year's
Come," published in the *New York Mirror* in 1841.[3] He died in
1869.[4]

Far more famous than Jonas Phillips was John Howard Payne,
born in New York City, on June 9, 1791, to a Jewish woman
named Sarah Isaacs. As a young man Payne went to London,
where he wrote plays and appeared as an actor. His greatest
success, written in collaboration with Sir Henry Bishop, the
British conductor-composer, was the opera *Clari*, which opened
in London on May 8, 1823. The opera's principal song was
"Home, Sweet Home," performed as the closing to the first act.

The English public loved Payne's nostalgic musical remembrance of hearth and home, and as the *London Quarterly Musician*
stated, no ballad ever became "so immediately and deservedly
popular." Payne's song was heard in America for the first time
on November 12, 1823, at the Park Theater in New York, with
the same critical and popular response. The *New York Mirror* of
November 22 called it "the most beautiful and tender [song] we
have ever heard. . . . There was something inexpressibly tender." The song's success was phenomenal. It is claimed that
100,000 copies were sold in the first year of publication; the
critics panned it, but millions of people loved it.[5]

"Home, Sweet Home," written when Payne was in England,
expressed the sense of depression often experienced by those
separated from home and family. As nineteenth-century music
critics well understood, the wide appeal of "Home, Sweet
Home" derived from the universality of its emotional sentiments. Payne himself later told "of a time when he stood on a
Christmas Eve in a London street, penniless, hungry and cold,
and heard with incredible feelings of loneliness 'Home, Sweet
Home' played in a rich man's parlor."[6] As Charles Hamm has
commented,

Certain of these songs of sentiment outlive those of more artistic
composition simply because they touch the hearts of the people. Each

and every word is understood because it has been written for them, and the music usually is simple enough to be readily grasped. America has produced much music of this kind, songs that will never die because they essentially vibrate in the home life of the nation. Such a song is "Home, Sweet Home."[7]

Sadly for Payne, he did not benefit financially from the enormous appeal of this song. He wrote in his diary, "How often have I been in the heart of Paris, Berlin, London or some other city and have heard persons singing or hand organs playing 'Home, Sweet Home' without having a shilling to buy myself the next meal or a place to lay my head."[8] Money never did come his way, for the protection of lyricist and composer by copyright laws was long in the future, but honor did. In 1850, two years before he died, he was invited to the White House by President Zachary Taylor to hear Jenny Lind sing his song.

Payne died in 1852 while serving as United States consul in Tunis, North Africa. When his body was brought back to America to be interred in Oak Hill cemetery, the funeral cortege included the President, his cabinet, and many high-ranking military and public officials. Newspapers throughout the country repeated the theme that Payne had finally come home. Twenty-one years later another tribute was paid to Payne and his ballad when, with money raised by a series of benefit performances of the opera *Clari*, a statue of him was erected in Prospect Park, Brooklyn, complete with a thousand voices singing "Home, Sweet Home."

Henry Russell, the most significant mid-nineteenth-century composer of sentimental ballads, was far more important than Payne in the history of American popular music and lived a happier life. Russell was born in Sheerness, England, on December 24, 1812, and came to America when he was twenty-one. He wrote his first ballad while working as organist of the First Presbyterian Church in Rochester, New York, and eventually went on to compose some 800 popular songs, including the famous "Woodman, Spare That Tree." Russell's songs, especially in his own renditions, clearly captured the popular fancy. More will be said about him in Chapter 6.

Because the songs of the 1840's were so often bought and sung by women, they were carefully expurgated. In fact, to quote the words of the editor of *The Parlor Companion*, "nothing in them could tinge the cheek of modesty with the slightest blush."[9] Stephen Foster's compositions exemplify the songs that were sung in parlors around America at this time. His "Beautiful Dreamer," "Jeannie with the Light Brown Hair," and "Come Where My Love Lies Dreaming," for example, were all tender, almost maudlin songs fit for the ears of proper ladies and for family singing.

Maudlin is a perfect description for the type of ballad that was popular in the 1840's and 1850's. Most commonly, songs of this genre described the untimely death of some sweet young girl. In 1848, for instance, Thomas Dunn English wrote "Oh Don't You Remember Sweet Alice" who, the song goes on to say, now "lies under a stone in an old churchyard in an obscure corner." "Lily Dale," written in 1852 by H. S. Thompson, tells of the sadness of loved ones over the death of "Sweet Lily, sweet Lily dear, over whose grave blossoms the wild rose in a flowery vale."[10]

Popular songs in the 1840's and 1850's had the power to elect as well as the power to entertain. Political campaigning as we understand it began in 1840, when William Henry Harrison ran against President Martin Van Buren, who was seeking a second term. Horace Greeley was largely responsible for the growth in the importance of campaign songs, for he included a new lyric in each issue of his paper, the *Log Cabin*. Harrison won the election of 1840 partially through the persuasive force of songs that praised his heroism and mocked his opponent, "that queer man Van Buren." When a jeweler from Zanesville, Ohio, Alexander Coffman Ross, wrote "For Tippecanoe and Tyler, Too!" the Whig party recognized a catchy phrase. It was so popular, according to the *North American Review*, that "it sang Harrison into the Presidency."[11]

Popular demand for a song could be created in various ways in the era before the advent of mass communications. Some lyrics were published in newspapers and magazines; songs could also be introduced at political rallies, as during the presidential campaign of 1840, or in minstrel shows.

The distinctively American type of musicale known as the

minstrel show began in the year 1843,[12] its creation partially necessitated by economic factors during and after the depression of 1842. Because of the depression, the performers of the day, who were already mainly engaged in blackface shows, found that it made good sense to band together in groups rather than continue as singles. The first of these groups, the Virginia Minstrels, had its premiere performance on February 17, 1843. (In the minstrel-show era, by the way, greasepaint had not yet been invented and performers had to use hamfat as the base for their makeup; hence the origin of "ham" in referring to actors.)

One of the men involved with the Virginia Minstrels was Daniel Emmett, famous today for having written "Dixie." Emmett began his show business career with a circus in Cincinnati, Ohio, for which he wrote "Bill Crowder," his first "nigger song." Emmett took the melody from an old song by "Daddy" Rice called "Gumbo Chaff." The lyric tells the story of poor old Bill Crowder, a black living in Cincinnati, who is cheated and gets into a fight with a Jewish old-clothes man. Like many minstrel songs, "Bill Crowder" was sung in blackface.[13]

The most famous of the minstrel shows was founded by Ed Christy in New York. Its first performance was on April 27, 1846. Christy formalized the tripartite minstrel-show schema. First came the humorous dialogue between the middle man, "Interlocutor," and the end men, "Bones" and "Tambo," followed by the "Olio," or what would today be called the variety show. Here the performers, made up in blackface and costumed in frock coats and white gloves, sat in a row and performed ensemble music. The second part of the show, the "Free Fantasy," showcased the special talents of the individual performers. Almost anything was acceptable in this section, ranging from song to gymnastics. The last segment of the show was the "Burlesque." Here the performers would parody what had gone on in the first two sections. The minstrels claimed that the Burlesques were original each night, since the performers, at least theoretically, did not know what would eventuate in the first sections, but in actuality the Burlesque was the most carefully orchestrated and choreographed portion of each performance.

Ed Christy's minstrels performed more than 2,500 shows in

the six years of their active creative life in the United States and then moved to England to introduce minstrelsy there. They were so successful, and minstrelsy was so prevalent by the early 1890's, that Gilbert and Sullivan regarded the Christy Minstrels as a fit subject for parody.[14] Other popular groups included the Kitchen Minstrels (1844), the Ethiopian Minstrels, the New York Minstrels, the New Orleans Serenaders, who parodied other minstrel groups (1843), the White Serenaders (1846), and the Bryant Minstrels (1857), for whom Stephen Foster wrote.

Minstrels did not concentrate solely on entertaining people; they were very active in political and social causes as well. In the late 1840's the Hutchinson family, the most prominent of the family minstrel groups, toured the United States with songs of reform as their major repertoire. They were against drinking and war, and strongly supported women's suffrage and the emancipation of the slaves. Some of the songs in the anti-alcohol campaign were "Temperance and Liberty," "Speed the Temperance Ship," "Young Man Shun That Cup," and "Father's a Drunkard—and Mother's Dead"; the most widely known temperance song was "King Alcohol—Pro Abstinence." The drinkers had their own songs, the most popular of which was "We're Pro Drink, There's Nothing Like Grog."[15] In the 1850's, the feminists, too, came up with a song to voice their point of view, entitled "Let Us Speak Our Mind If We Dare It."

However, in the late 1850's, the country was confronting an issue more urgent than such perennial concerns as alcohol and suffrage. The country was gearing up for war, and the issue that inflamed Americans most was slavery. Many singing societies were formed to further the emancipation of the slaves. Some of these singing societies had important supporters and contributors, among them the abolitionist leader William Lloyd Garrison, who wrote new anti-slavery lyrics for popular songs of the day. A number of these songs were collected in an anthology entitled *The Anti-Slavery Harp* (1851).

The most famous example of a song being borrowed by the abolitionists is provided by a popular hymn written by William Steffe, a Sunday school teacher in Charleston, South Carolina. Later on, with lyrics by Julia Ward Howe, the melody became

"The Battle Hymn of the Republic," but first, in the years just before the Civil War, it gained currency as "John Brown's Body Lies a Mouldering in the Grave." The anti-slavery movement assumed that the hero of the song was the famed abolitionist who had made the ill-fated raid on the arsenal at Harper's Ferry, Virginia, in 1859, but in reality the lyrics were composed by the soldiers of an infantry battalion stationed in the Boston area to mock one of their number, a Scotsman, who was known for his penury and his pro-Southern leanings.

Daniel Emmett's "Dixie" was also totally misinterpreted. By origin and purpose it was a "walk-around" (a minstrel show number, following the Olio, in which each member of the cast individually "strutted his stuff" before taking his seat for the Free Fantasy). Emmett wrote the song over a weekend in 1859 while working for the Dan Bryant Minstrel Show, and it was premiered by Bryant, the director and star, and one of the great performers of the late 1850's and the 1860's. "Dixie" soon became an enormous hit, and before long Southerners were treating it as if it had been composed intentionally as a patriotic hymn. When the touring company of the show *Pocahontas* first performed "Dixie" in New Orleans, for instance, the mayor and other municipal officials stood up, with the rest of the audience following suit. Southerners forgot, of course, that the song was a nostalgic look at a time that had really never existed, by a Northerner who had never been "in the land ob Cotton." Northerners similarly forgot the song's real intent. Emmett was assailed by anti-slavery newspapers, including William Lloyd Garrison's, as a traitor to the Union, and Dan Bryant's name was so tied to "Dixie" that he was persona non grata in most Northern cities during the early years of the Civil War.

Sheet Music of Marks and Stern

Courtesy of Harris Gilbert Family

2

CIVIL WAR TO GAY NINETIES

If the popular songs of the 1840's and 1850's expressed political emotions, they were tame in comparison to the more virulent songs which followed during the Civil War years. Music had become as important as the newspaper and the sermon in its power to move people politically and socially.

There were many great songs during the Civil War period. The popularity of "Dixie" in the South has already been mentioned. The second great song of the Confederacy, "Maryland, My Maryland," was written in 1861 by James Ryder Randall, a professor of English at Pydras College in Louisiana. Randall dedicated the lyrics to a Jewish friend, Henry J. Leovy, Esq. The music was borrowed from an 1824 Christmas carol, which had itself been borrowed from a twelfth-century Oxford University song.

The North also had its share of songs. Julia Ward Howe wrote "The Battle Hymn of the Republic" as a poem for the *Atlantic Monthly* in February 1862. Set to the melody of "John Brown's Body," it became the most frequently played song in the United States from the year of its introduction through the conclusion of the war, and its popularity has continued to this day.

The third composer of the Civil War period was George Frederick Root, a native of Sheffield, Massachusetts. He started out with popular songs, but on the outbreak of the conflict began to write stirring music to help the war effort. His initial effort, mildly successful, was entitled "The First Gun Is Fired." The second, however, to quote an anonymous Union soldier, "put as much spirit and cheer into the army as a splendid victory." The song was "The Battle Cry of Freedom."[1]

The music of the 1860's proved that the United States of America could produce good war songs even when temporarily divided, and that the martial spirit need not diminish the supply of honest sentiment and charming melody.

During the period from 1865, when the Civil War ended, to 1900, Jews came into their own as far as America and its music were concerned. These were the years of the great immigration. Whereas in 1880 there were approximately 250,000 Jews in America, by the turn of the century, there were 1,000,000, a large number of whom had been born here.[2]

In the late 1860's, music changed as the emotions of the people changed. The war was over, and with it went the overly sentimental, coy, and cloying songs of earlier days. There was less artificiality in the lyrics, and the propriety of the 1840's and 1850's gave way to fewer and fewer maidenly blushes as lyrics became more risqué.[3] Along with more colorful lyrics came a type of entertainment indigenous to America—the stage musical.

Musical shows began as "extravaganzas," the first important one being *The Black Crook* in 1866. It was entirely by accident that the new type of production occurred. Initially, a newly imported French ballet was scheduled. When the theatre where it was to be performed burned down, the producers approached the owner of a second theatre about the use of his facility. He had just purchased the rights to a melodrama entitled *The Black Crook*. An agreement was reached to combine the two shows in order to create an attraction that would, in the producer's words, "certainly arouse curiosity."[4] The show's major novelty was the fact that legs of the female performers were encased in pink tights, making it look as if they were wearing no tights at all. The Jewish composer Sigmund Romberg used the story of this first American musical as the plot for his *The Girl in Pink Tights*. *The Black Crook* turned out to be a gilt-edged investment, earning the producers about $2 million in profits and running for sixteen months.

Burlesque and vaudeville also made their initial appearances in the late 1870's and the 1880's. The series of "Mulligan" plays by Edward Harrigan and Tony Hart were among the most successful burlesques of the Reconstruction period. Although not Jews, Harrigan and Hart caricatured many ethnic groups, primarily the Irish and the Jews,[5] who were familiar to the lower strata of New York society. The music director and composer for Harrigan and Hart was David Braham, a Jew from London. Born in 1838, Braham arrived in America when he was eighteen after studying violin in England. He earned his living playing in the pit orchestras of various shows and in the 1870's became a composer, collaborating with various lyricists to produce such songs as "You're the Idol of My Heart," "Over the Hill to the Poorhouse," "The Eagle," a tribute to America's centennial, and "Money, the God of the Purse." In 1870, Braham moved to New York to assist Harrigan and Hart in their first "Mulligan" extravaganza. For the next several years, all of his songs had lyrics by Harrigan, who was not only his collaborator but his father-in-law, for Braham married Harrigan's sixteen-year-old daughter in 1876. When the team of Harrigan and Hart broke up in 1885, Braham continued to write songs with Harrigan. He died in New York on April 11, 1905.

The ethnic flavor of the Harrigan-Hart-Braham comedies was an important factor in their great popularity. This type of "localism," as it was called, became very prevalent in the 1880's and 1890's, mainly as a result of the influx of immigrants into New York and other East Coast cities. The easiest way to reach any audience was to present local customs on the stage in a humorous way; for example, Yiddishisms in a Jewish neighborhood,[6] such as the antics of a greenhorn Jew upon his arrival in America,[7] or the business dealings and misdealings of a "Dutchman," the disguised caricature of a Jew or any immigrant from Eastern Europe.[8]

Caricatures, complicated plots, memorable songs—all combined to assure the popularity of the "Mulligan" shows. There was one aspect, though, that had historical significance, for these shows were the first in American theatrical history to use as their settings places familiar to American audiences. Many great songs came from these shows as well as from their sister entertainment, vaudeville. Most of our best early songwriters, among them Irving Berlin, Irving Caesar, and Jerome Kern, had a background in vaudeville. Many fine performers also began their careers on the vaudeville circuit.

The dominant vaudeville house of the late nineteenth century was Tony Pastor's Opera House. He introduced Weber and Fields, Sam Bernard, Sophie Tucker, and his greatest star, Lillian Russell (Helen Louise Leonard). Miss Russell was married to a prominent English Jew named Edward Solomon, who came to America after beginning a successful songwriting career in England. Among his songs were "Billie Taylor," "All on Account of Eliza," and "Reward of Virtue," all written in 1881 upon his arrival in America.

One must ask how these songs became so popular. The answer is simple: the great publishing houses. In this area the Jews truly shone, and it was in the 1880's that the great publishing enterprises began, specifically the house of M. Witmark and Sons.

The story of the Witmark family dynasty reads much like the American dream. The firm was founded in 1886 by three brothers, Isidore, Julius (Julie), and Jay Witmark, aged seventeen, thirteen, and eleven, respectively. As they were too young legally to run a business, their father, Marcus, became the titular director of the company. Before the Civil War, Marcus had been a very prosperous businessman in Alabama and Georgia. Unfortunately for the family finances, he served as an officer in the Confederate army and lost everything as a result of the war.[9]

Isidore, Julius, and Jay came into the printing business in a small way when they received a printing press from their school as a prize. Their home at 402 West 40th Street became their factory,[10] and they began earning a modest income printing Christmas cards and advertising flyers.[11] While Isidore and Jay operated the press, Julius earned money as a boy-singer of ballads with Billy Birch's San Francisco Minstrels. He was headlined as the "wonderful boy soprano" and later as the "celebrated boy baritone."

Before very long the brothers decided to branch out and become music publishers. Their reason for taking this step was quite simple. The Willis Woodward publishing house had recently begun the practice of paying a percentage of the royalties to any singer who would work one of its songs into his act. Julius made a deal with Woodward, but after the song involved became a best-seller, the publisher reneged, attempting to buy him off with a twenty-dollar gold piece. The Witmark brothers were so angry that they opened their own publishing outfit to give Woodward some competition. Since Isidore, who knew how to play the piano and liked writing songs, had already had several efforts published, it was decided that he would quit his job in a water-filter business and write full-time to provide them with material.[12]

Needless to say, there were many difficulties. The Witmarks had no capital and no experience, but they did have certain important advantages. First there was Isidore, who could write new and creative songs; secondly there was Julius, who had the contacts and the voice to sing the songs; and lastly they had an office with a press on which they could print their songs.

The Witmark brothers began their publishing career with quite a coup. Rumor had it that President Grover Cleveland was about to marry Frances Folsom at the White House, so Isidore decided to write a wedding march for the President. The Witmarks printed several thousand copies. When the White House denied the rumors, they thought they were stuck with a worthless song. Three days later, however, the wedding was officially announced. The house of M. Witmark and Sons, of course, was the first with an appropriate song, making a great deal of money and establishing itself as a company with a good future.

As this incident demonstrates, the Witmarks introduced a new practice into the music business, that of writing songs about the front-page stories of the day and other specific events. They also took over the tradition of paying singers to present their songs. Since Julius was already a singer, he was able to find the talents to sing the songs. Isidore became the liaison between the talent and the business, thereby becoming what would later be known as a "song plugger." As the list of titles published by the Witmarks lengthened, they "placed songs with almost every topnotcher at Tony Pastor's."[14] They were so successful that they were forced to find larger quarters, and in 1888 they moved to 32 East 14th Street—the first of the many publishers to open shop in the Union Square area.

In addition to Isidore's songs the Witmarks were soon publishing songs by other writers. One of the earliest of these was "When the Sun Has Set" by Charles K. Harris, an unknown young Jewish composer from Milwaukee. Harris went on to write some of the smash hits of the later nineteenth century, but this was his first published song. Upon receiving a royalty check from the Witmarks for 85 cents, he was so enraged that he borrowed $1,000 from friends and opened his own publishing office at 207 Grand Avenue in Milwaukee. After only a year he had earned enough to repay the loan and move to more commodious quarters in Milwaukee's Alhambra Building. Later he opened a branch office in Chicago. In 1892, only four years after he began, Harris wrote his masterpiece, "After the Ball," the first song in America to sell more than 2 million copies. Within a short time, it reached sales of 25,000 copies per week, eventually totaling 5 million.

Several other Jews went into the music publishing business after the success of the Witmarks and Harris. Among them were Joseph Stern and Edward B. Marks, who formed a partnership and founded the Joseph W. Stern Company in 1886.[15] They had begun in entirely different professions, Stern as a necktie salesman and Marks as a traveling notions and button salesman,[16] but both wanted to be professional songwriters. Marks had always been in the habit of writing "occasional verses," and Stern, who had gained a good business grounding as well as musical skill, could turn out adequate songs on very short notice.[17]

Their first song, a poem by Marks with music by Stern, was "The Little Lost Child." This doleful little ditty was typical of the maudlin music mentioned earlier. It tells the story of a little girl who while lost meets a policeman. He returns her to her mother, who miraculously turns out to be the policeman's long-lost wife![18]

Marks, as the salesman for the company, tells of having to "lug around our music and songs in a briefcase. When meeting up with various singers or bands it was necessary to buy drinks for everyone to get them to play our songs."[19] The two men had named their firm Joseph W. Stern and Company because Marks did not originally intend to stay in the music business and expected to return to peddling notions. The sales of "The Little Lost Child" convinced him that music was a better, more lucrative profession.

The song's success was due in part to innovation. A Brooklyn electrician had invented a process that made it possible to flash a picture on the wall behind a singer to illustrate whatever lyric was being sung. Stern and Marks, recognizing a good thing when they saw it, provided the money necessary for the man to hire actors to produce slides illustrating "The Little Lost Child." The song, performed against the background provided by the slides, was introduced in 1894 to enormous popular acclaim. The innovation caught on, and before long many other songs were being "plugged" through the use of song slides. All told, "The Little Lost Child" was to sell over 2 million copies of sheet music.

Marks and Stern had an even bigger hit in 1896 with a song called "Mother Was a Lady; or, If Jack Were Only Here." It told the story of a waitress being taunted by a customer and responding, "you wouldn't talk that way to my mother for she was a lady. If only my brother Jack were here, he'd take care of you." This song was written in conjunction with William Fox, who went on later to found Fox Pictures Corporation.[20] "Mother Was a Lady" sold even more copies of sheet music than "The Little Lost Child."

Marks and Stern served as the inspiration for another great song publishing house, Shapiro and Bernstein. Maurice Shapiro and Lew Bernstein opened their doors in 1896 after also being in the retail sales business. Joining the others who had preceded them, they rented an office on Union Square. Harry Von Tilzer and his brother, Albert, Jews from Detroit, joined the business as songwriter/publishers.

Leo Feist also combined songwriting with publishing. He began in 1893 as a sales and field manager for the R and G Corset Company,[21] then decided that anyone who could sell corsets could also sell songs. Feist began his musical career by selling

"Those Lost Happy Days" to Stern and Marks. When it proved successful, he demanded a partnership. They refused, and to spite them he opened his own company with the famous slogan, "You can't go wrong with a Feist song."[22] Other songs he wrote and published were "Nobody Cares for Me," "Oh, Oh Miss Liberty," and "Smokey Mokes" (with the help of Harry Von Tilzer). Feist's importance to the music world was not as a composer or founder, but as a great organizer and publisher.

Why did so many song publishers aggregate in one place, Union Square? There were many reasons. Within two blocks were the Tony Pastor Vaudeville house, the Dewey Theatre, several burlesque houses, the Alhambra, where "extravaganzas" were staged, and five other legitimate theatres that gave live performances. Equally important was the area's collection of restaurants and eateries—it was here that the publishers could meet with potential buyers, wine and dine them, and sign them up.

The new publishers found that a method could be applied to the madness of songwriting. If songs were stereotyped, it would be possible to write, publish, and sell them all the more quickly—by mass production, as it were. That is exactly what happened. Various formulae were invented whereby composers, even those who could not read music, could write songs as the mood hit them. Immediately upon publication, the songs were presented to the public and "plugged."

Oftentimes, the songs were plugged by the same men who published them. "Julie" Witmark, Marks and Stern, and Leo Feist were all first-rate song pluggers. In addition, several top singers made their reputations in the plugging business. Two of the most important were Jews—Meyer Cohen, who gave up a career as a singer of ballads on the stage to become a plugger for Joseph W. Stern and Co., and Mose Gumble, who worked for Shapiro-Bernstein and later for Jerome W. Remick and Co.

The great singers of the day were the targets of the song pluggers' selling efforts, but of equal strategic value were managers, waiters, bandleaders—and almost anyone else who had an audience nearby. Soon it became fair game to accost the audience itself! A publisher who knew that one of his songs was to be sung in a show would place a plugger in the audience. After one or two verses, the plugger would stand up and, as if by magic, sing the new song, bringing the audience along. Gus Edwards, who became a producer and vaudeville star, made his start in this manner.

M. Witmark and Sons found another great hit which effectively made their fortune, "The Picture That's Turned Toward the Wall," by Charles Graham. In 1891, Graham had seen a play called *Blue Jeans* in which a farmer turns the picture of his daughter to the wall after she runs off with a lover of whom he does not approve. The scene provided a song lyric for Graham, and he sold it to the Witmarks for $15. They put the manuscript in a file and forgot about it. In time, however, when an Irish tenor needed a new song, they remembered "The Picture." He loved it and used it in his show; Julie Witmark, by then a topline entertainer, used it too. In his autobiography, Isidore Witmark remarked,

"The Picture That's Turned Toward the Wall" was more than a financial success for the Witmarks. It brought them a coveted prestige. Formerly they had sold sheet music by the hundred copies; now they knew sales in the thousands. . . . Jobbers who had scorned to deal with "children" were camping on their doorstep for copies. Dealers who had refused them displays now buried other songs beneath "The Picture." Singers whom they had been obliged to chase now chased them.[23]

Witmark hits were numerous in the 1890's: "Her Eyes Don't Shine Like Diamonds" (1894), "I Love You in the Same Old Way" (1896), "Honey, You're My Lady Love" (1897), "Just One Girl" (1898), "Just as the Sun Went Down" (1898), and "When You Ain't Got No Money—You Needn't Come Around" (1898). Their most successful song in this period, however, was "When You Were Sweet Sixteen," written in 1898 by James Thornton, an English-born composer.

The last song in the Witmark catalogue, and the one still popular today, was another sentimental ballad, "Sweet Adeline." Although published in 1903, it belongs to the type of music that was prevalent in the nineties. A very sentimental echo song (the title is echoed in every line of the lyric) it caught the fancy of singers, audiences, and barbershop quartets. It even played a role in politics, for John J. "Honey Fitz" Fitzgerald used it three times as his theme song when running for mayor of Boston. It was the last great song for the Witmarks.

Needless to say, the 1880's and 1890's produced a brand-new generation of songwriters, although the largest outpouring of music came from only a few men—Charles K. Harris, Monroe Rosenfeld, and Harry Dacre. These men, who combined writing with publishing, joined Marks and Stern, Shapiro and Bernstein, and Kerry Mills in a bustling new business.

More than just new writers, though, the public demanded new styles. Early in the 1890's love, and more specifically unrequited or disappointed love, was very popular with both songwriters and the public. The love songs expressed the morality of the day—a kiss and then immediately marriage. As the song hits soon made clear, true happiness could only be found in waltz tempo! Next to love in importance came virginity, at least the virginity of girls—a deep source of maternal and music-lyric solicitude. [24]

Following the love songs in popularity came the lachrymose songs. Tears were considered good, right, and natural. Charles K. Harris was the king of the tearful songs. Here are some illustrative Harris lyrics from songs that were the rage of the 1890's: "The pardon came too late, the letter was edged in black"; "the widower sat on his wife's grave, with blinding tears falling he sang of his lost pearl"; "the child asked the switchboard girl for heaven because her mother was there, and the wires seemed to moan"; "the soldier's last words were 'Just break the news to mother' "; and "the boy's last words were, 'Don't send me to bed, I'll be good.' " [25] Each was a famous Harris composition!

The songs of the 1890's, said one critic, "were more cruelly characteristic of their time than ever before. They were inexorable in their revelation of limited human understanding, commonplace emotions and the platitudes of social intercourse. More songs were written and published than in any previous decade yet few were very good. Many are remembered today as museum pieces and objects of ridicule. It is hard to believe that they were taken seriously, but obviously they were."[26]

A change was sweeping the country, however, and the popular music showed it. The year 1892 saw the music industry's first million-copy seller, but it was also the year that Coca-Cola ceased being advertised as a patent medicine, now to be proclaimed a pleasurable soft drink. Fun was taking the place of moral uplift.[27] No more would be heard the gushing, well-known mottoes, maxims, and proverbs that had characterized music from the 1870's through the 1890's. The theatre of the nineties came up with another type of music altogether.[28]

Weber and Fields' *Whirl-I-Gig*

*Courtesy of Billy Rose Collection
The New York Public Library at Lincoln Center
Astor, Lenox and Tilden Foundations*

3

THE RAGTIME ERA

In the period from 1890 to 1910, maudlin and melancholy songs were no longer the rage, and instead the emphasis was on humor. Like the lachrymose trend of previous years, however, this change in popular taste was in many ways forced and false. Up from the South and Midwest came the temper and tempo of the new music that restored life to the songwriting business and wrecked forever the rigidity of the waltz-time morality. The new immigrants also helped, for the American melting pot produced a great musical stew compounded of European sounds and African syncopation—it was called ragtime. As will be discussed later in the chapter, the new music was perfect for the hustling and bustling of turn-of-the-century America.

Opinions about ragtime differed. Anton Dvorák, on an American tour in 1892–95, wrote, "In negro melodies of America I discover all that is needed for a great and noble school of music."[1] A New England music critic who disagreed said,

Ragtime is a mere comic strip representing American vices. Here is a rude noise which emerged from the hinterlands of brothels and dives, presented in a negroid manner by Jews most often, so popular that even high society Vanderbilts dance to it. All this syncopated music wasn't American, it is unamerican. The Jew and the Yankee stand in human temperance at polar points. The Jew has oriental extravagance and sensuous brilliance. However, ragtime is a reflection of these raucous times; it is music without a soul.[2]

Either way, ragtime was seen as a unique musical form. Before we discuss it more fully, however, we must trace develop-

ments in the burgeoning music industry and consider the continuing popularity of sentimental ballad-type songs. By the
mid-1890's, many of the original publishers had outgrown their
offices and relocated. The first to do so was M. Witmark and
Sons. They moved from 14th Street, at the heart of the theatre
district, to an uptown area, around 28th Street. The others
followed, and by the late 1890's virtually every other publisher
was on or near the same street. Monroe Rosenfeld, a journalist-
songwriter, described the area in a magazine article on popular
music. Harry Von Tilzer, the songwriter turned publisher, had
wound pieces of paper over the strings of a piano to make it give
off a tinny sound that he was fond of. While visiting him to
research the piece, Rosenfeld heard the piano, which gave him
the title for his article, "Tin Pan Alley." From that time on, the
area, and eventually the American music business in general,
was known as "Tin Pan Alley." Later on, Von Tilzer claimed that
he had coined the name, but whether or not this is true, it was
Rosenfeld who made it stick by giving it large circulation.

> Sing a song of Tin Pan
> And Cock Robin, too;
> Who really scores the hit
> That magnetizes you?
>
> "I," says the lyricist,
> "With my words and patter;
> Take my lines away
> And the rest doesn't matter."
>
> "I," cries the composer,
> "With my tune and tinkle;
> Without them the song
> Would be dead as Van Winkle."
>
> The arranger looks on
> With a cynical frown.
> "He thinks up the tune
> But I set it down."
>
> "You?" sneers the plugger.
> "Go tell that to Grover.

You guys set it down,
But I put it over!"

Mr. Publisher smiles.
"And whose shekels stake it?
If it wasn't for me,
How could you fellows make it?"

From the wings speaks a ghost,
"How these kids run amuck!
Shall I tell them the truth,—
That it's me, Lady Luck?"[3]

Tin Pan Alley was symbolic of the creativity that filled the music world from the 1890's to the 1940's. From hundreds of offices in several closely situated office buildings came words, music, and chaos. From the windows of the Brill Building and others, flew out songs and words which often lasted no longer than the time it took to write them. The songs may have died, but the singing lived on.

Early in the days of the Tin Pan Alley publishers, the offices were humble, rather unpretentious rooms—dirty, filled with smoke, and furnished with a desk, a piano, a chair, and a spittoon. In those dingy quarters were first heard the melodies that would entertain America and the world. Theodore Dreiser, the American novelist and brother of songwriter Paul Dresser, described Tin Pan Alley this way:

In Twenty-seventh or Twenty-eighth Street or anywhere along Broadway from Madison to Greeley Square, are the parlors of the scores of publishers. . . . rugs, divans, imitation palm plants make this publishing house more bower than office. Three or four pianos give to each chamber a parlor-like appearance. The walls are hung with the photos of celebrities neatly framed. In the private music rooms, rocking chairs. A boy or two waits to bring "professional copies" at a word. A salaried pianist or two wait to run over pieces which the singer may desire to hear. . . . And then those "peerless singers of popular ballads" as their programs announce them, men and women whose pictures you will see upon every song sheet, their physiognomy underscored with their own "Yours sincerely" in their own handwriting. Everyday they are here, arriving and departing, carrying the latest songs to all parts of the land. These are the individuals who in their own estimation "make" the songs the successes they are. In all justice, they have claim to the distinction. One such, raising his or her voice nightly in a melodic interpretation of a new ballad, may, if the music is sufficiently catchy, bring it so thoroughly to the public's ear as to cause it to begin to sell. . . . In flocks and droves they come, whenever good fortune brings "the company" to New York or the end of the season causes them to return, to tell of their successes and pick new songs for the ensuing season. Also to collect certain prearranged bonuses.[4]

The success of the Alley depended on the public, and the public depended on the Alley; it was a mutual need. The men and women who worked on Tin Pan Alley were professionals in every sense of the word. They shared a heritage and a drive. Wrote one,

These are hard-boiled ladies and gentlemen, not in business for their health as they will assure you. "Staff notes into bank notes" might be their motto and their heraldic device a loud speaker rampant. The music business dealt in musical journalism in a way; the emotional tabloid which told of the day to day events that stirred the public. It was above all, opportunistic, and for that very reason, it is one of the truest indices of the public and its desires.[5]

The Witmarks, Charles K. Harris, Monroe Rosenfeld, Shapiro and Bernstein, the Von Tilzers—all were pioneers of popular music; each did his best to make and popularize a truly American industry. It was a trade which had no parallel in the rest of the world.

Not only did the publishers determine what songs would be published, but they had a hand in shaping the style of the songs. Through the reports of singers who were involved with the public, these businessmen could tell what was being accepted and what was not. On the basis of this information they would decide whether the public wanted familiar songs or new songs in a familiar style. Something of the methods and approach of the Tin Pan Alley publishers and songwriters can be gleaned from the words of advice that Charles K. Harris, the most successful songwriter of his day, wrote for songwriters just getting into "the business":

Watch your competition. Note their successes and failures; analyze the cause of either and profit thereby. Take note of public demand.

Avoid slang and vulgarisms; they never succeed.

Many-syllabled words and those containing hard consonants, wherever possible, must be avoided.

In writing lyrics, be concise; get to your point quickly, and then make the point as strongly as possible.

Simplicity in melody is one of the greatest secrets of success.

Let your melody musically convey the character and sentiment of your lyrics.[6]

With such directions from the master, it is no surprise that many of the songs came out sounding exactly alike. But the songwriters of Tin Pan Alley had other ideas as well. Just as comedians long to play *Hamlet,* so the Alleymen desired to elevate themselves into theatre music, the next area into which Tin Pan Alley spread.

It was Charles K. Harris's "After the Ball" which convinced the publishers of the power of the musical theatre. Interpolated by another composer into the score of the show *A Trip to Chinatown,* "After the Ball" became the hottest music property in America up to that time. If there was profit to be made, the Witmark Publishing Company would not be far away. In 1898 they purchased the entire catalogue of songs belonging to the vaudeville team of Weber and Fields, who by the mid-nineties, and into the turn of the century, had become what Harrigan and Hart had been: humorists who made light of ethnic differences and the trials of daily life.

Joe "Mike Dillpickle" Weber and Lew "Meyer Bockheister" Fields were Jewish comedian-producer-musicians who became famous as "Dutchmen" par excellence. They began in vaudeville in the late 1870's at only nine years old, doing as many as fifteen shows a day for the enormous sum of $6 a week. Later they played any house that would book them. In 1896, with $300 between them and $1,500 more borrowed from a brother-in-law, they purchased a property on 29th and Broadway which became the W. and F. Music Hall. Such stars as Lillian Russell, Faye Templeton, and many others played the house, and within two years, in 1898, they were taking in $5,000 per week.

Very quickly Weber and Fields augmented their musical talents by hiring staff composer John Stromberg away from the Witmarks. By 1899 they were so successful that they hired Lillian Russell for a "run-of-the-show" contract in a Stromberg musical entitled *Whirl-I-Gig*. In the show were such luminaries as David Warfield, who had starred as a Jewish comedian in the previous Weber and Fields show, Peter Daily, and of course Weber and Fields (as themselves). The interest in the show was so enormous that on opening night seats were auctioned. From this single performance Weber and Fields realized a net profit of $10,500, with Stanford White and William Randolph Hearst bidding as much as $750 for the best seats.

What was it that made these two Jewish talents so popular? Both men were cast as comic "Dutchmen," the euphemism for Germans. Weber was short and fat; Fields, tall and thin. Both men sported small tufted beards under their chins and dressed in oversize checked suits and derby hats. Their conversational routines hilariously butchered the English language. "I am delightfulness to meet you," Weber would say to Fields, to which Fields would respond, "Der disgust is all mine." Fields was the bully and Weber inevitably was the hapless victim; it was a perfect shlemiel-shlemazel situation. One of the most famous pieces of stage dialogue was created by Weber and Fields. "Who was the lady I seen you with last night?" said one. "That was no lady, that vas mine wife." Visual jokes, pratfalls, ludicrous songs, and dialogue were their stock and trade.[7]

Had Weber and Fields achieved nothing else, they would be remembered for their creativity and producing skill. However, Fields also became the founder of a great Broadway theatre family. His daughter, Dorothy, was one of the twentieth century's most famous and prolific lyricists, working with such greats as Jerome Kern, Gershwin, and Arthur Schwartz. Her brothers, Herbert and Joseph, became famous as librettists, playwrights, and directors. The family's culminating achievement was the script for Irving Berlin's *Annie Get Your Gun*.

Weber and Fields, as noted earlier, recognized that publishing their own music was more than they could handle, so they sold their catalogue of songs to Witmark and Sons for $10,000. Weber and Fields broke up their partnership in 1904 after performing in the extravaganza *An English Daisy*, with music by the Jewish composer Maurice Levi. The split became an immediate national event and topic of conversation. According to the *New York Herald*,

An audience which filled the large new theatre and composed of representatives of society clubdom, the world of first night, the theatre in every walk of life, called for the curtain to rise again. Then in response to demands, speeches were made by members of the company in which the two men who had made Weber and Fields household words were told that they were committing business suicide; were told that they were making a grievous mistake, amid cries of "Right, right!" A Broadway audience is not particularly sentimental, but the tears that streaked the painted and powdered faces on the stage were multiplied many times in the audience as "Auld Lang Syne" became the final number.[8]

As it happened, that night in 1904 was not their last performance together; Weber and Fields were reunited in 1912 and 1913 in nostalgic looks at the old-time theatre of the nineteenth century.

Very quickly Tin Pan Alley's music had penetrated all parts of America. Within a few years, some of the songs from Tin Pan Alley had become oral tradition. People no longer remembered who had written them, and instead it seemed as if they had always been around. Tin Pan Alley did not draw on traditional music, it created the music.

The originality and innovative spirit of the founders of Tin Pan Alley, these early publishers and composer-lyricists, would be totally eclipsed by the achievements of the men and women who were to come on the scene in the next few years. The sophistication of the theatrical music they produced would have been impossible if not for the firm basis provided by the men discussed so far. In this new era about to dawn, Tin Pan Alley would now introduce complete musical scores where before it had created songs; in the past the hits had been individual and disconnected, now they would be tied together as musical units, their identities interwoven with the plot of the show in which they were used. Tin Pan Alley had come of age.

Coming of age meant different things to different people. To the publishers it meant selling music. More than ever, on Tin Pan Alley, 28th and Broadway, songs were produced as if on an assembly line. To keep up with the demand, publishers hired armies of composers, lyricists, arrangers, and orchestrators. Some of our greatest songwriters began as arrangers and orchestrators. Song pluggers were another source of new talent.

Creativity was not a strong interest among publishers at the turn of the century. What they wanted was songs that would sell. If songs with girls' names in them were selling well, there would be a spate of them. If specialty numbers were big for the moment, there would be a great outpouring of more of the same.

The only way of telling whether a song was successful was from the sheet music sales—the sole source of income for publisher and writer. As Charles K. Harris proved with "After the Ball," a fortune could be made from a song. By 1900 million-copy songs were no longer unusual; between 1900 and 1910 there were one hundred such songs. Medium-selling songs were in the 600,000 range. The price of sheet music dropped according to the sales figures and the economy. In 1890 a copy of sheet music cost 40 cents, by 1900 about 25 cents, and in 1910 generally 10 cents.[9] Even with the drop in prices, a publisher could realize a $100,000 profit from a million-copy sale of a hit song.[10]

Several songs in the first decade of the twentieth century sold more than two million copies, among them Harry Von Tilzer's "A Bird in a Gilded Cage" (2,000,000 in 1900) and Leo Friedmann's "Let Me Call You Sweetheart" (5,000,000 copies in 1910). Some of Friedmann's other songs were "Coon, Coon, Coon—I Wish My Color Would Fade" (1900) and "Meet Me Tonight in Dreamland" (1909).[11] Composers and lyricists who had songs in the 600,000- to 2,000,000-copy range in this period included Gus Edwards, Charles K. Harris, Ted Snyder, Irving Berlin, Joseph W. Stern, Ed Marks, Jean Schwartz, and Leo Edwards.[12] If the publisher was also the song's author, he could earn twice the

$100,000 amount. In other instances, the composer and lyricist would split the $100,000.

To make their songs more accessible, publishers sold them in department stores and dime stores. Wherever people were likely to be, sheet music was available. To assure good sales, publishing houses would send song pluggers to stores, theatres, and amusement areas. Song pluggers were originally called "boomers" because they had to be able to sing their wares. Around 1900 the Lower East Side synagogues were a prime source of boomers. The synagogues were canvassed for boys with large lungs and "rabbinic voices" who could be taught the music and planted in vaudeville shows or stores. They were trained to get up at the proper moment and sing the song along with the headliner.[13] Song pluggers such as Mose Gumble, the ace of pluggers, were joined by newcomers who would go on to great achievements of their own. Both Harry Cohen, the boss of Columbia Pictures, and Jean Schwartz, a successful songwriter, began as boomers.

Jean Schwartz became a respected member of the Tin Pan Alley community on the basis of his song "Bedelia," which Mose Gumble promoted into a three-million seller. Schwartz was born in Hungary on November 4, 1878. When he was fourteen he came to America, where he worked as a song demonstrator in the sheet music department of a store in New York, Siegel-Cooper. Following this he became a song plugger for Shapiro-Bernstein. His first song was a piano cakewalk called "Dusty Dudes" (1889).

In 1901 Schwartz formed a partnership with William Jerome, a lyricist of great repute. They wrote such songs as "Rip Van Winkle Was a Lucky Man," "Any Place I Can Hang My Hat Is Home Sweet Home to Me," "Don't Put Me Off at Buffalo Anymore," and "When Mr. Shakespeare Comes to Town."[14] Most of Schwartz's best songs were interpolated into the scores of musicals of the early twentieth century, including several Weber and Fields extravaganzas.

After his partnership with Jerome broke up in 1914, Schwartz went on to write with other lyricists. His most fruitful collaboration after Jerome was with the Jewish team of Joe Young and

Sam Lewis. Together they wrote a song that became an Al Jolson classic, "Rock-A-Bye Your Baby with a Dixie Melody." Together with "Swanee," George Gershwin's greatest hit, "Rock-A-Bye Your Baby" was introduced in *Sinbad* (1918), a show that ever since has been famous in the history of American musical comedy. Schwartz contributed to various other revues and shows until his retirement in 1928. He died in Los Angeles on November 30, 1956.

By 1900, ragtime was the rage of Tin Pan Alley. This does not mean that ballads had lost their appeal, however. Songs in waltz-time dealing with timeless love sold millions of copies every year. "My Gal Sal" (1905), "Down By the Old Mill Stream" (1910), "Mother, A Word That Means the World to Me" (1915), and "Till We Meet Again" (1918) are examples. [15] Nostalgia was an important influence on the music of the early decade; people looked back on the simpler life of the 1890's with fondness and desired the old-time songs to return. "Bird in a Gilded Cage" (1900), "Good Old Summertime" (1902), "Sweet Adeline" (1903), "Shade of the Old Apple Tree" (1905), "I Wonder Who's Kissing Her Now" (1909), "Let Me Call You Sweetheart," and "Down By the Old Mill Stream" (1910) are all examples of the old songs coming back. [16]

Another master of the old-type song that was recognized as anachronistic even when it was written was Gus Edwards. Born on August 18, 1879, in Hohensallza, Germany, as Gustave Edward Simon, Edwards was brought to the United States in 1887. His family settled in the Williamsburg section of Brooklyn. During the day he worked in his uncle's cigar factory and at night he searched around the theatre district looking for work. Edwards learned the business as a song plugger and music salesman, and in 1896 he and four friends were booked as a vaudeville team. In 1898 he introduced his first song into their act, a "coon song" entitled "All I Want Is My Black Baby Back." [17] Since he was unable to write down his music, Edwards had his compositions transcribed for him, a common practice in the early days of the Tin Pan Alley era.

During the Spanish-American War, Edwards entertained the troops at various camps, and while at Camp Black he met Will

Cobb, who would serve as his lyricist. Their first big success was "I Can't Tell You Why I Love You, But I Do, Do, Do" (1900).[18] In 1901 they had another big seller: "Mamie, Don't You Feel Ashamie." Four years later Gus Edwards wrote three of his great songs—"In My Merry Oldsmobile," "He's My Pal," and "Tammany," which became the theme song of the New York Democratic political machine—and in that same year he opened his own publishing house.

In 1907, Edwards created a style of musical theatre with which he became totally identified. Capitalizing on the popularity of his song "School Days," which sold over 3 million copies of sheet music, he created a variety show entitled *School Days*, serving as emcee "Schoolteacher" to introduce new young talent. The *School Days* shows were so successful, and his search for talent so widespread, that the phrase was coined, "Pull your kids in, here comes Edwards."[19] Among the talents Edwards discovered were Eddie Cantor, George Jessel, Walter Winchell, the Marx Brothers, and the Duncan Sisters. Edwards wrote most of the songs for these revues himself. The most lasting of them were "Sunbonnet Sue" (1908) and "By the Light of the Silvery Moon" (1909). Edwards also wrote for the *Ziegfeld Follies* and various Weber and Fields extravaganzas. He retired in 1939 after a short career in movies and died in Los Angeles on November 7, 1945.[20]

It must be remembered that these old romantic songs were holdovers from the previous generation of songwriters. They never did fade totally from the scene, but they enjoyed a cyclical popularity. As was said at the beginning of the chapter, the time had come for the dominance of ragtime.

The word "ragtime" was first used in 1893 on the sheet music for "My Ragtime Baby" by Fred Stone. By 1897 the term had been copyrighted and was in common use. Although ragtime was primarily a song style associated with black composers, such as Scott Joplin and James Scott, several Jews used the genre very successfully. George Gershwin, long before he achieved any success in theatre or music, wrote "Rialto Ripples" in collaboration with Walter Donaldson in 1916. Joe E. Howard began his stardom career with the sentimental ballad "I Wonder Who's Kissing Her Now," but his first success as a composer was the ragtime song "Hello, My Baby," which he wrote with his wife, Ida Emerson, in 1899.

Howard was born in New York City on February 12, 1867. His father was a saloon-keeper on the Lower East Side, and Howard was born in a backroom of the bar. At eight years old, he ran away and found temporary shelter at a Catholic orphanage; he escaped from there to St. Louis, where he sang in saloons and brothels to earn a living. At seventeen, Howard organized a vaudeville act with Ida Emerson, a dancer, and they were soon married. By 1895 they were good enough to appear in a Chicago vaudeville house, and it was there that Joe E. Howard made it big. Following their success, they were invited to New York to appear at Tony Pastor's club. Ida Emerson was one of the nine women Howard married.

Between 1905 and 1915 Howard wrote the music for more than twenty different shows staged in Chicago. Several of these went on to greater success in New York. From the depression to the post–World War II era, Howard ran a successful nightclub, and occasionally did public appearances. He died on May 16, 1961, while doing a public benefit at the Lyric Opera House in Chicago, after finishing a chorus of "Let Me Call You Sweetheart."

Howard's greatest song, "I Wonder Who's Kissing Her Now," later became the subject of a major lawsuit. Howard claimed he had written it himself, but it turned out that the song had, in fact, been written by Harold Orlob, who worked for Howard in 1908–9 and gave him the completed song. This would not have been regarded as an unusual incident at the time, but contrary to the custom of the day, the actual author in this case received no compensation. Orlob did not demand credit for the song until 1947, when a screen biography of Howard was being prepared. He did not claim any damages, however. The case was settled out of court. Credit for writing the song was split between Howard and Orlob, but Orlob was not given any money from the royalties.

The music of ragtime was also enhanced through the efforts of L. Wolfe Gilbert, who was born in Odessa, Russia, on August

31, 1886. Gilbert's family left Russia as a result of the anti-Jewish pogroms of Czar Alexander III. Before too long Gilbert was so Americanized that he was writing songs about places in America he had never seen. His most famous song, "Waiting for the Robert E. Lee," was about a paddle-wheel steamer. It didn't matter that he had never been on one, or that there were no levees in Alabammy—what mattered was that the public liked the song. Gilbert wrote the lyrics while watching a group of black stevedores unloading freight from a Mississippi riverboat in Baton Rouge, Louisiana. The song was brought to Al Jolson by a song plugger working for the Mills publishing house. Jolson introduced it into his weekly Sunday evening concerts and helped make it a multi-million seller. A second song for which Gilbert is justly remembered is "Lucky Lindy." Gilbert's success was so great that he quickly opened a publishing house of his own.[21]

One can hardly talk about ragtime without mentioning the most famous of the so-called ragtime songs, "Alexander's Ragtime Band" by Irving Berlin. This Berlin hit truly helped to make ragtime the primary song style on Tin Pan Alley, even though it was not really a ragtime song at all. Except for one phrase it lacks the syncopation required for a true ragtime piece and is closer to a march. The public considered it ragtime, however, and Berlin did not disagree. The song made him the "ragtime king."

Berlin exhibited his interest in ragtime as early as 1909 when he wrote "That Mesmerizing Mendelssohn Tune," a ragtime version of Mendelssohn's "Spring Song."[22] In 1910 Berlin wrote "Yiddle on Your Fiddle Play Some Ragtime" and "Violin Ragtime." Both of these songs were incorporated into the act of an unknown performer named Eddie Cantor. "Alexander's Ragtime Band," written in 1911, made Berlin the dominant force in American music, a title he held for the next fifty years. The ragtime years culminated in Berlin's writing of a ragtime production, *Watch Your Step.* Billed as a "syncopated musical," it opened on December 8, 1914, at the New Amsterdam Theatre. After "Alexander's Ragtime Band," Berlin went into the publishing business as a partner of Waterson and Snyder, who had been his original publishers. It was the beginning of a fantastic business relationship and creative collaboration. By 1919, though, Berlin had become too big, and he left the partners to open his own company. After all, he had one of the most valuable collections of songs on Tin Pan Alley, the works of Irving Berlin.

The Vaudeville Stars

Lew Fields of Weber and Fields

Courtesy of American Jewish Archives

Al Jolson

Fanny Brice

**At Rehearsal for Jewish Theatrical Guild Dinner, Eddie Cantor and
Paul Whiteman Impersonate Each Other**

The Last of the Red Hot Mammas, Sophie Tucker

Courtesy of American Jewish Archives

Billy Rose

4

THE GOLDEN AGE

The era between the two World Wars was the golden age of music in America. Many talented songwriters and lyricists turned out hundreds of popular and brilliant songs that soon spread over the entire world. In addition to creative brilliance, these luminaries all had another characteristic in common. George Gershwin, Irving Berlin, Oscar Hammerstein, Richard Rodgers, Jerome Kern, Lorenz Hart, and many other major musical figures of this period were all Jews.

In the history of American popular music, each period of development has been dominated by a single group. For the years 1910 through 1940, that group was the Jews. Before the twentieth century, Jews played but a small part in the world of popular music, probably because of their small numbers, but problems in Russia and Europe at the turn of the century soon brought about an increase in Jewish immigration to America.

By 1910 there were about a million Jews in New York City alone. These new immigrants saw the theatre as a way to become Americanized. It was a school as well as an entertainment.[1] Moreover, while the immigrants were often poorly educated, some of them were well trained as far as a skill was concerned. Although they encountered less anti-Semitism than in Europe, still it existed, so they went into trades and fields where Jews were already active. The music and entertainment industries are two major examples.

Many of the immigrants anglicized their names: Israel Baline became Irving Berlin, Billy Rosenberg became Billy Rose, Asa

Yoelson became Al Jolson. Harry Jolson wrote, "As Asa and Herschel we were Jew Boys, as Al and Harry we were Americans."[2] In addition to becoming Americanized, these immigrant Jews formed the music to suit themselves. Popular songs were soaked in the wailing of the synagogue cantorial. The Yiddish singing style, with the cry in the voice and the heart on the sleeve, was typified by Al Jolson, Norah Bayes, and Sophie Tucker, the vaudeville stars who made the Tin Pan Alley songs into hits. They fused Yiddishisms into all-Americanisms. "My Mammy" may have been a Yiddishe Momma, but she was also as American as apple pie.[3]

The vaudeville circuit—by 1910 already 2,000 theatres strong—was largely dominated by Jews. The Shubert brothers—Sam, Lee, and Jake—were the sons of a Lithuanian peddler named David Szemanski who came to America in the late 1880's. The nightclub business was invented by a Jew, Jack Levy, who in 1907 induced several restaurants at which he was a patron to accept singers as entertainers during eating hours. The nightclub became a new place for songs to be heard and another place where Jews played important roles.[4] Marcus Loewe, Adolph Zukor, and Martin Beck (Morris Meyerfeld),[5] who founded the Orpheum circuit, all were founders of the Hollywood movie industry as well. They were joined by Louis B. Mayer, Samuel Goldwyn, the Selznicks, William Fox, and the Warner brothers. The personal style and values of these entrepreneurs was aptly described by Irving Howe:

Often vulgar, crude and overbearing, they were brilliantly attuned to the needs of their business; they commanded and used to the full a profound instinct for the common denominator of taste; and they left a deep imprint on American popular culture. Trusting their own minds and hearts, shrewd enough not to pay too much attention to the talented or cultivated men they hired, the movie moguls knew when to appeal to sentiment, which twirl of fantasy, which touch of violence, which innuendo of sexuality, would grasp the native American audiences. It was something of a miracle and a joke.[6]

Why did Jews dominate the entertainment industry? First, in part, it can be attributed to talent. Also, Jews already were in the business, and this made it easier for other Jews to enter—anti-Semitism was not so difficult a problem. As Irving Howe has noted:

> Just as blacks would later turn to baseball and basketball knowing that there at least their skin color counted less than their skills, so in the early 1900's Jews broke into vaudeville because here too people asked not, who are you? but what can you do? It was a roughneck sort of egalitarianism, with little concern for those who might go under, but at best it gave the people a chance to show their gifts.[7]

No matter how one views the American song industry, the Jews cannot be left out. Jews were certainly prominent among songwriters, lyricists, performers, and publishers of songs. They contributed a distinct Jewish flavor and style that added much to the flavor of popular music. As early as 1903 performers were taking the songs of the day and adding Yiddish dialect to them.[8] Irving Berlin ably represented the newcomers, but there were many others as well, among them Jerome Kern, Berlin's contemporary. Gershwin, Richard Rodgers, Harold Arlen, Oscar Hammerstein, and many others continued the trend and contributed to the glory that is Tin Pan Alley. Alexander Woolcott, summing up the contribution of Berlin and other Jews to American music, said: "And if anyone, on hearing Jerome Kern say that Irving Berlin IS American music, is then so fatuous as to object on the ground that he was born in Russia, it might be pointed out that if the musical interpreter of American civilization came over in the foul hold of a ship, so did American civilization."[9]

Not quite so high class, but just as important musically, was the contribution of Jews to burlesque—not the minstrel shows mentioned earlier or the type of burlesque in which Weber and Fields or, earlier, Harrigan and Hart had starred, but the burlesque that showcased beautiful females in various states of undress involved with dance and fancy sets. From this type of entertainment came the striptease and off-color shows known as burlesque today.

By the early years of the 1900's the format of burlesque had been set. This included "blackouts"—quick skits followed by a short period of darkness in which to change the scenes—then "German" or "Jewish" comedians, followed by slapstick, dancing, and lots of girls.

Al Shean of Gallagher and Shean got his start in burlesque (he was the uncle of the Marx Brothers). Eddie Cantor first received public attention by performing in one of the amateur nights that became a burlesque tradition. Sophie Tucker changed from being a "coon caller" in blackface to performing in whiteface with the advent of burlesque.

Fanny Brice also started as a coon singer. In 1910 she asked Irving Berlin to provide some specialty material for her. Let her tell the story:

Irving took me in the back room and he played "Sadie Salome" . . . a Jewish comedy song. . . . So, of course, Irving sang "Sadie Salome" with a Jewish accent. I didn't even understand Jewish, couldn't speak a word of it. But I thought, if that's the way Irving sings, that's the way I'll sing it. Well, I came out and did "Sadie Salome" for the first time ever doing a Jewish accent. And that starched sailor suit is killing me. And it's gathering you know where, and I'm trying to squirm it away, and singing and smiling, and the audience is loving it. They think it's an act I'm doing, so as long as they're laughing I keep it up. They start to throw roses at me.[10]

The song changed Fanny Brice from a balladeer to a comedienne, as well as the outstanding interpreter of Yiddish comedy songs. As a result of this performance, Florenz Ziegfeld signed her for the *Follies of 1910.*

Although not as important as the songs in other genres of show business, the songs that were used in burlesque received great exposure. As Alex Wilder notes in his history of American popular music, "To place a song in a burlesque show was the infallible method of establishing a hit and insuring great profits. The runs were long and by the time one show after another presented a song, the whole country knew the tune by heart."[11]

Florenz Ziegfeld played an enormous role in the history of burlesque and its higher-class sister, the Broadway revue. The more successful he became, the less popular he seemed to be. "To know him was to dislike him" became the music world's pet phrase when describing Ziegfeld.[12] There is a question as to Ziegfeld's religion. Several sources claim he was Jewish, others deny it; there is no question, however, that Ziegfeld's first wife was Jewish and that he provided the beginning for many Jewish talents. For that reason if no other, he is included here.

Born on March 21, 1868, in Chicago, Ziegfeld was the son of Dr. Florenz Ziegfeld, president and founder of the Chicago Musical College, which he had begun the year before his son's birth. Ziegfeld Senior's contemporary, George Ade Davis, referred to him as "one of the most picturesque figures in the history of musical development in America, a pioneer who has lived to see the successful combination of his labors, to watch the growth, the budding and the blossoming of musical development and even to see the matured and ripened fruit as well. His autograph across the pages of musical history will never be defaced."[13]

Florenz Ziegfeld the younger began his impresario career at the 1893 Chicago Columbian Exposition, where he assisted his father in importing acts for the main show. His first efforts were enormous disasters, costing him his job. He regained his position by signing an act called "Sandow the Great," a handsome young muscle-builder able to lift automobiles and houses and to withstand three elephants walking across his chest. Ziegfeld achieved a major public relations coup when he invited Mrs. Potter Palmer, Chicago socialite and grande dame, to visit Sandow after the show to inspect his musculature. The news of her favorable reaction created a sensation, providing Ziegfeld with a ten-times-improved box office.

Ziegfeld's next achievement was the signing of the Gallic idol Anna Held, a Polish Jew by birth, but the quintessence of French spice and personality. Her great success in American theatre and music included a song called "It's Delightful to Be Married," which she wrote for her show *The Parisian Model* (1906). Anna Held was married to her producer, Florenz Ziegfeld. When publicity was waning, Ziegfeld invented the story that she took daily milk baths to improve her beauty and skin tone. Immediately dairies noted an increase in milk sales, and the publicity carried both Held and Ziegfeld to great notoriety with the public.

Using the *Folies-Bergère* as his model and his French wife as the impetus, Ziegfeld decided to create an American follies to rival the famous French version. In 1907 he achieved this dream, and with only three exceptions, a *Ziegfeld Follies* would brighten the stage of New York for each of the next twenty-five years. Ziegfeld set out to make the "Follies girls" synonymous with taste and beauty, but he did not skimp on sets, costumes, or talent. He always hired the best, and his shows attained such prestige that his booking of Ed Wynn, W. C. Fields, Fanny Brice, Harry Ruby, Irving Berlin, Leo Edwards, and Eddie Cantor gave their respective careers a push no one else could have given. Such songs as "My Blue Heaven," "A Pretty Girl Is Like a Melody" (by Irving Berlin), which became the *Follies* theme song, "Peg O' My Heart," and "Mr. Gallagher—Mr. Shean" were all *Follies* numbers. Jerome Kern, Rudolf Friml, Gus Edwards, Louis A. Hirsch, and Jean Schwartz were among the men who wrote for Ziegfeld.

When something was popular, there were always those who would borrow on the success and create their own. The directions for writing commercial popular music said, "one should fashion a song around a previous hit; to use the model as a take off. Then the chances would be that you'll finish up with something different enough to be choice, but not avant garde."[14] Similarly, Ziegfeld provided the model for the theatre-music world's most successful entrepreneurs, the brothers Shubert.

Levi, Sam, and Jacob Szemanski, who became Lee, Sam, and J. J. Shubert, came from the most poverty-stricken of backgrounds. Their father, David Szemanski, was a Lithuanian peddler who fled from his hometown of Shervient to England and then to the United States.[15] The most difficult problem for David was his drinking—most of the profits from his peddling went to buy whiskey.[16] Nonetheless, within a short time he earned enough money to bring his family of six children (Fanny, Sarah, and Dora were the other three) and his wife to America.

Upon the family's arrival in New York in 1882, an immigration officer somehow recorded the name of David Szemanski from Shervient as David Shurbent. Apparently the script was hard to read, and various other officials subsequently changed it to Shurbart, then to Shobart, and finally to Shubert.

The Shubert brothers individually were men of great intelligence, humorlessness, and drive. Each handled a different part of their operation. J.J. was the producer-businessman, Lee the producer-artist, and Sam the international traveling real estate agent and talent scout. Although most of their productions were labeled the "Messrs. Shubert," it was largely the results of Lee's efforts which the audience viewed on stage. Fred and Adele Astaire began their careers in a Shubert show, the revue *Over the Top,* with music by Sigmund Romberg. In 1912 the Shuberts opened their competition to Ziegfeld's *Follies,* the *Passing Show.* They attempted to hire away various Ziegfeld talents, including Ed Wynn, the composers Hirsch and Schwartz, as well as the aforementioned Sigmund Romberg. Ziegfeld eventually lost the competition, as did anyone who challenged the Shubert domination of musical theatre, when the brothers bought him out and began presenting *The Shubert Ziegfeld Follies.* In 1924, due to competition from the new musical comedies as well as other more modern and innovative revues, the *Follies* and *Passing Show* revues went out of business. By the late 1920's, the revue format passed from public favor.

The Shuberts were the most powerful force in the theatre-music world in the first fifty years of the twentieth century. There was hardly a city in the country which did not sport a Shubert theatre; New York had more than six, Chicago, three. With enormous booking power came artistic power. By the beginning of World War I, virtually all the great theatrical musical talent in the United States was under Shubert control. Tin Pan Alley was the most famous Alley in New York; Shubert Alley was second.

Another theatrical opportunity for music was the "extravaganza." The Shuberts contributed greatly to the extravaganzas when they built the Wintergarden Theatre in 1911. The production that opened the building began with a Spanish ballet, followed by a Chinese opera; but what made the evening really historical was the third piece—"La Belle Paree," written by a newcomer to the theatre, Jerome Kern.

Another debut in "La Belle Paree" was Asa Yoelson, by then known as Al Jolson. He was born in Srednicke, Lithuania, in 1886, the son of Moses Yoelson, a chazan who later worked in New York, then in Washington, D.C.[17] As a young man Al once sang along with the audience when Eddie Leonard was doing his rendition of "Ida, Sweet as Apple Cider." The resulting appreciative applause told him that he had found his profession.

By 1909 Al Jolson had become the chief attraction of the Lew Dockstader Minstrels, and the next year he was a headliner at Hammerstein's Victoria in New York. Even at this young age, he was a polished performer. He would stop in the middle of a show and come downstage to ask the audience if they wouldn't rather hear some of his own favorites instead of the songs in the show—more often than not, they agreed. The newspapers noted the innovation, as did the audiences, and Jolson's performances became very popular.

This crowd-pleasing technique was made into a permanent attraction when Shubert's Wintergarden Theatre began Sunday afternoon concerts where Jolson could sing whatever songs he chose. Although originally a blackface performer, he would appear at these concerts in whiteface. During one of his performances in the Jean Schwartz musical *The Honeymoon Express*, Jolson was suffering from a painful ingrown toenail. To relieve the pain, he went down on one knee and threw out his arms for balance. To the audience it appeared as if he was embracing the entire group and they loved it. The gesture became a Jolson trademark.

Jolson wrote some of the songs he made famous, most notably "California—Here I Come," and introduced several all-time greats, such as "Swanee," "Rock-A-Bye Your Baby with a Dixie Melody," "Toot, Toot, Tootsie, Goodbye," and April Showers." Born to poverty and begging for nickels, he left an estate of $4 million when he died in 1950.[18]

One of Jolson's favorite lyricists was the German-Jewish refugee Gus Kahn. Born in Koblenz on November 6, 1886, Kahn came to the United States in 1891 and grew up in Chicago. He began publishing specialty material in 1908 and in 1927 wrote his most famous show, *Whoopee*, for Eddie Cantor. "Love Me or Leave Me" came from *Whoopee*, but Kahn was responsible for many other hits, including "Toot, Toot, Tootsie," "It Had to Be You," "Yes, Sir, That's My Baby," and "Ain't We Got Fun."[19]

Kahn wrote several of his songs with composer Walter Donaldson, the two most famous being "My Buddy" and "Nothing Could Be Finer Than to Be in Carolina in the Morning." The story is told that Kahn and Donaldson were in the Kahn living room one day attempting to write songs. Suddenly, when Kahn's son, Donald, started yelling "dada, dada, dada," their concentration was interrupted. Kahn angrily stomped into the room where the boy was playing, calling to Donaldson, "I'll stop him, Walt, don't worry!" "No wait, Gus!" shouted Donaldson. He sat down at the piano and repeated the phrase the boy had played on his toy guitar. The two men listened as if with new ears, and in short order the simple phrase was turned into the basis for the ever-popular "Carolina in the Morning."[20] Little Donald later became a well-known songwriter in his own right.

Gus Kahn was once asked why so many "songboys" wrote about the South, as he had with "Carolina in the Morning." He replied that Southern place- and state-names lent themselves to rhyming, but more than that, "Our song boys are of the North. Paradise is never where we are. The South has become our never, never land, the symbol of the land where the lotus blossoms and dreams come true."[21]

If blossoms and lotus were unnatural to the surroundings of Broadway, so was the operetta. Conceived originally in Europe, this musical genre had great success in America. Its original sources, ranging from Gilbert and Sullivan to Offenbach, invaded America, gaining musical success and sheet music sales.

Before long so-called Americans were creating domestic versions of the European imports. Sigmund Romberg, mentioned earlier, was the greatest of the operetta composers, but there were others. Emmerich Kalman, a Jew who was born in Siofok, Hungary, in 1882, blended his native Hungarian music with the grace of the Viennese operetta. His best works in America fused the classical and jazz styles; *The Duchess of Chicago* and *The Violets of Montmart* were the most successful. His original American effort was *Parisian Love*. The show opened at the Shulman and Goldberg Public Theatre in New York. Though it played only on Friday, Saturday, and Sunday evenings, and Saturday and Sunday matinees, this was enough to make a profit and Kalman's reputation.[22]

Another composer who began in operetta but went into regular Tin Pan Alley popular songwriting was Gustave Kerker, born in Herford, Westphalia, Germany, on February 28, 1857. His family settled in Louisville, Kentucky, in 1867, and Kerker began writing a few years later. His most famous songs were "Forty Miles from Schenectady to Troy," "The Belle of New York," and "The Telephone Girl." He died in New York on June 29, 1923.

By the 1930's operetta was passé. The Broadway musical had taken its place. The greatest of the operetta composers, Romberg, died in 1950, the last of the operetta composers in America.

The second decade of the twentieth century was much faster than the first. The auto was already the established means of locomotion, and motion pictures were beginning to compete with the shows people could see on stage. Ragtime, which had already affected melody as well as rhythm as a syncopation device, suddenly created a new musical experiment, jazz.[23] Harry Von Tilzer wrote "I'll Lend You Everything I've Got Except My Wife (And I'll Make You a Present of Her)." Jean Schwartz and Bert Kalmar continued the Hawaiian craze by writing "Hello Hawaii, How Are You." Suddenly all the hits were Oriental- or foreign-sounding songs. "Siam," "Bom Bombay," and Rudolph Friml's "Allah's Holiday" were the songs of 1915.

All these songs had one thing in common, they were danceable, for the period from 1910 to 1920 was a time when America went dance mad. Earlier, the most popular songs had been waltzes, and the crooners often accented and lengthened the songs so that they became difficult to dance to. Songs had many choruses and several verses because they had to tell a story. By the mid-decade, though, if you couldn't dance to a song, it couldn't achieve any success. The year 1911 even saw the first "Castle Walk" wedding, named after the two greatest dance partners in America, Irene and Vernon Castle. It all took place at the wedding of an Eizendrath to a Stein![24]

Sophistication was in, the natural life was out. There were always a few jeers at the hicks; New Yorker–Russian Irving Berlin wrote about "Farmer Brown raising the dickens, in a cabaret far from cows and chickens. . . . This is the Life!" (1914). Even the stately dances of the 1880's attended by high society returned as a source of musical inspiration: "At the Ragtime Ball," "At the Old Maids' Ball," even "At the Yiddish Society Ball."[25]

Sadly, the idyllic simplicity and classic sophistication of those years did not last. With the assassination of Archduke Francis Ferdinand of Austria by a Serbian nationalist in 1914, political events got in the way. War broke out between Austria and Serbia. It didn't take long for Germany, England, France, and Russia to be drawn in; and with their involvement came a series of changes in the music of Tin Pan Alley.

First there was a spate of patriotic songs, such as Harry Von Tilzer's "Under the American Flag" and Edgar Leslie and Archie Gottler's "America, I Love You." Tin Pan Alley was in a bit of a quandary, however. There was an enormous need for music, yet despite the desire to "make the world safe for democracy" there were many on the Alley who were convinced that the Central Powers, Germany and Austria-Hungary, would be the victors. Furthermore, they recognized that many American favored the Germans, perceiving them as a "comfy people" who made and enjoyed the comforts of life, like beer, hot dogs, and hamburgers. Germans were seen, as well, as friendly, cheerful, and even as lovers. No one was more "all-American" than Irving Berlin, yet in 1914 he wrote, "Oh, How That German Could Love."[26]

Still others on Tin Pan Alley were distinctly pacifist, using music as an outlet for their political views with such songs as "I Didn't Raise My Boy to Be a Soldier" and "Our Hats Off to You, Mr. President" (which praised President Wilson for his 1916 campaign promise to keep America out of war). In opposition were the more martial songs. Several of these parodied the pacifist songs. "I Did Not Raise My Boy to Be a Coward" and "I Didn't Raise My Boy to Be a Soldier, I'll Send My Daughter to Be a Nurse" are good examples.

April 2, 1917, saw President Wilson, who had vowed to keep us out of war, ask a cheering Congress for a declaration of war against the Germans. Recognizing the martial value of songs, the War Industries Board allowed supplies of paper to be provided for the music publishers. As an economy measure, however, the long sheets on which music had formerly been printed were replaced with shorter ones; moreover, instead of the art work of peacetime, now there were war slogans: "Eat more fish, cheese, eggs and poultry. Save beef, pork and mutton for our fighters."[27]

It is interesting and not surprising that the songs of the war years had many of the same themes as the prewar songs, transposed to a different setting. The ballad songs of separation were the most popular. Lew Brown and Albert Von Tilzer wrote "I May Be Gone for a Long Time" and "Au Revoir But Not Goodbye, Soldier Boy." "Hello Central, Give Me No Man's Land," by Lewis, Young, and Jerome, told about a young child calling her daddy, who is stationed overseas. The similarity to Charles K. Harris's "Hello Central, Give Me Heaven" was intentional.

Of course there were specialty numbers during the war years, songs of humor and lightness. The musical *Sinbad*, from which George Gershwin and Irving Caesar's "Swanee" came, as well as "Hello Central, Give Me No Man's Land," also included "How'd You Like to Be My Daddy" by Sam Lewis, Joe Young, and Ted Snyder.

Sam Lewis was born in New York on October 25, 1885. After working days as a runner for a brokerage house while singing in cafes at night, he turned to writing his own material as well as songs for Lew Dockstader's Minstrels and Van and Schenck. His partner, Joe Young, was born in New York on July 4, 1889. Young began his show business career as a card boy in a vaudeville house, placing the name cards of the different acts on the marquee, and then worked as a song plugger. He died in 1939. Some of the songs Lewis and Young wrote together rank among the standards of Tin Pan Alley, including "Rock-A-Bye Your Baby with a Dixie Melody," "Five Foot Two, Eyes of Blue," "How You Gonna Keep 'Em Down on the Farm," "My Mammy" (with Al Jolson), "Dinah," and "I'm Sitting on Top of the World."

Ted Snyder, the third partner, was born in Freeport, Illinois, on August 15, 1881. He began as a cafe pianist and opened his own publishing house in 1908. Later he merged with Irving Berlin's publishing house and retired to California to run a nightclub. His most famous songs were "The Sheik of Araby," which he wrote with Billy Rose in honor of Rudolph Valentino, and "Who's Sorry Now?"

Harry Von Tilzer wrote another comedy-type song with "Buy a Liberty Bond for the Baby," but the master of the comedy song was Irving Berlin. "They Were All Out of Step Except Jim," "Oh How I Hate to Get Up in the Morning," and "I'm Gonna Pin My Medal on the Girl I Left Behind" all came from Berlin's primary musical contribution to the war effort, the show *Yip Yip Yaphank*. Berlin's music was parodied by some of his competitors—for example, the song "When Alexander Takes His Ragtime Band to France," written by Cliff Hess and Edgar Leslie in 1918. The lyrics ran as follows:

> When Alexander takes his ragtime band to France,
> He'll capture every Hun, and take them one by one.
> Those ragtime tunes will put the Germans in a trance;
> They'll throw their guns away, Hip Hooray,
> and start right in to dance.
>
> They'll get so excited they'll come over the top,
> Two step back to Berlin with a skip and a hop.
> Old Hindenburg will know he has no chance,
> ("I haff nein Chaaance!")
> When Alexander takes his ragtime band to France.[28]

Together with E. Ray Goetz, Irving Berlin's brother-in-law, Leslie also wrote one of the most popular songs of the war years, "For Me and My Gal."

Leo Feist was the chief publisher of war songs. When the war was almost over, he began to look for another enemy to replace the Kaiser and the Germans. He chose the so-called enemy within the country. Feist songs encouraged citizens to "Knock the bull out of the Bolsheviki. With anarchy and bloodshed, our freedom's at stake, so let's wipe out each cause of it and trample on the snake."

Feist was not the only composer-publisher planning for the aftermath of the war. Jack Yellen and George Meyer wrote a series of songs dedicated to the return of "the boys." "Everytime he looks at me, he makes me feel so unnecessary. Oh, just think of it Clarice, he spent two months in Paris, and Oh! Oh! Johnny's in town." It soon became clear that the public wanted no more war songs or righteous morality songs; the twenties were coming and with them the "normalcy" of Warren Harding. But not before Billy Rose wrote a stirring epitaph to the returning soldiers.

Rose was born William Rosenberg, on the Lower East Side of New York, on September 6, 1899.[29] He began his career as a stenographer, becoming chief of the stenographic department of the War Industries Board. His first song, "Barney Google" (with Con Conrad), was an enormous hit, allowing him to produce and write for others as well as himself. His songs included "That Old Gang of Mine," "It's Only a Paper Moon," "Me and My Shadow," which he supposedly wrote with Al Jolson (in truth Jolson got credit because he had successfully plugged the song and it was a legal way to pay him off), and "I Found a Million Dollar Baby in a Five and Ten Cent Store." After becoming a producer, critic, and newspaper columnist, Rose went into the nightclub business. He died in 1966.

It is fitting to conclude the discussion of World War I and its music with Rose's lyrics. His songs sounded the death knell for the one-finger composers of early Tin Pan Alley. Soon they were replaced by more creative composers and lyricists who were better versed in classical formal music and words. It was not a coincidence that Romberg, Kern, Gershwin, and Rodgers were thorough musicians as well as tune men.[30] Their time was to come.

> There's a grave near the White House
> Where the unknown soldier lies,

And the flowers there are sprinkled
With the tears of mothers' eyes.

I stood there not so long ago
With roses for the grave
When suddenly I thought I heard
A voice speak from the grave.

"I am the Unknown Soldier,"
The spirit voice began,
"And I think I've got a right
To ask some questions, man to man.

"Are my buddies taken care of?
Was their victory so sweet?
Is that big reward you promised
Selling pencils in the street?

"And that baby that sang
'Hello Central, Give Me No Man's Land,'
Can they replace her daddy
With a military band?

"I wonder if the profiteers
Have satisfied their greed?
I wonder if the soldier's mother
Ever is in need.

"I wonder if the kings
Who planned it all are satisfied?
They played their game of checkers
And eleven million died!

"I am the Unknown Soldier
And maybe I died in vain,
But if I were alive and my country called
I'D DO IT ALL OVER AGAIN!"[31]

Harold Rome's *Pins and Needles*

Courtesy of International Ladies Garment Workers' Union

5

BETWEEN THE WARS

The war to end all wars was over and Americans wanted no more songs that would depress them or remind them of the years they had just suffered through. The warmth, sentimentality, and remembrance of things past of the prewar years suddenly became a mad desire to do anything, absolutely anything, that was new. To live for today was the theme of the decade known as the "roaring twenties." Morality, at least the morality that had been the norm in the first decade of the twentieth century, was gone, and in its place came the flappers and the so-called flaming youth. Love was free, and as the greatest of the non-Jewish composer-lyricists, Cole Porter, said in 1934, "Anything Goes." Hedonism was the way; fads came and went; there seemed to be no end to the prosperity people were enjoying. Movies became an entertainment norm, and film stars became the gods and goddesses of the day.

With all these drastic changes, Tin Pan Alley, as always, also changed. The first big change was the introduction of "jazz." This was not an immediate or overnight phenomenon, any more than ragtime had been; rather, jazz gradually substituted for ragtime, merely carrying the distortions of ragtime a little bit further.[1] The man who came to personify jazz was George Gershwin. His contributions made jazz a popular music form with serious classical underpinnings. By 1922 Gershwin was recognized as a musical and jazz genius.

Gershwin's life story appears in Chapter 12, but one incident is worthy of mention here. On November 1, 1923, at a concert in the Aeolian Hall in New York, concert singer Eva Gauthier performed a concert of classical music by Bellini, Byrd, Purcell, and some more modern composers, such as Hindemith and Schoenberg. She also included music by some modern American masters of popular song, including Irving Berlin and Jerome Kern, as well as three songs by George Gershwin, accompanied by Gershwin himself. Deems Taylor, reviewing the concert in the *New York World*, said, "The jazz numbers stood up amazingly well, not only as entertainment but as music. . . . Young Mr. Gershwin began to do mysterious and fascinating rhythmic and contrapuntal stunts with the accompaniment."[2]

Gershwin continued writing jazz for the theatre with his 1922 *George White Scandals*. Included in this score was a black opera entitled *Blue Monday*. The opera never appeared after the first night, because White feared it was too depressing for the audience, but the seeds were planted for Gershwin's masterpiece, *Porgy and Bess*.

The beginnings of jazz were not the only changes in the music industry with the onset of the 1920's. The music world was spreading out, and a geographic place called Tin Pan Alley no longer existed. Just as the Witmarks had moved their quarters when things became too crowded, so the other music publishers spread out, going into the higher-numbered streets around Broadway. The theatre district was moving into the neighborhood it inhabits today, between 42nd and 50th Streets, and with it came the publishing houses. Irving Berlin, who had just opened his own publishing firm after splitting up with Waterson and Snyder in 1919, transferred his offices to the Strand Building in the West 40's. Remick's and Feist's moved to West 40th Street, Harms was on West 45th, and Charles K. Harris moved to West 47th. Many of the smaller publishers found space in the Brill Building, 1619 Broadway.

Why the move to follow the theatres? It is an easy question to answer. By the middle 1920's, the Broadway show had become the prime vehicle for Tin Pan Alley songs. Vaudeville was in its last few years, totally disappearing by the early 1930's, and even the revue was showing signs of change, as was noted in the previous chapter.[3] If a song could be interpolated into a hit show, it too would become a hit; if a composer had the good fortune to write a hit show, the sheet music sales would be guaranteed. Oftentimes, though, the reverse was true. A popular song could save an otherwise doomed Broadway show.

Several songwriters made their debuts in the early years of the 1920's; like so many before them, each had learned the trade by working in the publishing business. Sammy Fain, born in New York on June 17, 1902, began as a song plugger and pianist for the Jack Mills publishing house. Soon afterwards he toured the vaudeville circuit and went into radio entertaining. His first song, written in 1925, was "Nobody Knows What a Red-Headed Mama Can Do."

In 1927 Fain met Irving Kahal, who had been born in Houtzdale, Pennsylvania, on March 5, 1903. Kahal began songwriting at the same age as Fain, eighteen. When they met, Kahal was a vaudeville singer performing with the Gus Edwards Minstrels. Together Kahal and Fain wrote several standards, including "Let a Smile Be Your Umbrella," "Wedding Bells Are Breaking Up That Old Gang of Mine," and "I'll Be Seeing You." Together they also wrote one of the most successful musical comedies of the 1930's, *Hellzapoppin*, with Olsen and Johnson. Their other shows included *Sons O'Fun* and *Boys and Girls Together*.

Con Conrad was born on New York's Lower East Side as Konrad A. Dobert on June 18, 1891. By age sixteen Conrad was a seasoned vaudeville performer, but he left the footlights for the dingier offices of Tin Pan Alley. A natural piano player, he entertained on the side at silent movie houses. His first song, "Down in New Orleans," was interpolated into the *Ziegfeld Follies of 1912*. After its success, he formed a publishing company with Sam Waterson (later Irving Berlin's partner).

In 1920, Conrad enjoyed a major success with the publication of "Margie," named for Eddie Cantor's daughter. Cantor continued Jolson's method of interpolating songs into shows, using "Margie" in a Winter Garden concert. Other Conrad hits included "Ma, He's Makin' Eyes at Me," "Barney Google" (written with Billy Rose), and "Memory Lane."

The 1920's was a time of almost hysterical enjoyment and silliness; the music reflected these feelings. Gus Kahn wrote of this in his "Ain't We Got Fun" and "Carolina in the Morning," and so did Lewis and Young in "I'm Sitting on Top of the World," made famous by Al Jolson. It was a difficult time for the less flexible writers on Tin Pan Alley, for the public wanted certain quite specific types of songs.[4] Nonsense songs, songs about places exotic or otherwise, even domestic political issues were the subjects of the day. The comic strip "Barney Google" inspired two great songs; one, already mentioned, was "Barney Google," with music by Sammy Fain and lyrics by Billy Rose. Among other Rose hits were "Come On, Spark Plug" (Barney Google's horse) and "That Old Gang Of Mine," both written in 1923.

Political songs came back into popularity as they had been in the late nineteenth century. In 1920 Harry Von Tilzer and William Jerome wrote "If I Meet the Guy Who Made This Country Dry," and Irving Berlin composed "I'll See You in Cuba," both of which dealt with the nation's animosity toward Prohibition. Imagine the surprise and anger of the returning troops when they found that the wine they had become accustomed to in Europe was no longer available in the United States. Canada and Cuba became very popular places! Gus Kahn wrote very movingly about the returning boys, as well as those who did not return, in "My Buddy." The bitterness and sorrow felt by many in this country helped propel the song to national prominence.

Enrico Caruso's death in 1921 fostered a real triumph of bathos when "They Needed a Songbird in Heaven, So God Took Caruso Away" was written by the non-Jewish team of George Walter Brown, George A. Little, and Jack Stanley. As in Charles K. Harris's day, crying was still a popular emotion.[5] Irving Berlin fostered emotional songs, as always, when he wrote in 1921, "All By Myself" and "Say It With Music." Rodgers and Hart wrote of love in "Poor Little Ritz Girl," as did Vincent Youmans and a young man known as Arthur Francis with "Two Little Girls in Blue." Arthur Francis had a more famous name when he wasn't writing lyrics—Ira Gershwin.

By far the most famous and outlandish song of the 1920's was "Yes, We Have No Bananas." The lyrics were written in 1923 by Irving Cohen and Frank Silver, who apparently took the title from a conversation they overheard between a Greek fruit seller and a customer. However, another story was spread claiming that "yes, we have no bananas" was a password used in the Philippines during the Spanish-American War! Still another "midrash" has the title coming from a comic strip character in the newspaper.

As to the music, we know the answer. "Yes, We Have No Bananas" was the most successful song ever written by a committee! The entire staff of the Shapiro and Bernstein publishing firm got together to write it as a joke. These men included Hanley and McDonald, who had written "Indiana" and "Trail of the Lonesome Pine," Lew Brown, who later joined with DeSylva and Henderson to write "The Best Things in Life Are Free" and "Button Up Your Overcoat," and finally Shapiro and Bernstein themselves.

The song the "committee" came up with contained snippets of various other songs contributed by the several composers, including the "Hallelujah Chorus" from Handel's *Messiah*, "My Bonnie Lies Over the Ocean," "An Old-Fashioned Garden," "The Bohemian Girl," "I Dreamt That I Dwelt in Marble Halls," and finally "Aunt Dinah's Quilting Party." It was introduced in a restaurant but did not become a hit until Eddie Cantor interpolated it into one of his shows. The audience reaction was terrific, and the song became a permanent addition to Cantor's repertory.

For Jews, the 1920's were a good time to be in the music business, at least as far as working on Tin Pan Alley was concerned, but out on the road, things were much more difficult. Even so great a theatre personage as George M. Cohan, the great "Yankee Doodle Boy" and Irish Catholic, was barred from a hotel because he was presumed to be Jewish.[6] The management of New York City's Claridge Hotel offered a five-dollar bill to any Jew who would willingly leave after registering. This action caused the hotel's closing. In addition to such instances of actual discrimination, the image of the Jew in the songs of the day was not terribly flattering. Jews were presented as money-grubbing, hand-rubbing old men who wore crepe hair and ran pawn shops. Sadly, the Jews of Tin Pan Alley helped to perpetuate this stereotype. A popular song mentioned earlier, "At the Yiddishe Society Ball," typified the rather anti-Jewish stereotypes of the period. The lyric told of Abie Stein ordering some wine when he knows he is broke, and when the waiter brings it, Stein says, "Can't you take a joke?" Louie Fink, who thinks he's smart, says, "Bring me some more a la carte," and all the guests go around the hall "trottin' for nothing."[7]

But the 1920's also saw some big changes on Tin Pan Alley, for a new form of entertainment had begun sweeping the country, the movies. Soon movie companies began purchasing the great publishing houses; for example, Warner Brothers purchased Remick and Company, obtaining all the songs Remick had published, and all the staff composers as well. Harry Warren and Al Dubin, who went along in the deal, helped to create several of Warner's greatest movie musicals with such songs as "42nd Street" and "I Only Have Eyes for You."

At the same time that Tin Pan Alley was spreading into New York's theatre district, much of the Alley's talent was moving out west to California. By the end of the 1920's, with the advent of the "talkies," the movie industry began to undergo a revolutionary transformation that greatly increased the role of popular music in film-making.[8] Tin Pan Alley had been important to the movies before then, however, for silent films had needed the services of tunesmiths who could turn out the mood music and melodic underscoring needed to take up the attention of audiences in the absence of sound tracks. Even so great a talent as Victor Herbert provided music for the "flickers." At times the music was more memorable than the movie itself. One such example was Herbert's score for D. W. Griffith's sequel to his masterpiece *Birth of a Nation*, entitled *The Fall of a Nation*. A critic for *Musical America* wrote, "It is not only synchronized with the picture but its rhythms are in absolute accord with the tempo of the action. Mr. Herbert's stimulating score clearly indicated the marked advance that music is making in the domain of photoplay and should prove encouraging to composers who have not yet tried their hand at this type of work."[9]

Song pluggers from Tin Pan Alley recognized that the movies represented an as yet untried field for selling their songs. Song slides, amateur nights, anything which could sell songs was attempted. "Ramona," the most successful song from a movie in the twenties, was written by L. Wolfe Gilbert in 1927. In the film of the same name, it was sung by Dolores Del Rio, the star and title character, accompanied by Paul Whiteman's orchestra. The recording of "Ramona" sold over 2 million discs. With this song came changes that altered the popular music industry forever.

Al Jolson was the first performer to benefit from the screen's conversion to sound. His famous movie *The Jazz Singer*, a film version of the Broadway play by Samson Raphaelson, was the first talkie. The story is by now famous. A young man gives up his father's dream that he become a synagogue cantor and instead chooses a career as a jazz singer. On the evening of Yom Kippur, when the elderly father is lying on his deathbed, the wayward son returns to chant Kol Nidrei. *The Jazz Singer* was an enormous success and proved beyond doubt that sound films were to be a permanent entertainment feature. It grossed over $3 million, an unheard-of sum in those days.

Within two years, in 1929, came the first composer and lyricist team who wrote just for the movies. Irving Thalberg, the director of production at Metro-Goldwyn-Mayer, decided to have original music for his film *The Broadway Melody*. To write the lyrics, he chose Arthur Freed.

Freed was born Arthur Grossman in Charleston, South Carolina, on September 9, 1894. He began his education at one of America's best private schools, the Exeter Academy in New Hampshire. After working as a piano demonstrator for a Chicago music house, he became a songwriter. This resulted in his association with the Gus Edwards revues and the Marx Brothers, who were touring the country in a vaudeville show accompanied by their mother, Minnie.

With Louis Silver, Freed wrote songs and shows for New York restaurants. After World War I Freed and Silver went to Seattle and then to Los Angeles, where they managed a theatre. It was in this position that Freed began writing his own material for shows which he himself produced. He went on to become a lyricist, author, and motion picture producer of great fame and repute. His name generally meant a class production with great attention to style.[10] His song lyrics, such as "You Were Meant for Me," "Singing in the Rain," and "You Are My Lucky Star," exhibited the same characteristics. Eventually Freed became the producer directly in charge of all MGM movie musicals.[11]

Sigmund Romberg, the Gershwins, Rodgers and Hart, Jerome Kern, even Maurice Ravel, went to Hollywood to write for the movies. Gus Kahn, Howard Dietz, and Leo Robin also moved from the stage to the screen. By 1929, even the king of Tin Pan Alley, Irving Berlin, had traveled westward. His influence was all-encompassing; he contributed several of the greatest hits ever recorded for films, including "Cheek to Cheek," "I've Got My Love to Keep Me Warm," "White Christmas," "The Easter Parade," and "The Night Is Filled With Music." His talent was recognized in the first movie to feature the music of only one composer, *Alexander's Ragtime Band*. All the great Berlin hits from the stage were included, which allowed an entirely new group of people to hear and enjoy them.

George and Ira Gershwin went to Hollywood in 1930 but soon returned to New York. They went back two years later. At the insistence of their old friend Fred Astaire, they were hired to write several musicals. The songs for these movies rank among the finest written by the pair: "They Can't Take That Away from Me," "Let's Call the Whole Thing Off," "A Foggy Day in London Town," "Love Walked Right In," and lastly, "Our Love Is Here to Stay." George Gershwin died while working on his fourth movie.

A composer who wrote primarily for the movies was Harold Arlen. Born in Buffalo, New York, on February 15, 1905, Arlen, whose original name was Hyman Arluck, was the son of a cantor. He reached the top of the songwriting business with movies like *The Wizard of Oz* and *Cabin in the Sky* and stage musicals like *Bloomer Girl* and *St. Louis Woman*.

Arlen's partner and lyricist, E. Y. "Yip" Harburg, was equally successful in Hollywood and on Broadway. Harburg was born in New York City on April 8, 1898, and was educated in the public school system. After graduating college he wrote poetry for popular magazines and edited the magazine of New York's City College. Subsequently, he worked in South America as an agent for a firm that went bankrupt soon after his arrival. Harburg held down several more jobs in South America and in 1921 returned to the United States, where he opened an electrical supply company. When his business failed during the depression, he turned to songwriting. He said later, "I had my fill of this dreamy abstract thing called business and I decided to face reality by writing lyrics."[12]

Write lyrics Harburg certainly did. First, for the stage, he wrote several revues and shows, including *Finian's Rainbow*, *Bloomer Girl*, *Life Begins at 8:40*, and *Flahooley*. His greatest success was in the movies, where he wrote the lyrics and/or screenplays for *The Wizard of Oz*, *Cabin in the Sky*, and *Gold Diggers of 1936*. Among his numerous great song hits were "April in Paris," "Brother, Can You Spare a Dime?" "Old Devil Moon," and "How Are Things in Glocca Morra?" His career also encompassed stage directing and film producing.

It should not be thought that the growth of the movies in the twenties caused the Broadway musical to die. Nothing could be further from the truth. In 1924 and 1925 alone there were forty-six musicals on Broadway, each of them a variation on the "gals and gags" theme of burlesque and the revue. The 1920's, in fact, was the golden age of Broadway. The revue, which reached maturity through the efforts of Florenz Ziegfeld, enjoyed its full glory, although the *Ziegfeld Follies* of the 1920's were not as bright as the earlier versions, and competition set in. Along with the Shuberts came other revue-type shows, most notably George White's *Scandals of 1919*. It was White who gave George Gershwin his start, allowing him to write the *Scandals* of 1920 through 1924. Among the more than forty songs in these shows were two of Gershwin's greatest: "I'll Build a Stairway to Paradise" and "Somebody Loves Me."

Gershwin left the *George White Scandals* in 1924 to write musical comedy and more serious music, and he was replaced by the team of De Sylva, Brown, and Henderson. Lew Brown, born in Odessa, Russia, on December 10, 1893, came to New York with his family at age five. He was educated in the New York public schools and for fun wrote parodies of popular songs. His first hit as a songwriter came in 1912 with "I'm the Loneliest Gal in

Town." The music was by Albert Von Tilzer. After several years with Von Tilzer, Brown met Ray Henderson, and the two men went into partnership in publishing as well as songwriting. Buddy De Sylva was the third member of the team. After a period of success in the publishing business they sold their firm and left for Hollywood. Among their top songs were "Life Is Just a Bowl of Cherries," "The Best Things in Life Are Free," "Don't Sit Under the Apple Tree," and "You're the Cream in My Coffee."

Irving Berlin continued to have a great influence on the stage musicals of the period. His *Music Box Revue* was housed in an entirely new theatre that he and Sam H. Harris built especially for it. All the songs for the first show in 1921 were written by Berlin, and they were brilliantly received. The most outstanding was "Say It With Music." Three editions of the *Revue* followed, with such songs as "What'll I Do" and "All Alone."

The most innovative and witty musical revue of the pre-1940 years was *As Thousands Cheer* in 1933, with book by Berlin and Moss Hart. The story line was based on the pages of a newspaper, with news stories and features represented in song. Berlin wrote "The Easter Parade," "Heat Wave," and "Supper Time" for this show. The characters included Franklin D. Roosevelt, Gandhi, Douglas Fairbanks, and John D. Rockefeller, Sr.

Very interestingly, the revue saw another change in the usual ethnic makeup. In 1928, Dorothy Fields and Jimmy McHugh wrote the songs for an all-black revue entitled *Blackbirds of 1928*. Among the songs in this show were "Doin' the New Low Down," "I Can't Give You Anything But Love, Baby," and "Diga, Diga Doo."

Dorothy Fields, born in Allenhurst, New Jersey, on July 15, 1905, was the daughter of Lew Fields, of Weber and Fields fame, as well as the sister of Joseph and Herbert Fields, who became famous as librettists for musicals. She began her professional career as an art teacher in a New York high school, and also wrote poetry for magazines, but was directed into songwriting by composer J. Fred Coots.

Although Fields's first efforts were, by her own admission, terrible, she did not lose faith and continued her work. She met her first partner, Jimmy McHugh, while working for the Mills publishing company. When their initial assignment proved a failure, they were given another, to write the *Blackbirds* show mentioned above. Although the show was not an immediate hit with the critics, Fields and McHugh waived their royalties to help it continue. Only after the institution of a Thursday midnight show did the revue catch on and become the biggest hit of the season. "I Can't Give You Anything But Love" went on to sell 3 million copies of sheet music.

Dorothy Fields became famous as a librettist, book writer, and lyricist. She collaborated with some of the most famous names in Broadway history, among them Jerome Kern, Sigmund Romberg, Harold Arlen, Arthur Schwartz, Burton Lane, and Cy Coleman. Her songs included "On the Sunny Side of the Street," "I'm in the Mood for Love," "A Fine Romance," and "The Way You Look Tonight."

Always "au courant," as she liked to describe herself, Fields wrote hit shows in every decade from the 1920's through the 1970's, all in the style of the day. Undoubtedly her greatest achievement was the book and libretto she and her brother wrote for Irving Berlin's *Annie Get Your Gun*. Though the show is thirty-five years old, it is still regarded as the quintessence of the Broadway musical. Also active in civic and Jewish philanthropies,[13] Fields never retired, and she died while in the midst of writing a new set of lyrics for a show to follow her last hit, *Seesaw*. She was far and away the most famous woman to write for the Broadway musical or for Tin Pan Alley.

Appropriately, one of Dorothy Fields's collaborators began his career very soon after she did. Arthur Schwartz was a successful lawyer and author before he decided to contribute to a new kind of revue which made its debut in 1922–23. Called the *Grand Street Follies*, it was a slimmed-down show with little or no scenery or fancy costumes, relying instead on wit and satire. The show was advertised as "A Lowbrow Show for Highbrow Morons." Far from that, it was so successful that it moved from off-Broadway to a regular theatre and ran through several different "editions."

Schwartz was born on November 25, 1900, in Brooklyn,

where he lived most of his early life. He attended Brooklyn public schools and received both his B.A. and his law degree from New York University. Before becoming a lawyer, Schwartz taught English literature at a high school and wrote songs for NYU. From 1924, when as a Phi Beta Kappa he was accepted into the bar, until 1928, Schwartz was a fairly successful lawyer. In 1928 he began writing songs professionally. He was also a librettist and producer of movies and plays. Among his shows were *The Band Wagon, Stars in Your Eyes, A Tree Grows in Brooklyn,* and *Inside U.S.A.,* which he also produced. His songs were equally numerous: "Dancing in the Dark," "You and the Night and the Music," "I Guess I'll Have to Change My Plan," and "Something to Remember You By."

Schwartz's talents were seen in many avenues; but more than his own ability, he fostered a type of show which affected all of Broadway. The big musical revues, with enormous sets, costumes, and budgets, were on the way out. In their place came smaller, more intimate shows like those written by Schwartz. For instance, a group of young members of the Theatre Guild collectively wrote the *Garrick Gaieties of 1925.* Among the songs and skits were parodies of Broadway plays and of prominent actors and actresses. Herbert Fields served as the choreographer, and two of the new contributors who enjoyed hearing their first songs on Broadway were Richard Rodgers and Lorenz Hart. "Manhattan" and "Mountain Greenery," the great Rodgers and Hart hits of the first two *Garrick* shows, were a taste of the brilliant theatre songs this team was to produce. The team of Rodgers and Hart set the pace for Broadway from that day until fifteen years later when they split up.

The *Little Shows* were sophisticated small revues much like Gus Edwards's earlier *School Days.* They helped introduce Fred Allen, Libby Holman, and several other unknowns to the world of Broadway by highlighting their special talents. The experienced performer of the troupe was Clifton Webb. All of the sketches and songs were written by Howard Dietz, who was later to achieve fame as Arthur Schwartz's lyricist.

Dietz was born in New York on September 8, 1896. He went to public school and then to Columbia University, where his classmates included Oscar Hammerstein II and Lorenz Hart. Dietz became a contributor and editor of the Columbia news-paper and also wrote for several local New York papers. After winning a $500 prize, Dietz went into the advertising business. In 1924 he became advertising director and promotion manager for MGM, where he stayed for thirty years, eventually becoming vice-president. All during these years he wrote lyrics, first with Jerome Kern, and most successfully with Arthur Schwartz. His songs included "Body and Soul," "Dancing in the Dark," and "Louisiana Hayride." He is also remembered for his English lyrics to the Strauss operetta *Die Fledermaus*, the standard translation in use even today.

Vernon Duke, whose original name was Vladimir Dukelsky, was a unique man who combined classical training with Tin Pan Alley. Born in Pskoff, Russia, on October 10, 1903, Duke studied composition and eventually entered the Kiev Conservatory of Music. As a result of the Russian Revolution, he left Russia in 1920 and went into classical music professionally. He began in Constantinople at the YMCA, where he came across the music to "Swanee" by George Gershwin and Irving Caesar. He was so interested that upon his arrival in New York, he called Gershwin, who then became his mentor. Gershwin even helped Dukelsky to anglicize his name to Vernon Duke. By 1932 Duke had written his most famous song, "April in Paris," with lyricist E. Y. Harburg. His other great songs include "Autumn in New York," "Taking a Chance on Love," and "Cabin in the Sky." His numerous classical compositions, which he wrote under the name Vladimir Dukelsky, ranged from concerti to symphonies, with music for the piano, cello, flute, and bassoon.

The 1920's and 1930's saw musicals by the men who today are viewed as the masters: Jerome Kern, Oscar Hammerstein, George and Ira Gershwin, Richard Rodgers, Lorenz Hart, Lew Brown, Irving Berlin, and Kurt Weill. Weill was born in Dessau, Germany, on March 2, 1900, and received a thorough education in classical music both privately and at the Berlin College for Music. His major musical activity was writing serious operas. Most of them were well received by the critics. They ranged in subject matter and style from a surrealistic opera, *The Protago-*

nist, to *The Rise and Fall of the City of Mahagonny*, which dealt with a fictional town in Alabama run by three ex-convicts as a socialist state in which everything was either pardonable or permissible.

The Threepenny Opera, patterned on the original opera by John Gay, and written with Bertold Brecht, was Weill's greatest success. It took Germany by storm, and by 1929, a year after its premiere, it had been performed over four thousand times in one hundred different theatres around the country. Within five years it has been translated into eighteen languages and was exported to the United States and around the world. *The Threepenny Opera* enjoyed its greatest success in America. Following its 1954 revival, the song "Mack the Knife" became a hit-parade success, selling over 3 million records.[14]

In 1935, two years after the Nazis gained power, Weill was forced to leave Germany. After a short stay in Paris, he came to the United States, where he wrote the music for Franz Werfel's tribute to Jewish history, *The Eternal Road*. This show did not appear on Broadway until two years later. In the interim, another Weill production, the anti-war musical *Johnny Johnson*, was presented. All-American in style, it exhibited Weill's ability to change his music to suit the public taste. By 1938, Weill was writing truly American musicals with patriotic settings. *Knickerbocker Holiday* was typical of his work in this vein. Using New Amsterdam of the 1600's as the setting, Weill wrote about fascism as he saw it developing in Europe. His famous "September Song" came from the score of *Knickerbocker Holiday*.

With George Gershwin, Weill is held in higher critical esteem than any other American composer.[15] His death in 1950 was a great blow because he was just finding an American idiom. George Gershwin was his close friend and Ira was his best lyricist. Their feelings about liberty and freedom profoundly affected Weill's work. In "How Can You Tell an American," written for *Knickerbocker Holiday*, Weill identified what he regarded as the essence of true Americanism: loving and supporting liberty. Weill made that love his theme.

Often, what makes a man great in the eyes of his peers is his ability to look into the future. Weill certainly had that ability, for he predicted the civil and social unrest of the 1930's several years before it occurred. On October 29, 1929, "Black Thursday," Wall Street "laid an egg," as *Variety* put it. By 1931, nearly 30,000 businesses had folded, 2,500 banks had failed, and 10 million people were out of work. Depression was everywhere, and the songs of Tin Pan Alley recognized the emotions and fears of the masses. Money was something no one had, so all of a sudden there was a spate of songs promising that money wasn't needed for love. "I Found a Million Dollar Baby in a Five and Ten Cent Store," by Mort Dixon, Billy Rose, and Harry Warren, was typical. Rodgers and Hart wrote "I've Got Five Dollars," with "debts beyond endurance" and coats and collars "which moths adore." The most representative song of the depression era was Harburg's "Brother, Can You Spare a Dime?" This song, and many like it, lamented the depths to which America had sunk, but others were written to cheer up the populace. "Happy Days Are Here Again" is the best example; it was used as Franklin Roosevelt's theme song, later by Harry Truman, then by John F. Kennedy, and finally it became a Democratic Party anthem. Written by Jack Yellen and Milton Ager, it was introduced on the evening of Black Thursday and became an almost "hysterical" hit; everyone in the room needed cheering up. In a similar vein was "On the Sunny Side of the Street," written by Dorothy Fields and Jimmy McHugh (1930).

As mentioned, Kurt Weill was a stern social critic. His songs were the precursors of two very important revues in the history of American theatre. The first of these shows was entitled *Pins and Needles*. Originality and fresh spirit were combined in a unique way; everyone in the cast was a member of the International Ladies Garment Workers, and naturally the show was a union production. With a leftist point of view, its desire was to "Sing me a song with social significance, all other songs are taboo."

The composer and lyricist for the show, Harold Rome, was new to Broadway. Born in Hartfort, Connecticut, on May 27, 1908, he was educated in Hartford, later going on to Yale University, where he received a degree in arts and architecture. While still a student, Rome played with the Yale Orchestra and toured Europe with the group. He also played piano with jazz bands in an attempt to earn extra money. Following his graduation, he went to New York. He accepted a nonpaying job in architecture in order to get some experience and earned his living by writing popular songs and playing piano in bars. For three summers he was musical director of Green Mansions, an adult camp in the Adirondacks, where he was required to write three complete musicals each summer. All told, Rome composed ninety songs for these various camp shows.

Rome's camp-show collaborator was Charles Friedman. When Friedman was commissioned to write a musical revue for the ILGWU, he asked Rome to compose the songs, and this brought about Rome's introduction to the professional theatre. *Pins and Needles* had been intended as a show for union members and their friends, but it was so well received by critics and public alike that it continued for 1,108 performances, one of the longest runs in Broadway history to that time. In order to keep the "social significance" updated, new material was introduced every few weeks. Rome continued to write for left-leaning musical revues and later wrote several complete Broadway shows, including *Destry Rides Again*, *Wish You Were Here*, and most successfully, *Fanny*.

Rome's success fostered the second political-satire revue mentioned earlier. This one was far more politically oriented. The composer-lyricist was Marc Blitzstein, born in Philadelphia, Pennsylvania, on March 2, 1905. Blitzstein was educated at the University of Pennsylvania and the Curtis Institute of Music, and enjoyed several years of study under the best music teachers Europe had to offer, among them Nadia Boulanger and Arnold Schoenberg. Upon his return to America, he was a soloist with the Philadelphia Symphony Orchestra and soon became involved in the popular music business. He also lectured at Vassar, Columbia, the Brooklyn Institute for the Arts, and the New School for Social Research.

Blitzstein's popular-music orientation was strictly in the socialist tradition, for he wrote about the masses getting trampled on, and the class struggle in America. His crowning achievement in the musical area, clearly reflecting the influence of Kurt Weill in its songs and lyrics, was *The Cradle Will Rock*, presented on June 15, 1937. The plot, which takes place in a night court, sets steel workers against employers. The capitalist, Mr. Mister, who controls the entire community, including the school, the newspaper, the church, and the court, has formed a Liberty Union to break the union started by the workers, but he fails and the workers are victorious.

The story of the show's production is quite interesting in its own right. Originally written in 1936, *The Cradle Will Rock* was accepted for production by the WPA–Federal Theatre, whose producer was John Houseman and whose director was Orson Welles. Several civic groups, angered by the play's anti-capitalist, anti-government libretto, brought about the closing of the Federal Theatre on opening night. The audience were already in their seats when the closing was announced. While the cast attempted to entertain them, the producer frantically searched for a new place in which to present the play The nearby Venice Theatre was procured, and cast and audience went there. As it was impossible to move the costumes, sets, and orchestra to the new theatre, Blitzstein and his cast proceeded to do the show without them, with Blitzstein at the piano explaining the scenes as they came along. Judged by the reviews, this unique presentation enhanced rather than detracted from the show's effect. Brooks Atkinson wrote, "*The Cradle Will Rock* is the most versatile artistic triumph of the politically insurgent theatre."[16] In addition to being the theatrical event of the season, it proved to be a great financial success.

The popular songs of the depression era reflected the split in society. On the one hand there were the politically conscious songs, for the decade of the 1930's was largely spent in recovering from the excesses of the previous decade. On the other hand, the depression lay heavily on people's minds and pop-music became less bouncy and original. More often than not, the arranger became the creative force in the Tin Pan Alley world. Composers left it to the arrangers to create new and jazzy treatments of fairly pedestrian songs.[17] While the Hollywood movies were being brightened by the musicals of Busby Berkeley, the musical theatre tackled subjects of current concern. George and Ira Gershwin indicted World War I profiteering in their musical *Strike Up the Band*. The show was so politically potent that it had to be rewritten in a less virulent manner. Even Irving Berlin dealt with serious issues when he condemned police corruption in *Face the Music*.[18]

In the 1930's, radio changed the music business greatly. Songs could be played on the air and thus did not have to be plugged in individual theatres or shows to gain popularity. Moreover, sheet music sales were no longer the marker that made a song a hit. Record sales and radio were the key factors. In line with these developments the publisher-producers invented the "Hit Parade," a radio program that played various recordings and then rated them by sales and popularity.

By 1935, Tin Pan Alley had been so thoroughly infiltrated by the new breed of theatre composers that most of the top twenty songs of the year were written by Kern, Rodgers and Hart, Gershwin, Cole Porter, Irving Berlin, Harburg and Arlen, Vernon Duke, and Howard Dietz. The top two songs of the year were Kern's "Lovely to Look At" and "I Won't Dance," with Gershwin's "Soon" coming third. The next year Irving Caesar's "Is It True What They Say About Dixie" headed the list, continuing the tradition of songs about the South written by Jews who had never been there![19]

The year 1938 saw an event that was quite interesting as far as Jews were concerned. The most popular song of the year, and almost of the decade, had originally come from the pen of Sholom Secunda and Joe Jacobs, two men who wrote for the Yiddish theatre. The song was recorded on November 24, 1937, by Patti, Maxine, and Laverne Andrews—its name, "Bei Mir Bist Du Schoen."

Two different stories are told about the origin of this song. One has it that the agent Lou Levy, thinking that an all-Yiddish song sung by three gentile girls would be an amusing hit in New York City, brought the song to the attention of the Andrews Sisters. Supposedly they cut the demonstration record in Yiddish, but Jack Kapp, the president of Decca Records, insisted that English words would have to be used.

Another story is told by Sammy Cahn, the creator-lyricist of the English version (along with Saul Chaplin), in his autobiography, *I Should Care*. Cahn says that he heard two black performers singing the song in Yiddish at the Apollo Theatre in Harlem. Though the audience couldn't understand a single word, they seemed to enjoy the song. Cahn was impressed, so he went out and bought the sheet music. He aroused the interest of the Andrews Sisters, and they tried to convince Jack Kapp of Decca to let them record it. He agreed, but only if Cahn would translate the words into English.

The record earned $3,000,000 for Decca, and Cahn and Chaplin attempted to repeat the success with another Yiddish song, "Joseph, Joseph," by Nellie Casman and Samuel Steinberg. It became a second hit of the 1938 record year.

Sammy Cahn, originally Cohn, was born in New York on June 18, 1913. His parents helped in the founding of a synagogue upon their arrival from Galicia, and it was at this synagogue in New York that Sammy was Bar Mitzvah. As a boy he had been trained in the violin, and for light entertainment, as well to earn spending money, he organized his friends into a dance band. One of his friends was Saul Chaplin, with whom he began writing song lyrics.[20] Most active in the film industry, Cahn wrote such movie musical classics as *Anchors Aweigh*, *Three Cheers for the Boys*, and *Toast of New Orleans*. His stage musicals include *High Button Shoes* and *Look to the Lillies* (a flop). Cahn's list of songs is enormous, but among his best are "Three Coins in the Fountain," "Let It Rain, Let It Rain, Let It Rain," "Papa, Won't You Dance with Me," and "Be My Love."

As the 1930's drew to a close, and another major war in Europe became imminent, Americans turned inward, and patriotic songs came back into vogue. Harold Arlen and E. Y. Harburg wrote "God's Country" for the anti-war musical *Hooray for What!* Al Jacobs wrote the lyrics for a song that became an American standard, "This Is My Country," introduced by Fred Waring and his Pennsylvanians.

The song that led the way, as far as patriotism is concerned, belonged to Irving Berlin. It was originally written as the second-act closing for the World War I show *Yip Yip Yaphank*, but

Berlin cast it aside when he decided that having soldiers sing about their love for America as they marched through the audience on the way to war was simply gilding the lily.

In 1938 Kate Smith, who had decided to present a radio broadcast dealing with patriotism and her pride in being an American, approached Berlin for a suitable song. He remembered the one he had discarded two decades earlier. He gave Kate Smith the rights to the song without any payment, but stipulated that any profits it might accrue should be given to the Boy Scouts, the Girl Scouts, and the Campfire Girls. All told, the song earned them over half a million dollars.

Berlin's song became almost a second national anthem, so much so that on February 18, 1955, President Eisenhower honored Berlin with a gold metal engraved "GOD BLESS AMERICA." It is for that song as much as any other that Irving Berlin will be remembered.

PROGRAM

MEYER W. WEISGAL *and* CROSBY GAIGE

present

MAX REINHARDT'S PRODUCTION
of

THE ETERNAL ROAD

Play by
FRANZ WERFEL

Music by
KURT WEILL

Settings, Costumes and Lighting by
NORMAN BEL GEDDES

Production Supervisor
CHARLES ALAN

Dances and ensembles staged by
BENJAMIN ZEMACH

Associate Director
FRANCESCO von MENDELSSOHN

Musical Director
ISAAC VAN GROVE

Artistic Adviser
HARRY HORNER

Entire production conceived and directed by
MAX REINHARDT

(Program subject to change without notice)

PROLOGUE

A SYNAGOGUE

"This is a black night in Israel"

The Rabbi	Myron Taylor
The Adversary	Sam Jaffe
The Timid Soul	Mark Schweid
The Rich Man	Anthony Blair
The Estranged One	Harold Johnsrud
The Estranged One's Son	Sidney Lumet
President of the Congregation	David A. Leonard
First Pious Man	Robert Harrison
Second Pious Man	Edward Fisher
Third Pious Man	Baruch Lumet
Fourth Pious Man	Leslie Austen
Fifth Pious Man	Bennett Challis
Sixth Pious Man	Cassius C. Quimby
Seventh Pious Man	Harry Hammill
Eighth Pious Man	Hal Kingsley
Ninth Pious Man	Kurt Kasznar
Fanatic	Roger De Koven

Kurt Weill and Franz Werfel's *The Eternal Road*

Courtesy of Richard C. Norton, Jr.

PROGRAM Continued

Adversary's Follower .... Abner Biberman
Watchman .... David Kurlan

Elders .... {
Al Clifford
Charles Homer
Gustav Stryker
}

Women of the Congregation .... {
Edit Angold
Elizabeth Carpenter
Alberta Chauncey
Mildred Dunnock
Miriam Elias
Lea Wardell
}

Boys of the Congregation .... {
Nat L. Mintz
Dickie Van Patten
}

Jesse—A Young Man .... Herbert Rudley
The Alien Girl .... Eliebe Lynn

Synagogue Choir .... {
Antoinette Allen
Ruth Virginia Lewis
Eva Ortman
Angela Schopp
Eleanor Searle
Molly Taylor
Michael Bataeff
Albert Cazentre
Carroll Howes
Lucien Rutman
Harold Sternberg
Sam Sternberg
James Spivak
Sol Tisman
}

The Voice of God is sung by Ben Cutler

Part II

Henry Russell

6

HENRY RUSSELL

Henry Russell was probably the most popular songwriter in the British Isles during the first half of the nineteenth century. Without question, he was the most influential writer of American songs before Stephen Foster. In fact, Russell was the first songwriter to spend his formative years in America rather than come here after having made a reputation.

Russell was born in Sheerness, Kent, England, on December 24, 1812; he made his debut on the stage at the age of three and began piano lessons at the age of six. His ability and talent allowed him the opportunity to play in a children's opera company managed by the director of the Drury Lane Theatre in London, Robert W. Elliston. Russell recounted in his autobiography, *Cheer, Boys, Cheer,* that while in this production he was brought before King George IV, who took him on his knee and kissed him.[1]

Two major events in Russell's life were pivotal in his decision to go into the world of theatre and music. The first was his meeting with the great tragedian Edmund Kean when he was ten years old. Russell reported in his autobiography that Kean said, "My dear boy, you will never become either a great actor or great singer unless you learn to speak every word you utter distinctly and clearly. Unintelligibility and slovenliness in speech are the curse of the profession."[2]

Apparently Russell took Kean's words to heart, for he began taking speech and music lessons. In 1825, when his voice had changed, so that he was a baritone instead of a child soprano, he took off to Bologna to master Italian opera, which had just become the rage in England. There he studied with Vincenzo Bellini, the opera and bel canto composer, and also became acquainted with Donizetti and Rossini.

After a brief stay in Paris, where he met Meyerbeer, Russell returned to England. Though he was thoroughly versed in the musical style of Italian opera both as a singer and as a composer, earning a living proved more difficult than he had expected, and he decided that opportunities might be better in the New World. In the early 1830's he sailed for Canada. When his luck still did not improve, he moved on to Philadelphia, where he appeared in the opera *La Sonnambula* as the character Elvino. After this role ended he accepted a job as organist for the First Presbyterian Church in Rochester, New York. About two years later he was appointed "professor of music" at the Rochester Academy of Music. The title was honorary at most.

Russell remained at the church for eight years, and it was during his tenure there that the second of the pivotal events in his life took place. He heard a speech by the great orator and politician Henry Clay. Although not moved by Clay's ideas, he was impressed by Clay's ability to motivate and grip the audience. Russell later wrote, "That speech of Henry Clay affected me to a singular extent. It may sound a strange statement, but I don't think I should be talking extravagantly, if I declare that the orator Henry Clay was the direct cause of my taking to the composition of descriptive songs."[3] Indeed, Russell claimed, he left the speech asking himself, "Why should it not be possible for me to make music the vehicle of grand thoughts and noble sentiments, to speak to the world through the power of poetry and song?"[4]

Profoundly motivated by these thoughts, Russell wrote a new composition in the ballad style he was to make so famous and popular. It was entitled "Wind of the Winter's Night, Whence Cometh Thou?" "All through the night," he later recounted, "I paced up and down in my room arranging the music for the poem and I remember that the notion uppermost in my mind was to infuse into my music the subtle charm, as it were, of the voice of Henry Clay."[5] The poem was set in a type of music familiar to Russell, for it had many of the attributes of an Italian opera. Containing mood changes to match the lyrics, the song resembled a dramatic prelude to an aria with a rich and extremely melodramatic piano accompaniment. The vocal part demanded a very considerable range.

In 1836, at the age of twenty-four, Russell went to New York to establish himself as a singer of ballads. He had, said the critics, "a pleasing but light baritone voice." More importantly, he carried a collection of his own songs. As a musical competitor, John Hill Hewitt, recollected, "Russell's voice was a baritone of limited register. The few good notes he possessed he turned to very good advantage."[6] In his book *Shadows on the Wall*, Hewitt described Russell's appearance and performing style. "He was rather stout, but not tall. His face was prepossessing, of the Hebrew cast, dark and heavy whiskers and curly hair. He was an expert at wheedling applause out of audiences and adding to the effect of his songs by a brilliant piano accompaniment. With much self-adulation he often used to describe the wonderful influence of his descriptive songs over his audiences."[7]

After making his first New York appearance in October 1836, Russell toured around the country. He came back to New York in the spring of 1837, billed as "the Popular Ballad Singer." Within a year, a contemporary reviewer wrote, "His fame was now fully established and devoting his whole attention to composition and singing, he traversed the States of America from extremity to extremity with a rapidity without parallel, singing at all places and at all times to multitudes that all but idolized him."[8]

Russell's songs came off the press with amazing speed; he wrote ten major songs in the next three years. In the same operatic style as his "Wind of the Winter's Night" was "The Maniac," written in 1840. This song told the story of a man who is wrongly committed to an insane asylum and is being driven mad by the situation in which he finds himself.

The Hutchinson Family singers, a famous New Hampshire singing group, had enormous success with "The Maniac." John Hutchinson himself described the effect its lurid portrait of an insane man had on audiences. "I sang it alone to the accompaniment of the brothers. Judson and Asa would commence a prelude. Meanwhile I would be in my chair behind them with the finger of each hand raising the hair on my head and bringing it in partial dishevelment. Then I would rise, with the expression of vacancy inseparable from mania and commence." According to Hutchinson, the delivery of the refrain, "No, by heaven, I am NOT mad," was always calculated to make the blood of the audience freeze. Said a friend of the Hutchinsons, "John performed it with appalling power."[9]

More typical of Russell's songs, and more important to the development of music in America, were his simple ballads and romantic lachrymose songs, which filled the country's concert halls long before the advent of Stephen Foster. "Woodman, Spare That Tree," his most successful song in this genre, was written in 1837 with words by George P. Morris, a writer for the *New York Mirror*. The song was inspired by an incident that took place near Morris's country home. While the two men were out for a ride, Morris recalled a tree his father had planted and in curiosity suggested that they go to see whether it was still standing. Russell agreed, and when they arrived at the site, they found a farmer readying himself to cut it down. Morris persuaded him not to fell the tree, and Russell found a suitable theme for a song.

"Woodman, Spare That Tree" enjoyed enormous popularity well into the twentieth century, but its original success was in large part due to Russell's presentation. Wrote an eyewitness to a Russell concert:

He had finished the last verse. . . . The audience was spellbound for a moment, and then poured out a volume of applause that shook the building to its foundations. In the midst of this tremendous evidence of their boundless gratification, a snowy headed gentleman, with great anxiety depicted on his venerable features, arose and demanded silence. He asked in a tremulous voice, "Mr. Russell, in the name of heaven, was the tree spared?" "It was, sir," replied the vocalist. "Thank God, thank God, I breathe again!" and he sat down overcome by emotion.[10]

The second of Russell's popular songs in a similar vein was "The Old Arm Chair," written in 1840. Considered the first of the "mammy" songs that were to become so popular in the years that followed, it had a musical range of only five notes! "I love it, I love it, and who shall dare, to chide me for loving that old arm chair, . . . for my mother sat there," the song began recounting how the singer, through different stages of his life, had seen his mother seated in her favorite chair.

> I've treasured it long as a holy prize,
> I've bedewed it with tears, and embalmed it with sighs.
> 'Tis bound by a thousand bands to my heart;
> Not a tie will break it, not a link will start.
> Would you learn the spell—a mother sat there,
> And a sacred thing is that old arm chair.

Finally the song concludes in a torrent of tears when the singer "Learnt how much the heart can bear, When I saw her die in that old arm chair."[11]

With songs like that, Russell gained renown not only as an expert performer, but as an expert in wheedling tears from his audiences.[12] Like many of the writers on Tin Pan Alley years later, Russell had discovered the nostalgic power of the word "old." He wrote such classics as "The Old Family Clock," "The Old Spinning Wheel," "The Old Bell," and "That Old Gang of Mine." A jokester once sent him a lyric entitled "The Old Fine Toothcomb," and a Boston critic wrote that Russell's programs had every antique but "The Old Boot Jack!"[13]

Russell wrote over 800 ballads, most with his own lyrics. Not all were sentimental or dramatic, however. Some espoused such causes as temperance or the abolition of slavery, while others presented downtrodden characters worthy of respect. Such a song was "The Indian Hunter," written in 1837. It is credited with being the first American popular song to demand equal justice for the Indian.[14]

Russell also had much success with songs of the religious variety. An example is "Our Way Across the Mountains, Ho," based upon words from the psalms. Russell dedicated it to Mordecai Manuel Noah, an outstanding American Jew of the period, who had been gracious to him when he first arrived in New York.[15]

Within five years of his New York debut in 1836, Russell was an extremely popular performer throughout America. As early as 1838, the *New York Commercial Advertiser* commented that "His vocal exertions to please are always rewarded with a full attendance; and it is not surprising, for his voice and style are eminently qualified for general popularity."[16] Although concerts presenting several performers were the general rule at the time, audiences would not tolerate other singers on the same program as Russell. Thus the paper continued, "Mr. Russell is the only singer we have ever known, who could sustain a concert alone. Madame Caradoni Allen and all the other stars, have to introduce other voices to vary the scene and help keep the interest. But if Mr. Russell introduces any other person, the audience soon grows impatient and are glad to get rid of this interruption."[17]

Abraham Lincoln was one of the many theatregoers who loved Russell's songs. Lincoln's favorite was "The Ship on Fire," with music by Russell and words by Charles Mackay. The song told about a tragedy at sea. The extended piano introduction sketched a picture of a violent storm. The lyrics began with a description of a driving gale in which a helpless ship is being tossed and twisted. Aboard the ship, a mother with her small child in her arms falls to her knees and asks God for mercy. Next to her is her husband, dreaming of the peace and quiet of their cottage by the shore should they survive the storm. Suddenly fire breaks out and they realize the ship is doomed. The mother, father, and child are lowered into a lifeboat, "a mere speck on the wave." Suddenly cries of joy rise from the other people in the lifeboat, for in the distance a ship is approaching to rescue them. With that knowledge, the mother stands up and cries, "Thank God, Thank God, We're saved!"

Another maritime song by Russell was "A Life on the Ocean Wave," with words by Epes Sargent. This song achieved such popularity that the British Royal Marines adopted it as their official march in 1889. Stephen Foster is said to have been inspired by this song to write several of his own in a similar style.

In 1841 Russell journeyed to New York again, this time to form an ensemble of fellow English performers to give concerts around the East Coast. After the ensemble broke up, he continued his solo touring. He returned to England in 1842, presenting his first concert in London on March 8, 1842. After a brief trip back to America, he returned to England and attempted to reestablish himself there. He finally retired from the music business and became a very successful moneylender and bill broker.[18] Having made his fortune, Russell devoted himself to charity concerts for the poor, for temperance, and for other causes.

In the days before royalties were paid, it was not the writing of songs that gained a composer his livelihood. Russell sold his songs outright to publishers, usually for the sum of 10 shillings, and all told earned only £400 from song sales. More often than not, the publisher made a fortune from the songs, but Russell made his money from the concerts he gave. "Had it not been that I sang the songs myself, the payment for their composition would have meant simple starvation." He earned over $50,000 from his last three-season American tour, for example, all of which was lost when his New York bank failed.

Russell was married twice. His first wife was the daughter of a gentile banker named Lloyd. They had two sons, William Clark Russell (1844–1911), a novelist and biographer, and Henry Russell (1871–1937), who became the manager of the Royal Opera House, Covent Garden, and founder-manager of the Boston Opera Company.

Russell's second wife, a Miss De Lara, was Jewish, and their son was Sir Landon Ronald (Russell). Born in 1873, he was famed as a conductor of symphonic and opera music. He conducted at Covent Garden in 1894, toured America with the great Australian concert singer Dame Nellie Melba, and gained renown for his interpretation of the music of Sir Edward Elgar. He further conducted for British musical theatre and was the principal of the Guildhall School of Music in London from 1910 to 1937. Knighted in 1922, he died in 1938.[19]

Henry Russell died in 1900 and was buried according to the rites of the Christian church.[20] He paved the way for sentimental balladry in America. Many fellow Jews would follow in his footsteps, for in many ways, the American popular song began with him.

The Movie Moguls

William Fox of Twentieth Century-Fox

Louis B. Mayer of MGM

Sam Goldwyn of MGM

Courtesy of American Jewish Archives

Marcus Loew of Metro Pictures and Adolph Zuckor of Paramount Pictures

Courtesy of American Jewish Archives

Jack L. Warner of Warner Brothers

Monroe Rosenfeld's "Those Wedding Bells Shall Not Ring Out"

Courtesy of Harris Gilbert Family

7

MONROE ROSENFELD

Cincinnati can claim many favorite sons and daughters, but in the music world the first of them to gain prominence was Monroe Rosenfeld. Born in Richmond, Virginia, Rosenfeld was given his first job in music while living in Cincinnati. In addition, a Cincinnati publisher provided him with the impetus to become a professional, and his first songs were published in Cincinnati.

Monroe Rosenfeld had many vocations, including newspaperman, press agent, lyricist, short story writer, and arranger-adapter of popular songs. He left Cincinnati in the early 1880's on the advice of the publisher Frank Harding,[1] going to New York, where he began as a newspaperman.

Unlike many of his fellow songwriters, Rosenfeld was not a drinker; his intemperance ran to poker and horse racing.[2] As a result he was very popular, known up and down Broadway and the street he named Tin Pan Alley. All the bookies knew him; the racetrack owners and jockeys were both his personal friends and his downfall. If he wasn't at the track himself he bet heavily, and when he bet he usually lost.

Rosenfeld's penchant for betting had a significant influence on his songwriting career. Whenever he lost all his money, he would hunt up a publisher and sell a song to cover his immediate needs. Under extreme financial pressure he had another tactic, equally effective. He would create a title for a song and present it to a publisher, receiving a $10 or $15 advance, and then would farm the assignment out to one of the many hack writers who filled Tin Pan Alley. After the hack wrote the song for him, he would collect the rest of the fee and split the payment.[3]

Sometimes Rosenfeld would even sell the same song to two publishers and let them fight out the question of ownership. If all else failed, he was not averse to passing bad checks. On one occasion, with the police closing in on him, he jumped out of a second-story window and permanently injured his leg. As a result he walked with a limp, and for the rest of his life he wore bell-bottom sailor pants to cover the disfigurement.

Rosenfeld began his songwriting career in 1881, working for T. B. Harms,[4] but later on he wrote for any publisher who would purchase his songs or titles. He was a tearjerker specialist as well as a comic journalist for the *New York Herald*.[5] As a result of a series of articles he did for the *Herald* he became a well-known character in music circles,[6] writing songs under several pseudonyms, including F. Heister, F. Belasco, and Monroe Roosevelt, depending on the type of music he was composing.[7]

The year 1886 saw Rosenfeld's first big hit, "Johnny Get Your Gun," written in jig time, but with a melody borrowed from an earlier song entitled "Johnny, Get Your Hair Cut." George M. Cohan, in turn, later borrowed some of Rosenfeld's words, using the opening lines in "Over There." But that is not all, for it seems that the composer of "Johnny, Get Your Hair Cut" borrowed his melody from "The Arkansas Traveller," or as it is known today, "Turkey in the Straw," written originally in 1852.

Like many songwriters of the period, Rosenfeld churned out numerous topical songs about events in the news. In 1884, for example, he wrote one about the failure and bankruptcy of the Marine Bank of Brooklyn. The bank had been headed by Ferdinand Ward, Jr., whose chief financial backers were former President Ulysses S. Grant and his son; with the bank's closing the Grants lost their entire fortune. The title page of the sheet music presented a well-dressed man, carrying a suitcase filled with money, standing in front of a bank emblazoned with the Marine Bank name. The caption read, "Take the next boat to Canada, free passage to bank presidents."

Another Rosenfeld song about a current scandal was "Ma!

Ma! Where's My Pa?" which he wrote under the name of H. R. Monroe. While campaigning for the presidency, Grover Cleveland admitted that he had fathered an illegitimate child. The rest of the lyric answered the title's question with, "up in the White House, darling, making the laws, working the cause, up in the White House, dear."[8] As will be seen later, Rosenfeld also wrote a famous topical song of the year 1898, "Let Me Shake the Hand That Shook the Hand of Sullivan," a tribute to John L. Sullivan, heavyweight boxing champion of the world.

It was not the humorous topical songs that proved to be Rosenfeld's forte, however. His greatest hits were maudlin melancholy ballads of the genre so popular in the 1880's and 1890's. These ballads reflected the pious attitudes of women at home and men's concepts of how their wives, sisters, and daughters should behave. Monroe Rosenfeld fed this market with tear-drenched ballads and verses.[9] In 1884 and 1885 he gained great success with two such songs, each written under a pseudonym. First was "Hush Little Boy, Don't You Cry," initially published under the name of F. Belasco, and the second was, "Goodbye, Boy, Goodbye."

The early 1880's also saw the composition of Rosenfeld's "Climbing Up the Golden Stairs," an all-time minstrel hit usually sung in Negro dialect. Rosenfeld wrote this song in 1884 under the pen name of E. Heiser. All of these songs were fairly popular when they appeared under pseudonyms, but sales jumped enormously when the song-buying public learned that the popular Rosenfeld was the real composer.

A fellow composer-publisher, E. B. Marks, described Rosenfeld as "a vulpine thin faced man with a silky moustache and a hypnotic line. He was a most persuasive salesman and a melodic kleptomaniac."[10] "Melodic kleptomaniac" does not adequately describe Rosenfeld. As indicated by "Johnny Get Your Gun," he was not the least bit reluctant to "borrow" someone else's melody. This was so even if the original composer was likely to hear about it. For example, consider the 1888 song "With All Her Faults, I Love Her Still." Rosenfeld pilfered the melody from a German song entitled "Mein Himmel auf Erden" ("My Heaven on Earth"), by Theodore Metz, the composer of "Hot Time in the

Old Town Tonight." Rosenfeld had heard Metz play the song at Wilson's Pavilion in Harlem. Metz, who was the director of the Primrose and West Minstrels, first learned about the uncredited "borrowing" when someone handed him a copy of Rosenfeld's "With All Her Faults." Despite his justifiable anger, Metz and his company introduced the ballad, and singer Dick José of the Minstrels made it popular.[11] Rosenfeld and Metz were very close friends. They got together soon after this incident to collaborate on a new show. When Rosenfeld was told of Metz's anger about his use of the melody from "Mein Himmel auf Erden," he simply remarked, "Teddy has his German up!"[12]

As an example of an "echo" song, where the title is repeated several times in the course of the verses, "With All Her Faults, I Love Her Still" has become a classic. It also enjoyed great popularity among barbershop quartets and schools. The moralizing slant of the lyrics does not seem to go far enough in specifying the faults of the man who was jilted by his girl. In fact one critic of the day wrote that the girl did herself a favor by leaving the self-appointed hero. In any case, the jiltee's lament makes up the body of the song, and the chorus begins and ends with a heart-breaking echo of the title:

> With all her faults I love her still,
> And even though the world should scorn;
> No love like hers, my heart can thrill,
> Although she's made that heart forlorn.
>
> No love like hers, my soul can thrill,
> No other love can win my heart.
> I love her still! I love her still!
> With all her faults I love her still.

Rosenfeld wrote other songs in the waning years of the 1880's but they are musically and historically of little consequence. It was in the decade of the 1890's that Rosenfeld really hit his stride, turning out several of the greatest song sensations of the day: "I Was Once Your Wife," "Don't Ask Me to Give Up Mother," "Don't Say I Did It, Jack," "Those Wedding Bells Shall

Not Ring Out," "Take Back Your Gold," and "She Was Happy Till She Met You."

Since Rosenfeld was a newspaperman as well as a lyricist and composer, and therefore, presumably, something of a hard-boiled realist, he was often asked whether he wrote his lyrics sincerely or with tongue stuck "derisively" in his cheek. He regularly claimed that the sentiments were genuine, but it is difficult to believe this of his 1894 hit, "Her Golden Hair Was Hanging Down Her Back." The sheet music credited Rosenfeld with composing it, but the melody was in fact the creation of Felix McGlennon, for whom Rosenfeld did the arrangement. It might be added that there is some question whether Rosenfeld had *anything* to do with the song besides arranging it. Some credit McGlennon with both words and music. In any case, the lyrics dealt with a "simple maiden" and her first trip to New York.

> There was once a simple young maiden
>   Came to New York on a trip,
> And her golden hair was hanging down her back.
> Her cheeks were like the roses,
>   She'd a pout on her lip,
> And her golden hair was hanging down her back.
>
> When she landed at the station here,
>   She took a little stroll,
> At ev'rything she wondered
>   Till she lost her self-control.
> Said she, "New York is quite a village,
>   Ain't it? Bless my soul!"
> And her golden hair was hanging down her back.

Rosenfeld undoubtedly wanted his audience to accept the song at its sentimental face value. It is equally clear, though, that he provided a bit of humor and satire in the last two lines: "But alas and alack, She's gone back, With a naughty little twinkle in her eye." It seems she wasn't the only one with a twinkle in her eye! In this period songs were so popular that often a single good one could launch a publishing house. "Her Golden Hair" was such a song, providing the impetus for the Leo Feist publishing empire. "You can never go wrong with a Feist song" was first emblazoned on the cover of sheet music because of the Rosenfeld-McGlennon song.[13]

As has already been intimated, Rosenfeld would do just about anything to earn the money he needed to pay his gambling debts. Along with songwriting he worked as a journalist-reviewer for the *New York Herald* and the *New York Clipper*. From 1891 to 1898 he worked as a poet-reviewer for the *Clipper*. While on this assignment, he wrote many pieces of sentimental doggerel. Again the cynicism of the "Golden Hair" song is easy to recognize:

> Oh dear little maid so demure
> Has eyes that are filled with devotion;
> That other you scarce can endure
> So spiteful she is to your notion.
>
> Alas see them when they are wed,
> How strangely deceived was each lover;
> There's only one word to be said,
> You can't tell a book by its cover![14]

Rosenfeld also supplemented his income by editing and correcting manuscripts of other composers. Sometimes, whether from a sincere desire to help or because of a promised share of a new song's royalties, he would add his own name to another's creation. On one occasion, it is said, he unwittingly aided the career of a future theatre great. A young man of twenty named John Golden once showed Rosenfeld some of his lyrics and asked if he would set them to music. Rosenfeld demurred, thoughtfully stroking his moustache, and said, "John, my boy, you'll never make a fortune writing songs. Stick to the theatre and if you've got the stuff, you'll never regret it." Golden went on to become a major producer.[15]

In 1895 Rosenfeld joined forces with his old friend and musical competitor, Theodore Metz. Together they wrote an Indian operetta entitled *Poketa*, Metz composing the music, and Rosenfeld the libretto. The show was a colossal disaster. Nonetheless, Metz later commented that he had great respect for Rosenfeld's ability. "You could stretch out a topic for Rosenfeld to work on and he'd have the job done before you were through talking. As for *Poketa*, that's just how we did it. I outlined the plot, situations, and the rest, and that very night the libretto was finished in Rosenfeld's room."[16]

Whether to placate the critics who claimed that he falsely took credit for the work of others or, more likely, because he wanted to reward the singer who had introduced a new ballad he had written, Rosenfeld gave half the royalties and lyricist credit for "Take Back Your Gold" to Louis W. Pritzkow. The song was written in 1897 entirely by Rosenfeld, but he shared the credit with Pritzkow to pay him for introducing it in the Primrose and West Minstrel show.

In light of this, it is ironic that Pritzkow was not the performer who made "Take Back Your Gold" famous. The plugger who really sold the song was Emma Carus, a shouter who prefaced her shows with the statement, "I'm not pretty, but I take care of my family!" Carus plugged "Take Back Your Gold" often in her act, perhaps as a way of repaying Rosenfeld for discovering her and giving her her first break. He had liked the quality of her speaking voice and urged her to become a song plugger. Her delivery was perfect for the song's sentiments, especially in the defiant ending, "She spurned the gold he offered her and said, 'Take back your gold, for gold cannot buy me!' " Rosenfeld did everything he could to make sure "Take Back Your Gold" would be well received; in addition to sending the song to a popular singer, he even reviewed it for the *New York Herald* in his own column![17] The song became so popular that it helped launch another great publishing house, Joseph W. Stern and Co.

Actors, singers, in fact almost everyone liked Rosenfeld and would scramble to introduce a Rosenfeld song if it needed plugging. In 1897, for example, there were plenty of performers who wanted Rosenfeld's newest song, "I Don't Care If You Never Come Back," but he gave it to Bert Williams, the black vaudeville star and half of the team of Williams and Walker. The same year saw the introduction of another great Rosenfeld hit, "Just for the

Sake of Our Daughter." It enjoyed enormous popularity during the last years of the 1890's, probably because of the high drama in its story line. There were three lengthy verses about a night of tragedy involving a policeman, his faithless wife, their maiden daughter, and a burglar who turns out to be the wife's lover!

The year 1898 saw the last two big hits from the pen of Monroe Rosenfeld. The first was "Gold Will Buy Most Anything But a True Girl's Heart." Here the story was about a wealthy man offering jewels fit for a queen to a poor girl in order to tempt her not to marry the man she really loves. She responds proudly, "I'd rather have my Jack than all your gold, for gold will buy most anything but a true girl's heart."[18] The second was the topical song "Let Me Shake the Hand That Shook the Hand of Sullivan," a farcical look at the popularity of the famed prizefighter. In light of the sophisticated wit shown in songs like this one, it is hard not to question Rosenfeld's sincerity in writing such maudlin and corny songs as "Gold Will Buy" and "Take Back Your Gold." Sincerity aside, however, Rosenfeld recognized that his audiences wanted ballads, and it was ballads that he continued to compose. Sadly for Rosenfeld, though, he sold most of these songs for a pittance simply to pay gambling debts; the ones who made the fortunes were his publishers. In the case of "Gold Will Buy Most Anything But a True Girl's Heart," the publisher was Howley and Haviland.

Rosenfeld's last song, "Down Where the Silv'ry Mohawk Flows," was presented in 1905 and attained a minor degree of success. By then he had become an elder statesman, giving encouragement to new composers and lyricists. This is exemplified by a review he wrote for the *St. Louis Globe Democrat* in 1903: "St. Louis boasts of a composer of music who, despite the ebony hue of his features, has written more instrumental successes than any local composer."[19] The new talent was the ragtime master, Scott Joplin.

Monroe Rosenfeld's songs graced the catalogues of many of the best publishing houses on Tin Pan Alley. He died bankrupt, but his creativity left the popular music world richer. Rosenfeld was one of the first Jews to play a role in the music business and one of the earliest composers on Tin Pan Alley.[20] His contribution to the world of popular music will be remembered as long as the term "Tin Pan Alley" is remembered, for it was Rosenfeld who coined it while reporting for the *Herald Tribune*.[21]

Charles K. Harris's "A Rabbi's Daughter"

8

CHARLES K. HARRIS

Perhaps more than any other songwriter, Charles Kassel Harris represents the attitudes and methods of the first generation of Tin Pan Alley composers. Harris was one of nine children.[1] Born in Poughkeepsie, New York, on May 1, 1867, he grew up in East Saginaw, Michigan, where his family settled a year later.

As a young boy Harris was very interested in minstrel shows and their music. In his autobiography, *After the Ball,* he tells how he constructed himself a homemade banjo from an empty oyster can and some old wire and ran errands for a minstrel musician in exchange for banjo lessons.

When Harris was fourteen his family moved to Milwaukee. He began to earn spending money by playing banjo and singing minstrel songs in several small clubs and variety theatres around town. He soon became very adept at the banjo and after a while decided to write his own songs rather than buy someone else's. Harris's first songs, "A There, Stay There," "If I Were the Chief of Police," "I Heard Her Voice Again," and "Bake That Matza Pie," were written for some singer friends who needed material for a show they were doing at Milwaukee's Phoenix Club.[2]

Obviously quite pleased with himself, the teenage Harris rented a room and hung a sign on the door announcing: "Banjoist and Song Writer. Songs Written to Order." Yet he was totally self-taught. According to a contemporary, "C. K. Harris could not distinguish a note of music from a cuckoo's egg!"[3] Harris said much the same thing in his autobiography, though in a more serious way:

93

The reader will naturally wonder how it was possible for me to write music to a song when even to this day I cannot distinguish one note from another. The answer is simple. As soon as a melody occurred to me, I hummed it. Then I would procure the services of a trained musician for the purpose, hum or whistle the melody for him and have him take it down on paper with notes. He would then arrange it for piano.[4]

Harris's chutzpah knew no limits. He began giving private concerts and banjo lessons without the slightest knowledge of music. Apparently he learned all he knew by talking with performers, hanging around theatres, and studying the *George C. Dobson Banjo Book*![5]

Hanging around theatres also gave Harris the big break he needed. When he was sixteen he attended a performance of *The Skating Rink*, a musical starring Nat C. Goodwin. Harris was convinced that he could write songs better than the ones in the show. In collaboration with his best friend, Charles Horowitz, Harris wrote "Since Maggie Learned to Skate" and somehow managed to convince Goodwin to use it as a replacement for one of the less distinguished songs in the show. Harris admitted later that it was a "dreadful number," but even so it was a beginning. Other early numbers by Harris were "Creep, Baby, Creep" and "Let's Kiss and Make Up." Both of these songs were also specially composed for performers visiting Milwaukee whom Harris then persuaded to perform them.

By 1891 five Harris songs had been interpolated into shows; in addition he had been a bellhop, a pawnbroker, and a banjo player.[6] In that year he finally became a published songwriter when the new company of M. Witmark and Sons printed his "When the Sun Has Set." Harris earned all of 85 cents from this creative effort. When he received his first royalty check from Isidore Witmark six months after the song was published, Harris wrote back that he would frame it as a souvenir of the smallest royalty statement on record. In his answer to Harris's letter, Julius Witmark told him, "Hang up your music. Yours is the only song we ever published that didn't sell."[7]

This experience led Harris to conclude that there was more money to be made from publishing songs than from writing them. As a result, he started his own publishing house in 1891, operating out of a $7.50 per month rented office at 207 Grand Avenue in Milwaukee.[8] Harris had borrowed $1,000 from three friends to finance the business and in the first year made a $3,000 profit. The next year, 1892, he bought them out.

Only twenty-five years old, Harris was the only printer-publisher-songwriter in America.[9] What was the source of his success? Harris had hit upon an entirely new idea in the field of popular music. He decided to write songs that fit specific situations. Previously songs had been thrown into shows promiscuously, the sole criterion being whether they provided the performer with an opportunity to display vocal and dramatic prowess. Harris wrote, "My idea was to never write a song which didn't fit some situation," a shrewd gimmick resulting from the principles he had learned as a young man in Milwaukee.

One of the first songs Harris wrote for his own company was "Alderman Michael O'Rourke," which earned him $10. He hired a friend to sit in the audience and applaud wildly when the song was presented. Perhaps the first plugger, the friend fell asleep, but the song was a hit anyway! Another early Harris song was "Thou Art Ever in My Thoughts," contracted to another publisher, which earned him $16.75 in royalties.

In time Harris decided that there were greener pastures than those in Milwaukee, so he traveled to Chicago. While there he met and befriended Will Rossiter, a prominent Chicago songwriter. It was Rossiter who instructed Harris in the copyright laws, introduced him to printers and publishers, and essentially showed him the ropes of the publishing business. Rossiter also introduced Harris to the manager of the Chicago Opera House, who invited him to write songs for the extravaganza *Ali Baba*. In payment Harris was given an envelope with the instructions, "Don't open this until you are on the boat to Milwaukee." Harris forgot to open it at all. When his mother later came across the envelope and found that it contained four fifty-dollar bills, she promptly fainted. It was the biggest single payment Harris had ever received.

In 1891, while beginning in the publishing business, Harris

also became a performer. Angered by the shoddy presentation of his songs, he decided he could do better. Although it was difficult, there were a few bright spots. Harris recalled one in his autobiography. He had been invited by his brother to play a concert in Oshkosh, Wisconsin. Song after song was greeted by enormous waves of applause, more than he had ever experienced. He finished with John Howard Payne's "Home, Sweet Home." At dinner after the performance Harris asked the doctor who was his table companion the name of the college he had just played. The doctor replied, "College? This is no college. This is the Northern Hospital for the Insane!"[10]

The first song Harris published was "Hello Central, Hello." He intended it to serve as payment for some banjo lessons he had been given, but was cheated by the plate maker who engraved the sheet music covers and internal pages. Harris learned a lesson, though, and attempted from then on to hire his own people for all the different phases of the publishing process instead of contracting outsiders.

In 1892 Charles K. Harris made history and took the music business a major step forward by writing and publishing the first popular song to sell several million copies of sheet music. The story for the song, "After the Ball," was inspired by an incident that took place while Harris was in Chicago. A friend of his broke his engagement after a big party and escorted another girl home in order to make his former fiancée jealous. The fiancée, with tears in her eyes, tried to cover her sadness with a smile. Seeing all this, Harris suddenly thought of the line, "Many a heart is aching, after the ball." Upon his return to Milwaukee, he was approached by his tailor, Sam Doctor, an aspiring singer, to write a new song. Harris remembered the incident in Chicago as well as the line he had thought of, and "in one hour's time I wrote the complete lyric and music of 'After the Ball.' "[11] He described the piece as a "song story" because the lyric was a long, sad tale of confused identity, told in three long verses, after which the chorus is repeated.

The type of story-ballad represented by "After the Ball" was a Harris specialty written for middle-class ladies to perform at home on their pianos (at this time the piano was played mostly by women or by touring performers from Europe, for men who were musical were thought to be effeminate).[12] Its story and melody were typically Victorian. A little girl climbs upon her old uncle's knee. "Why are you not married and why have you no home?" "I had a sweetheart once, but I caught her kissing another man at a ball," says the old man, explaining that he has never forgotten her or forgiven her. It turns out that the man she was kissing was her brother. "I never married because I broke her heart, After the Ball."[13] The technique of the old man talking to his niece was particularly inspired, for it allowed Harris to use the word "pet" whenever an extra syllable was needed to complete a line. It is used several times in the verse with great success. The chorus has become one of the most familiar of nineteenth-century music.

> After the Ball is over
> After the break of morn,
> After the dancers' leaving
> After the stars are gone.
> Many a heart is aching,
> If you could read them all,
> Many the hopes that have vanished,
> After the Ball.

The first performance of "After the Ball" was a disaster, for tailor-minstrel Sam Doctor forgot the third verse and had to leave the stage in great embarrassment.[14] Harris decided that he would never again permit an amateur to introduce his songs. He showed "After the Ball" to May Howard, who was appearing in Milwaukee, but she and her husband thought the song ridiculous and suggested that Harris dispose of it. When the Primrose and West Minstrel show came through Milwaukee, Harris offered the song to Dick José, who said he preferred one of Harris's earlier songs, "Kiss and Let's Make Up."

The next big show to come to Milwaukee was *A Trip to Chinatown*, important historically because so many of its songs have remained active parts of our musical heritage.[15] Already one of the most successful shows of the decade, *A Trip to Chinatown* had opened in New York on November 9, 1891, and was now touring the country. It included several songs by Percy Gaunt, among them "The Bowery."

Harris knew the shows's manager, Ben Singer, and through him was introduced to J. Aldrich Libby, the show's star and one of the most popular ballad singers in the country. Because of his popularity, Libby was in a position to interpolate any songs he wanted into the score. Harris didn't just show Libby his song. He also claimed that he was the Milwaukee correspondent for the *New York Dramatic News* and could guarantee a brilliant review if Libby would sing it, sweetening the deal further with an offer of $500 as well as a piece of the royalties.[16] Libby accepted, and the leader of the touring show's band, Frank Palma, orchestrated the song in return for a good cigar.

Libby introduced "After the Ball" at a matinee.[17] When he finished the first verse and chorus, "not a sound was heard. I [Harris] was ready to sink through the floor. He went through the second verse and chorus and still complete silence reigned. I was making ready to bolt, but my friends held me tightly by the arms. Then came the third verse and chorus. For a full minute the audience remained quiet, and then broke loose with applause. The entire audience arose, and, standing, wildly applauded for five minutes."[18] All told, they demanded more than six encores of the chorus.

Julius Witmark immediately offered Harris $10,000 for the rights to "After the Ball," but Harris recognized that if it was worth that much to the Witmarks, it would be worth twice that amount to himself. Within a very few days, the song was being presented in three cities around the country by three leading ballad-singers. The Oliver Ditson Company wired Harris from New York for 75,000 copies of the sheet music: 25,000 for Boston, 25,000 for New York, and 25,000 for Chicago. The song had not yet been printed and no Milwaukee press could handle so large an order, but Harris managed to find a Chicago printer who could, and within ten days the orders were filled. Ditson's sent Harris the first of many checks for "After the Ball," amounting to $14,250, along with an order for 100,000 more copies.

The success of "After the Ball" proved to be phenomenal. It sold over 5 million copies and earned $25,000 per week for the

Harris firm. By publishing his own song, Harris, who for the time being was the king of the ballad, had cut himself into the lion's share of the music business profits, showing the way for future composers.[19]

Harris's success with "After the Ball" provided some extra dividends as well. In 1892, while in Chicago to set up arrangements with a printer and open a branch of his publishing company, he was introduced at a party to Cora Lehrberg from Owensboro, Kentucky. She later became his wife. He also went to the Chicago World's Columbian Exposition, where his song had become the favorite. John Philip Sousa reported to Harris that people invariably requested it over and over; "Confound you, Harris, the playing of your song has tired me out."[20] Perhaps so, but Sousa included "After the Ball" in each of his Exposition programs and also in his concerts for years afterward,[21] doing much to popularize it around the country.

Because of Harris's unprecedented success, the people of Milwaukee referred to the late nineties as "the Harrisian Age." With "After the Ball" their city basked in the double fame of its flowing Schlitz and its flowing melodies.[22] Curiously, Harris's family seemed quite unaware of how much money "After the Ball" was making. Harris didn't tell his mother, with whom he lived, but one Saturday sent her to a matinee show and had a decorator come in to measure the house for totally new furnishings. The next Saturday he sent her to another matinee and had the entire house refurnished; each room was redone in the best velvets and heavy woods that Milwaukee could provide. When Mrs. Harris returned she thought she was in the wrong house and went back outside to check the number on the door. Her newly hired maid assured her that indeed she was in the right place. Harris wrote that this was the most meaningful moment in his life.[23]

With "After the Ball," Harris became a pillar of the popular music establishment. He transferred his center of operations from Milwaukee's Alhambra Building, where he had moved when he bought out his original investors, to New York's Union Square around 14th Street, following several other publishers whose stories have already been told.

"After the Ball" so typified the songs of the 1890's that Oscar
Hammerstein and Jerome Kern used it in *Show Boat* as the
perfect period piece.[24] This gigantic hit and tearjerker seemed
the ideal way for Magnolia, the romantic singer of the showboat
Cotton Blossom, to conquer an unruly crowd on New Year's Eve.
Perhaps that is the finest tribute of all.[25] To the day he died,
Harris was convinced that "After the Ball" was the musical
masterpiece of the nineteenth century.

Although Harris never had another success to match "After
the Ball," several of his songs were great hits. In 1897 he introduced "Break the News to Mother," which he wrote while
sitting in a barber's chair. The subject matter concerned the
death of a fireman. Set during the Civil War, the song seemed
very out of date until Harris changed the fireman to a soldier.
This increased the song's popularity, but Harris still couldn't get
it off the ground. Finally he sent it to Julia Mackey. She introduced the song the night after the battleship *Maine* was blown
up in Havana harbor, and it immediately caught the public's
fancy. A rival publisher is said to have commented: "Harris'
luck, it took a war to make his song popular."[26] "Break the News
to Mother" contained one of Tin Pan Alley's favorite rhyming
sequences, "mother" and "love her"!

Harris had an uncanny knack for picking successful songwriters to publish and for knowing in advance how many copies
a song would sell.[27] One of his close friends was Paul Dresser,
the brother of author Theodore Dreiser. Harris had predicted
the enormous success of Dresser's greatest song, "On the Banks
of the Wabash," and had influenced a publisher to present it in
New York. Dresser predicted that "Break the News to Mother"
would be an equal hit. Fortunately for the music world, Dresser
was a better composer than he was a prognosticator. Later in the
same year Harris attempted to have lightning strike twice by
writing a sequel to "After the Ball." Entitled "While the Dance
Goes On," it tells the story of a mother who is enjoying herself at
a dance while her baby is dying at home.

Now that Harris was a success, he no longer had to approach
others to sing his songs, and instead famous singers came to him
for help. Among them was J. Bernard Dyllyn, one of the most

popular baritones of the 1890's. For him Harris created the song "Just Behind the Times," the true story of an elderly minister who had served his congregation for many years and then was ousted by young people who wanted someone more up-to-date. Harris wrote in his autobiography, "Here was a man who had given the best years of his life to the members of his congregation, soothed their sorrows, married them and buried their loved ones for ever so many years, and who was now to be cast aside, like an old worn out glove, for a younger man."

> A party of young people gathered
> In their little church,
> A meeting of importance there to hold.
> They then decided that their minister,
> Although they loved him well,
> He must resign, for he was growing old.
> They sent to him this message,
> He read it through and through,
> While burning tears fell on the cruel lines,
> For it was written in that message
> That his sermons were too dry.
> It also read, "You're just behind the times."

CHORUS

> Behind the times, so they told him;
> He's just behind the times.
> His voice has lost its sweetness,
> Like bells that no more chime.
> He cannot hold their attention,
> He faltered o'er his lines;
> His power has gone, though few will mourn,
> For he's Just Behind the Times.

> On Sunday morn the church was crowded
> For t'was rumored round the town
> A younger minister was going to preach;
> And in that same old dusty pulpit
> Where the old man reigned for years
> Another man had come his flock to teach.

He spoke of love and politics;
He spoke of fashion, too;
Of sights he'd seen in many different climes.
The old man sat alone and listened,
Then he sadly shook his head—
"I guess they're right, I am behind the times.

And so at last the sermon ended
And the old man slowly rose.
"Just let me say a few words ere you go."
Then slowly up the aisle he staggered,
To his pulpit as of yore,
With trembling limbs and face as white as snow.
"I've buried all your loved ones,
I've wept beside their graves,
I've shared your joys and sorrows many times."
Just then he gave a start, for his poor heart
Had broken from its pain.
His last words were: "I am behind the times."[28]

Harris persisted in the habit of writing songs based on incidents or events of the day. Yet for a while he ran a dry spell. After writing three flops in a row because he was suffering from exhaustion, Harris, accompanied by his wife, took a trip to Washington, D.C., and Louisville. Upon their return, refreshed, he wrote three smash hits in a row. Harris's comment: "My advice to anybody, not only song writers, is: Don't try to write love ballads while suffering from indigestion." Harris delighted in giving advice based on his success as a songwriter. In his book *How to Write a Popular Song*, he showed his pride in the "song manufacturing" business, telling his readers: "Look at newspapers for your story line, acquaint yourself with the style in vogue, avoid slang, and know the copyright laws."[29] Harris even published rules on how to write a "coon song." For example, "the introduction or prelude should be four, eight or sixteen measures finishing on a dominant seventh chord." No wonder he called his business "song manufacturing."[30]

Charles K. Harris was a very innovative man, and several

features of the music world are attributable to him. He invented the practice of printing photographs of popular singers on the sheet music of songs they introduced, a type of ego "plugging." For "Is Life Worth Living," sung by Joe E. Howard, Harris invented the illustrated song, using three backdrops painted with a scene to illustrate each verse. The enthusiastic reception spurred Harris on to new creativity. His "I Loved Her Just the Same" was illustrated with stereopticon slides of real actors presenting scenes from the song. These were of enormous advertising value, and as Harris said in his autobiography, his songs were easy to illustrate because they "always told a story based on incidents taken from life—and always contained a moral. The audience would follow along, and by the chorus, would find themselves singing along."[31] Harris was also the first composer to have a piano with a movable keyboard that could automatically transpose songs. He couldn't play the piano well at all, and what little he could, was exclusively on the black keys.[32]

Many of Harris's songs were so popular that there were requests to use them as the basis for melodramatic plays. Al Woods, the founder of the production company of Woods, Sullivan and Harris, asked permission to use several song titles for plays. Harris granted permission for any title except "After the Ball." In fact Woods, Sullivan and Harris used three, "Cast Aside," "Fallen by the Wayside," and "One Night in June."[33]

Not long afterwards, Harris met Lewis J. Selznick, who suggested that Harris write a scenario for the newly invented movie process. When Selznick reneged on his promise, Harris produced the script himself. Selznick later stated that if the film was good, he would pay all the expenses plus a large fee for the script and would give Harris half the eventual profit after the release. Harris went on to write sixteen movie scenarios, all of which were great financial successes.

Selznick was not the only famous person with whom Harris had business dealings. Early in Harris's publishing career, a new composer named Gustave Luders begged him to publish one of his songs, but Harris was too busy publishing his own music. It was a major mistake, for the score turned out to be the *Prince of Pilsen*, which ran on Broadway for several years and earned an enormous fortune for Luders and his publishers.

The four Cohans were also friends of Harris's. He and George M. Cohan once had an argument as to which type of music would last longer, George's "coon and comic" songs or Harris's ballads. George's mother took Harris's side! Later Harris offered Cohan a blank check in return for the right to publish his songs, but Cohan had already signed with a rival company. It was a great financial disappointment.

Harris was also responsible for introducing S. L. Rothafel, more familiar today as "Roxy," to Marks and Spiegel, with whom he joined to start the Roxy Theatre chain, which included the Strand, the Rivoli, and the Rialto. Roxy never forgot the favor and served as the backer for several Harris ventures.[34] One such venture was the production of the film *After the Ball*.

During the run of the movie a young man rushed into Harris's publishing office requesting a singer to do "After the Ball" during the changing of reels at the Gem Theater in the Williamsburg section of Brooklyn. The man apparently did not realize that he was speaking to the composer. He was new to the business, he explained, and only wanted to make good. Harris replied that he didn't know of a singer and certainly wasn't one himself, but that he would come anyway. The audience in the theatre went wild when Harris stepped out on the stage, introduced himself, and said: "When my movies appeared in Broadway theatres I have been offered $1000 or more to make personal appearances which I refused. But when a young Jewish boy just starting in the business as a manager of a motion picture theatre and eager to make good came to me and laid his cards on the table, I decided to help him out, and here I am." Harris continued: "Don't be ashamed to sit upstairs in the gallery. I sat up there many a time. In fact, I shined boots to pay my way up there. If you will work hard and be honest, you too will all be able to sit downstairs like the other folks."[35]

Harris was fascinated by certain themes. The most common theme in his music was children. His second most successful song, written in 1901, was "Hello Central, Give Me Heaven." It was inspired by a news item about a child:

I remember one morning at breakfast my wife called attention to an interesting item in a newspaper. It was the story of a coal dealer in Chicago who had lost his wife, leaving a little daughter, aged seven, to comfort him. As he was reading his evening paper, his little girl, who had been playing with some wooden blocks close by, suddenly threw them aside and climbed on a chair so as to reach a telephone hanging on the wall. Cranking the small handle of the old fashioned telephone then in use, she said: "Hello, Central, give me heaven, for my mama's there."

When the child's message reached the operator in the telephone exchange the latter was rendered speechless. She told the other girls to listen in, which they did.

"Gee, I don't know how to answer the kid," said the operator.

One of the girls said: "Just say you're her mother and console her. It will soothe her little heart."

The father then took the little girl upon his knee and kissed her; and with a smile on her face, the child fell asleep in his arms.[36]

This song was one of the first "Hello" songs, a genre that became very popular soon after it was introduced. An even bigger success was the World War I song "Hello Central, Give Me No Man's Land." Another Harris song capitalizing on the child theme, and the last of his big sellers, was written in 1903. It told the sad story of a neglected child, forgotten by his parents, who was "Always in the Way."

Harris also dealt with the sadness of youth in an 1898 composition, "The Rabbi's Daughter." Embodying all the favorite Harrisian themes rolled into one—love, sadness, parental disapproval and authority, death—it is a perfect example of Harris's art.

> A Rabbi sat one evening with Bible on his knee.
> His daughter knelt beside him for she loved him
>   tenderly.
> Come tell me child, the Rabbi said,
> Why do you weep and sigh? Don't be afraid to trust me,
>   dear,

Tell me the reason why.
She gazed into his dear kind face and said:
    Will you forgive?
I love a man with all my heart, without him I can't live.
The Rabbi looked down at his child, "One question
    answer me,
Is he of Jewish faith or not"—her head sank on his knee.

CHORUS

You are a Rabbi's daughter and as such you must obey.
Your father you must honor unto his dying day.
If you a Christian marry, your old father's heart you'll
    break.
You are a Rabbi's daughter, and must leave him for my
    sake.

The hour of midnight sounded, the world seemed all at
    rest.
The maiden kissed a picture and she held it to her breast.
I'm told I must not love you, dear, I ne'er must see your
    face.
And that you cannot marry me, for you're not of my
    faith.
But I shall have no other love and though my heart
    should break,
To you my love I'll faithful be, though I may never wake.
Her words came true that very morn, for on her bed so
    white,
The Rabbi found his only child had died for love that
    night.[37]

It is interesting to note Harris's curious detachment from his
songs. In his autobiography, he often wrote of how moved his
audiences were by his songs, but never that they moved him as
well. One thing he was moved by, however, was money. In 1908
he went to see President Theodore Roosevelt about a financial
issue that greatly troubled the songwriters of the day. At the
time there was only the outdated 1701 copyright law in America,
and Harris represented a group of writers, including Victor

Herbert, Reginald de Koven, and others, who wanted to see the situation corrected.

Roosevelt was very interested in what Harris had to say, and as Harris noted in his autobiography, gave him a forty-minute interview, one of the longest he ever granted.[38] The President provided Harris with written introductions to the heads of the two congressional committees examining the question, Senator Smoot and Representative Frank D. Currier, and also sent him to the copyright office for further information. These efforts helped to bring about the passage of the Copyright Act of 1909, which provided the basis for the foundation of the American Society of Composers, Authors, and Publishers (ASCAP) in 1918 as an organization to protect songwriters.

Even with ASCAP, however, Harris felt that his music was not receiving its just treatment, so in 1925 he came out of retirement and went into vaudeville to advertise his own songs and to try to clean up the lyrics found in the newer popular songs. According to Harris, the 1920's and 1930's were a time of ruin, and it was only in the 1890's that there had been geniuses on Tin Pan Alley. "Fellows then wrote music and the words while by the 1920's you saw two names for the words and two more for the music." So far as Charles K. Harris was concerned, the era of geniuses was gone.[39]

Harris died on December 22, 1930, and soon afterward his widow sold his publishing firm to the Southern Music Company.[40] By then, of course, the day of the Harrisian popular song had long been ended. The public was no longer interested in endless tales of woe recounted in triple verses centering about a repeated refrain—melodramas about villains, death, women wronged, and children abandoned, always ending with vice conquered and virtue triumphant.

Modern critics have treated Harris very harshly. Most of them tend to agree with Sigmund Spaeth, who described Harris's career as "convincing proof that one can become an enormously popular songwriter without ever writing a really good song," and maintained that his work "was a perfect reflection of the essential naivete of his period."[41]

Whether one likes Harris's songs or not, however, it cannot be denied that he, more than anyone else, initiated the style that dominated Tin Pan Alley for a generation. His songs are still sung today, almost ninety years after they were written. Thus it would seem that his dispute with George M. Cohan ended in a draw.

9

THE VON TILZERS

It was no coincidence that when Monroe Rosenfeld, in 1903, began his famous series of articles about the music business, he went to the offices of Harry Von Tilzer for his research. Von Tilzer was one of the most popular men in the business, and also one of the most successful. It was in Von Tilzer's offices that the unique sound of player pianos tinkling away reminded Rosenfeld of tin pans, leading him to coin the phrase "Tin Pan Alley," although in later years Harry Von Tilzer claimed it as his own![1] That Rosenfeld should have sought out Von Tilzer for information when Von Tilzer had only been in the business for a few years, and had been publishing for himself only one year, illustrates how quickly Von Tilzer's success came. For many years he was called "Mr. Tin Pan Alley." When Tin Pan Alley died, Harry Von Tilzer's career ended as well.

If quantity is the criterion for a composer's importance, then Harry Von Tilzer ranks as one of the top men in the field. He claimed to have written 8,000 songs, 2,000 of which were published.[2] More than a dozen of these songs sold over a million copies each,[3] and Von Tilzer estimated that several hundred million copies of his songs were sold during the whole course of his career.[4]

Born on July 8, 1872, in Detroit, Michigan, Harry Von Tilzer was originally named Harry Gumm.[5] His parents, Jacob and Sarah Tilzer Gumm, had five children. Four of the boys went into different phases of the music business. When Harry was a young boy the family moved to Indianapolis, where his father purchased a shoe shop beneath a loft where a theatrical troupe gave performances. Harry loved going to see this group, and when he could raise enough money, he would also go to minstrel shows and burlesque theatres. When he was broke, he would sit in a hotel lobby waiting to get a glimpse of his favorite performers.

At fourteen years of age, after preparing himself for several months by learning a tumbling act, Harry succumbed to the lure of the stage and ran away from home, joining the Cole Brothers Circus.[6] His parents soon apprehended him and brought him home, hoping that he would forget about show business. Not quite a year later, though, he ran away again, this time to Chicago, where he became a "spieler" for a medicine show; later, in an itinerant theatrical troupe, he became an actor, pianist, composer, and juvenile lead.[7] Fearing that he would never get anywhere with a name like Gumm, he adopted his mother's maiden name, Tilzer, and added a "Von" for good measure.

The itinerant theatrical company gave Von Tilzer a ready outlet for the songs which he was already writing in great profusion. The first of his songs to be published, "I Love You Both," served as his entrée to the world of vaudeville. The star Lottie Gilson liked it so much that she persuaded her publisher, Willis Woodward, to bring out the sheet music, and he did so in 1892. The song asked "Who do you love more?"

> I love you both, Papa with all my heart.
> I love you both, from Mama I never could part.
> Father, you've always been good to me.
> And a mama that's sweeter there never could be.
> So to answer that question, it's quite hard you see,
> I Love You Both.

By this time Von Tilzer had written several other songs that Miss Gilson liked, including "De Swellest Gal in Town," which was published soon after. She gave him some sound advice: there were far greater rewards in songwriting than in acting, and the place for songwriting was New York, not the "sticks."

Working as a groom for a trainload of horses, Von Tilzer made his way to New York. Arriving in 1892 with only $1.65 in his pocket, he found a cheap room near the Brooklyn Bridge and got himself a job playing piano in a saloon for $15 a week. Working at the saloon left him ample time to compose dozens of songs every month, and he sold them wherever he could, sometimes for as little as $2.

The diversity of Von Tilzer's early songs was amazing—they included waltzes, German-dialect and Irish-brogue songs, even minstrel-coon songs. Little by little his songs were becoming known; some even made it to the stage of Tony Pastor's Music Hall in Union Square, the future site of Tin Pan Alley. In June 1896, Von Tilzer himself became a performer, joining up with George Sidney in a German-dialect comedy act. Most of his early songs were quite forgettable, but when he had hits, they were enormous.

Von Tilzer shared a room with a lyricist named Andrew B. Sterling, and it was with him that Von Tilzer wrote his first smash hit. The year was 1898 and the song was "My Old New Hampshire Home." The two men wrote it late one night, in the top-floor room they shared on 15th Street. They had to work by the light of the street lamp outside because they owed three weeks' back rent and were afraid to turn their lights on, and they scrawled the words and music on the back of a rent bill for want of writing paper. The next day they made the rounds of the publishing houses around Union Square. No one wanted the song, but finally they were able to sell it to a local printer named William C. Dunn, who controlled the Orphean Music Company. Amazingly enough, "My Old New Hampshire Home" went on to sell over 2 million copies.[8]

Even before Dunn knew that it was going to be a hit, however, he bought another Von Tilzer song, "I'd Leave My Happy Home for You." It sold almost as many copies as "My Old New Hampshire Home," but as a "coon song" was somewhat different from what vaudeville audiences were used to. The song was based on the following real events. In 1897, while appearing in a show in Hartford, Connecticut, Von Tilzer was approached by a young girl who begged him to find her a job in the theatre; she came from a wealthy home, she said, and was ready to sacrifice everything in order to be on the stage. To rid himself of this nuisance, Von Tilzer told the girl that he would try to find her something after the run of the show ended. On closing night, the girl was waiting in the theatre, ready to follow him anywhere. She even said, "I'd leave my happy home for you." Von Tilzer got rid of the girl, but he took her statement to lyricist Will A. Heelan, who quickly scribbled out some words with a slight "negro flavor" to them, including the repetition of the nonsense syllables "oo-oo."

> I'd leave my happy home for you, oo-oo-oo-oo,
> You're de nicest man I ever knew, oo-oo-oo-oo.
> If you take me and just break me in de business, too, oo,
> I'd leave my happy home for you, oo-oo-oo-oo.

The song was first used in vaudeville by Annette Flagler and then was presented at Tony Pastor's Music Hall by Blanche Ring, who enjoyed enormous success with it.

These two songs made Dunn a very wealthy publisher and Von Tilzer a recognized songwriter. Dunn soon sold out his company to two newcomers to the music business, Lew Bernstein and Maurice Shapiro. Exhibiting great business sense, Shapiro and Bernstein took Von Tilzer off the vaudeville stage and paid him $4,000 royalties for "My Old New Hampshire Home" as an advance against the money they might earn from it, a gesture of good will since they owned the song outright and did not have to pay him anything. Soon after, Shapiro and Bernstein made Von Tilzer a staff songwriter and then a junior partner, changing the company's name to Shapiro, Bernstein and Von Tilzer.[9]

Their wisdom was rewarded two years later when Von Tilzer wrote a two-million-copy seller called "A Bird in a Gilded Cage," with lyrics by Arthur Lamb. Von Tilzer had originally refused to write the music for Lamb's lyrics until it was clarified that the song's heroine was *married* to the rich old man, not just living with him. Once Lamb had made the necessary changes, Von Tilzer went off to a party with the "poem" in his pocket. The party ended up in a "road house of unsavory reputation." There he composed the tune.[10] When some of the "women" at the road house broke down into tears upon hearing it, he exclaimed: "If these ladies weep real tears over my song, I have composed a hit!"[11]

"A Bird in a Gilded Cage" was typical of the early Tin Pan Alley style both in content and in music. The song pointed up a moral that was very fashionable in the 1890's—that gold does not buy love or happiness. Musically it was a lovely waltz— quite appropriate since the story was set at a ball.

> The ballroom was filled with fashion's throngs,
> It shone with a thousand lights.
> And there was a woman who passed along,
> The fairest of all the sights.

The rest of the story dealt with a young woman married to a wealthy old man. She does not outlive him as she had expected, and the chorus serves as a eulogy over her grave.

> 'Tis sad when you think of her wasted life,
> For youth cannot mate with age,
> And her beauty was sold
> For an old man's gold,
> She's a bird in a gilded cage.[12]

The similarity to several of the songs written by Charles K. Harris is obvious; although Von Tilzer was brilliant, it really cannot be claimed that he was original. Von Tilzer resembled Harris in another respect also. Though his bosses paid him handsomely for "A Bird in a Gilded Cage," he decided to follow Harris's lead and establish his own publishing firm. After working with Shapiro and Bernstein, Von Tilzer wrote many great hits, including "Shine On, Harvest Moon" and "Wait Till the Sun Shines, Nelly," but he enjoyed his greatest success in the year immediately after he started his own firm on 28th Street.[13]

Between 1902, when he started the firm, and 1906, Von Tilzer wrote seven major hits. Four of them were composed in the firm's initial year, 1902, and sold over 5 million copies of sheet music. The first was "The Mansion of Aching Hearts," a sequel to "A Bird in a Gilded Cage." Here Von Tilzer preached against the idea that diamonds and gold could buy happiness. Irving Berlin, as a little boy, earned pennies by singing this song on the streets of the Bowery. As will be seen later, his relationship with Von Tilzer was to become much closer.

The second of Von Tilzer's 1902 hits was "Down Where the Wurzburger Flows." He had originally intended it to be used as a German drinking song in the Broadway musical *Wild Rose*, but when it was not accepted, Von Tilzer attempted to arouse the interest of other singers. Nora Bayes, still a relative newcomer to the stage, accepted the song and premiered it at the Orpheum Theatre in Brooklyn. Von Tilzer was sitting in one of the boxes, and like any good song plugger, he rose and sang several refrains when Miss Bayes had finished.[14] He was so good a "stooge" that he was hired for a week to continue plugging the song![15] Miss Bayes sang it so many times that she became known as "the Wurzburger Girl." In 1903 Von Tilzer wrote a sequel entitled "Under the Anheuser Bush."

Another of Von Tilzer's hits in 1902, "On a Sunday Afternoon," started out as an idea he had at Brighton Beach in Brooklyn. While enjoying the sand and the view, he came up with the thought that "people work hard on Monday, but Sunday is one fun day." Von Tilzer gave this appealing concept to his lyricist, Andrew B. Sterling, who created a lyric for it, and then he gave the completed song to the singing team of Weber and Fields. With their help it was soon selling 10,000 copies of music each day in New York City alone. "On a Sunday Afternoon" was one of the first seasonal songs to be produced on Tin Pan Alley.[16]

The fourth of Von Tilzer's 1902 hits was "Please Go 'Way and Let Me Sleep," for which he wrote the lyrics as well as the music. This song became a success as a result of brilliant plugging conceived by Von Tilzer himself. When the minstrel Arthur Deming introduced it in vaudeville, Harry Von Tilzer was sitting in the audience, pretending to be asleep and snoring loudly. Deming stopped singing and ordered an usher to wake the rude fellow and escort him out. As Von Tilzer was being shaken, he drowsily began the chorus, saying, "Please go 'way and let me sleep."

The publicity gained by this "shtick" assured huge sales for "Please Go 'Way and Let Me Sleep." As a semi-coon song, it typified a style often used by Von Tilzer. His first big coon song was "Down Where the Cotton Blossoms Grow" (1901), with lyrics by Andrew B. Sterling. Two others were "Alexander, Don't You Love Your Baby No More?" and "What You Goin' to Do When the Rent Comes Round?"

"Alexander, Don't You Love Your Baby No More?" the song on which Irving Berlin based "Alexander's Ragtime Band," was created from personal experiences. While at a performance by the minstrel team of McIntyre and Heath, Von Tilzer noticed that the name "Alexander" always seemed to draw a laugh from the audience. He decided that it was a good name. Sometime later he overheard a black woman comment to her boyfriend, "Don't you love your baby no more?" Together these incidents were the impetus Von Tilzer needed.

"What You Goin' to Do When the Rent Comes Round?" was also inspired by a real-life incident. While standing in the railroad station in Miami, Florida, Von Tilzer heard a black woman berating her husband for his lazy ways. "What you goin to do when the rent comes round?" she asked. Von Tilzer used the question as his theme and named the fellow in the song Rufus Johnson Brown. [17]

Actually Von Tilzer wrote songs in many styles, including "mammy songs," such as "I Want a Girl Just Like the Girl That Married Dear Old Dad" (1911), and ballads, such as "Wait Till the Sun Shines, Nellie." The latter sold more than 1 million copies. Some say its title was derived from a reporter's remark to a family whose property had been destroyed in a storm. Others maintain that Von Tilzer overheard it while standing in a hotel lobby. Whatever the source, "Wait Till the Sun Shines, Nellie" was one of his most successful songs. After the San Francisco fire it was even used by relief workers to cheer up the survivors: "Wait till the sun shines, Frisco." [18]

Harry Von Tilzer wrote songs about Ireland, "A Little Bunch of Shamrocks," about the South, "Down Where the Cotton Blossoms Grow," and about telephones, "Hello, Central, Give Me 603," later known as "All Alone" (about thirteen years earlier than the Irving Berlin song of the same name), and the first song for which an actual telephone was used on stage as a prop. As late as 1905, with "Where the Morning Glories Twine," he was also still attempting to write the kind of song people had enjoyed in the 1890's. A fine example of sentimental balladry, this song spoke of a desire to return to the innocence of lost youth.

> Mother dear will come to meet me
> And a sweetheart's kiss will greet me,
> Where the morning glories twine around the same
>   old door.[19]

The fad of writing songs about popular dances of the day was another Von Tilzer innovation. His first venture in this genre was "The Cubanola." Originally intended to be interpolated in a musical called *The Girl from Rector's*, it was introduced in 1909 by Harriet Raymond and served as the vanguard for other dance songs, such as "The Bunny Hug," "The Grizzly Bear," and "The Turkey Trot." Von Tilzer's last hit, "Just Around the Corner," came out in 1925. He had not had any big ones for several years and the Broadway producer Elizabeth Marbury wrote him a letter to console him, saying, "Just around the corner the sun will shine for you." Inspired by this statement, and with the help of Ted Lewis and his band, Von Tilzer's last song became a success.

Harry Von Tilzer was probably the most prolific songwriter in the annals of Tin Pan Alley, but he would deserve a place in the history of American music even if he had never written anything. Why? Because he was the publisher of George Gershwin's first song, "When You Want 'Em, You Can't Get 'Em; When You Get 'Em, You Don't Want 'Em,"[20] and because he was the man who gave Irving Berlin his start in the music business,[21] employing him as a song plugger at Tony Pastor's club, advising him, and publishing his "Just Like the Rose."

More than a songwriter and publisher, Harry Von Tilzer was a family man. He was happily married on August 10, 1906, and lived with his wife until his death on January 10, 1946. He spent his last years as a companion for his friends, resting on his musical laurels. He was one of the few popular composers to show development in his songwriting; he wrote in all the styles found in the popular music world and helped to mold and satisfy the public taste. If the 1890's can be called the Harrisian age, then the first decade of the 1900's should be called Von Tilzerian.

While in his office at 1587 Broadway not long before he died, Harry Von Tilzer was asked where Tin Pan Alley was. "Where is it? Songs. The real songs were written in the old days when pluggers were pluggers. A team gets excited now when it turns out a song that sells a few hundred thousand copies, why I've had one-hundred-eighteen songs that sold over half a million copies a piece. Under that number I wouldn't dream of calling it a hit."[22] For many years they, Von Tilzer and Tin Pan Alley, were synonymous. When he died, it did too.

Albert Von Tilzer, Harry's younger brother, also played an important role in the history of American popular music. He was born in Indianapolis on March 29, 1878, and learned to play the piano as a young boy. While working as the music director of a small vaudeville troupe, he was called to Chicago by Harry and given a job with Shapiro, Bernstein and Von Tilzer. He soon became interested in songwriting, but left for New York, where he became a shoe salesman in a department store. In 1900 he wrote his first song, "Absent Minded Beggar Waltz." In 1903 Harry published a song for which Albert had written both words and music.

Albert Von Tilzer will be remembered for two reasons. First, in 1903, he and his brother Jack opened their own publishing firm, the York Music Company. Second, he wrote two very successful songs, "Take Me Out to the Ball Game" (1908), which has become the national anthem of the sport, and "I'll Be with You in Apple Blossom Time," made popular in vaudeville by Nora Bayes and later by the Andrews Sisters.[23] Albert Von Tilzer died in Hollywood, where he was writing movie songs, on October 1, 1956.

The Theatre Giants

Opera Impresario Oscar Hammerstein I   CULVER

Courtesy of American Jewish Archives

Sigmund Romberg

George Gershwin—The Musician

Ira Gershwin—The Lyricist

Irving Berlin

Special Medal for Berlin Presented by President Dwight D. Eisenhower

Richard Rodgers and Lorenz Hart

Richard Rodgers While Working with Oscar Hammerstein II

Jerome Kern's Greatest Collaborator, Oscar Hammerstein II

10

JEROME KERN

Jerome David Kern was the first and the best—the teacher and the master of American musical theatre composers. They all recognized this. As Richard Rodgers said, "If you were at all sensitive to music, Kern had to be your idol. You had to worship Kern."[1]

Kern's work towered over that of his contemporaries. Many "embryonic" artists, inspired by his songs, became his disciples. George Gershwin was profoundly affected by two Kern songs he heard at his aunt's wedding when he was sixteen. Impressed by the unusual quality of the music, he asked the bandleader to tell him the composer's name. The songs were "You're Here and I'm Here" and "They Didn't Believe Me."[2] Gershwin wrote later, "I followed Kern's works and studied each song he composed. I paid him the tribute of frank imitation, and many things I wrote at this period sounded as though Kern had composed them himself."[3]

According to lyricist Oscar Hammerstein II, his sometime collaborator, Kern would spend hours working on a single modulation of a song. Wrote Hammerstein, "Kern would almost frantically work to ferret out some attractive and unusual way for creating a bridge from a verse to a refrain. I have seen him take off his shirt and work in his undershirt, the sweat pouring off of him, forgetting completely that I was there and that he was using up my time as well as his own."[4]

From the early 1920's until his death in 1945, Kern created a strong base upon which theatrical music could stand. Although he was never convinced that show music should not be operatic in style, he provided a typically American style for what had been a European genre. The number of classic songs in the thirty-six shows Kern wrote is amazing. Their stylistic patterns conformed to the popular music of the day, and most of the themes were not unusual. What made the songs so special and great was the fact that each aspect of every song fit into the pattern Kern had decided upon.

Born on January 27, 1885, in New York City, Jerome David Kern was the youngest of nine boys, of whom three survived. His parents, Fanny and Henry Kern, lived rather well, especially in comparison to the parents of the other composers included in this book. Henry Kern was the president of a firm which served the New York sanitation department, sprinkling the streets. He also sold real estate. Fanny, a fine pianist, provided the family's culture and music.

As a youngster, in the family home on East 74th Street, Jerome Kern entered the world of music by studying the piano with his mother as teacher. She was a strict disciplinarian, but he learned effortlessly and soon was always doing exercises or improvisations. Although coming from a German-Jewish home, Kern often visited a nearby Episcopal church to hear the choir practice. At age ten he saw his first musical show, *The Wizard of the Nile*, by Victor Herbert. Already he was showing signs of musical genius, for upon his return from the theatre, he sat down at the piano and, without the sheet music, played most of the songs from the show.

In 1895, when Kern was ten, his family moved to Newark, New Jersey, where Henry Kern had purchased a merchandising house. At Newark's Barringer High School Kern was recognized for his musical achievements. Referred to as "the little genius" by the teachers, who were impressed with his musical ability, not his scholastic aptitude, he soon was involved in all the musical activities at the school. After graduating from Barringer in 1902, Kern went on to Normal College in New York to prepare for a career as a music teacher, concurrently attending classes at the New York College of Music. There he received his first in-depth training in piano and harmony. His first published song, "At the Casino," was presented by the Lyceum Publishing Company in September of 1902.

Although Kern was one of the most thoroughly trained musicians to work in the field of popular music, his method of composition was almost entirely the same as that of the unschooled composers. He used the elementary lead sheet method, where just the melody line was written in, filling in with chords underneath. Only once did he attempt something more technical. In 1942, three years before he died, he composed a concert piece, "Mark Twain—A Portrait for Orchestra." As the critics said, he should have stayed with popular songs.[5]

In 1903 Kern went to Europe for a year. After studying composition and harmony with teachers in Heidelberg, he went to London, where Charles Frohman hired him to contribute musical numbers as fillers for Frohman productions. At a salary of $10 per week, it wasn't a marvelous job, but it provided an extremely important dividend, for on one of his first songs, "Mr. Chamberlain," Kern collaborated with P. G. Wodehouse, just beginning as a journalist-lyricist. The two were brought together by Seymour Hicks, a popular actor at the time, and "Mr. Chamberlain" was composed for Hicks, who sang it as an interpolation to the show *The Beauty and the Bath*. Kern and Wodehouse were to renew their partnership several years later. Meanwhile, before returning to America, Kern also wrote four songs for the English musical *Mr. Wix of Wickham*.

Back in New York, Kern went to work for the Shapiro-Remick publishing house as a song plugger. He soon came to the attention of Max Dreyfus, who had taken over the directorship of T. B. Harms, the largest publishing house on Tin Pan Alley at that time. Recognizing Kern's talent, Dreyfus signed him as a staff pianist,[6] later commenting: "I decided to take him on and to start him off by giving him the toughest job I know, selling music."[7]

In addition to plugging songs at various department stores, Kern kept writing new ones for Harms to publish. One of these was his first American success, "How'd You Like to Spoon with Me." The lyrics were written by Edward Laska, who had been commissioned by a producer to do a song for a show and approached Kern for a melody. Kern provided one he had written while in high school. When the producer turned the song down because he didn't like the use of "spoon" in the title, Laska and Kern took it to the Shuberts, who gladly interpolated it into their musical *The Earl and the Girl,* which opened on November 4, 1905. Wrote Laska:

The Shuberts were then just starting as producers and had one show on and another in rehearsal. Their office was atop the Lyric Theatre on 42nd Street which had been built for them by the socialite composer, Reginald De Koven.

Sam Shubert, the leading one of the three brothers, came out to see us and up chirped Jerry, "We are proteges of Reginald De Koven and have a song for you to hear." I nearly collapsed at hearing who we were, and Shubert, impressed with our connection, led us to an adjoining room with a piano. Jerry played and I sang. They were enthusiastic and agreed to feature it. . . . The song was an enormous hit and swept the English speaking world."[8]

The practice of interpolating new songs into existing shows was quite widespread at this time, and it gave Kern plenty of opportunities to write for the musical theatre without having to endure the pressure of doing an entire score. Between 1905 and 1912 he placed more than one hundred songs in shows written by others, and all told more than thirty musicals benefited from his contributions.[9] By all accounts a humorless man, Kern once commented that "Interpolating was such a common practice that a producer could go to the rear of a theater to congratulate a composer on a show's opening night success and find a whole crowd of songwriters saying thanks."[10] Though he himself was frequently one of them during the early part of his career, Kern was to condemn this practice years later, especially in cases where songs that had no bearing whatever on a show's plot or theme were brought in simply to exploit the commercial potential. "Songs," he said, "must be suited to the action and the mood of the play. My mission is to do something for the future of American music which today has no class whatsoever."[11]

In 1912 Kern was called upon to write the entire score for *The Red Petticoat.* It was a terrible failure, as were his next two musicals, but in 1914 he achieved his first Broadway success with some songs he contributed to *The Girl from Utah,* a show imported from England. Among them was "They Didn't Believe Me," his most famous and earliest "standard," and the first of his songs to sell a great amount of sheet music, more than 2 million copies. Kern wrote "They Didn't Believe Me" expressly for Julia Sanderson, who played the show's title role. The words, by Herbert Reynolds, contained several musical surprises which helped to sustain interest in the song. As will be related in Chapter 12, another song from the same show, "You're Here and I'm Here," first awakened George Gershwin's interest in songwriting.[12]

Around this time, Elizabeth Marbury, the owner of the Princess Theatre, decided to experiment with a new kind of low-budget musical, utilizing a smaller orchestra and less elaborate sets, that could be produced comfortably in her small playhouse. She approached Kern and an English lyricist-liberettist, Guy Bolton. They accepted, and from 1915 through 1919 Kern wrote the music for a series of "Princess shows" (named, of course, for the theatre). Unlike the operettas he had earlier favored,[13] these turned out to be situation comedies about American life, with honeymoon couples, rather than royalty, as their characters. In many respects they reflected Kern's fascination with American culture. A highly assimilated German Jew, he pioneered the American school of music and aspired to write an American operetta.[14]

As the basis for their first Princess show, which opened in 1915, Kern and Bolton adapted an English musical of Bolton's entitled *Nobody Home.* The cast comprised a chorus line of eight women, the principals, and an orchestra of ten. A radical departure from what had been seen earlier in American theatre, the show was well received by critics and audiences alike, even earning a small profit. Its major song, "The Magic Melody," became a hit.

The second Princess show, *Very Good, Eddie,* also opened in 1915. Guy Bolton was the librettist, and the lyrics for Kern's songs were written by Schuyler Greene. The plot concerned two married couples who plan a trip on the Hudson River Day Line. Somehow they get mixed up, so that one wife is with the other husband, but to maintain appearances, they continue the charade. The reviews were excellent, commenting that this was a "kitchenette production" and a "pleasing parlor entertainment."[15] The songs included "Babes in the Woods," and "Nodding Roses." The show earned a $100,000 profit.

In 1917 Kern wrote *Oh Boy!* The show was the vehicle for one of his best-known songs, "Till the Clouds Roll By" (also the title of Kern's film biography), as well as for "Nesting Time in Flatbush," a parody of "When It's Apple Blossom Time in Normandy." Even more successful than *Very Good, Eddie, Oh Boy!* ran for 463 performances, a very long run in those days. Perhaps more important, it reunited Kern with P. G. Wodehouse, his collaborator of thirteen years before. Wodehouse had been sent to review the show. The two men were delighted to see each other, and Wodehouse agreed when Kern suggested that they work together again.

In addition to *Oh Boy!* Kern wrote four other musicals in 1917, *Have a Heart, Love o'Mike, Leave It to Jane,* and *Miss 1917.* Except for *Love o'Mike,* the lyrics were all by Wodehouse. The next year, Kern, Wodehouse, and Bolton wrote another successful Princess show, *Oh, Lady, Lady.* So great was the demand for tickets that a second company was formed at another theatre to run concurrently with the Princess theatre production. The show's songs included "Oh, Lady, Lady," and "Before I Met You." Another of the songs, "Bill," had to be dropped because it was unsuited to the voice of the star, Vivienne Segal, but it turned up years later, and much more effectively, in *Show Boat.*

In 1919 a curious incident took place which had a great effect on Kern's attitude toward his music. A ragtime pianist named Johnny Black had borrowed a melody from vaudevillian Felix Bernard, added some Middle Eastern embellishments, and presented it to publisher Fred Fisher, who added story and lyrics to produce the song known as "Dardanella." A few months later Fisher claimed that "the regal theatre composer" Jerome Kern had stolen "Dardanella" for his song "Kalua." Kern was furious and brought several musicians into court to defend his position. Leopold Stokowski and Victor Herbert both testified that Fisher could not claim ownership since the line of music in question was taken from a nineteenth-century classical song. The jury which heard the case awarded one dollar to Fisher for damages.[16] As a result of this incident, Kern became very concerned about even the smallest details of the publication, performance, and arrangement of his songs. When radio first came into prominence, he even attempted to keep his songs off the air waves.

Although Kern achieved great success with his low-budget, contemporary-setting Princess shows, it should not be thought that he totally ignored the enormous costume musicals of the day. In fact he wrote several of the most gaudy and beautiful of them all. In 1920 the first of these costumed pageants, *Sally*, was produced by Florenz Ziegfeld. As usual with a Ziegfeld production, the costumes and sets were designed by the best people available—in this instance the costume designer was the great Joseph Urban.

The star of *Sally* was Marilyn Miller, for whom Kern wrote one of his most beautiful melodies, "Look for the Silver Lining," apparently as a companion piece for his earlier "Till the Clouds Roll By." The lyrics were written by B. G. De Sylva, who later wrote with Gershwin and Lew Brown. The song's inspiring quality was derived as much from Kern's magnificent melody, however, as from the beautiful lyrics. Also included in the score were the songs "Whippoorwill" and "Wild Rose," each of which did very well. Music critic Alec Wilder wrote that in *Sally* Kern created the first "American Sound" by combining the best that non-American theatre music had to offer, mainly European, with American themes.[17] In addition, one may add, Kern hybridized elements of ragtime into a syncopated approach to music that was entirely his own but carried with it a strong flavor of American black music. It is no wonder, then, that he influenced Gershwin as he did.[18]

During the next seven years, Kern wrote nine more shows, all relatively successful. In 1923 came *Stepping Stones*, starring Fred Stone, his wife Allene, and their daughter, Dorothy. The score included "Once in a Blue Moon" and "Raggedy Ann." Kern's next very successful show was in 1925, *Sunny*, starring Marilyn Miller, who had been such a hit in *Sally*. For her Kern wrote a song that posed an extremely difficult problem for the lyricist,

Oscar Hammerstein. It started out with a single note which had to be held for nine beats, a very long time, and obviously several words could not be sung on only one note. Hammerstein came up with an ingenious solution by using the word "who" five times in the refrain. Kern said later that this was Hammerstein's greatest lyric.[19] The next year, 1926, Kern wrote *Criss Cross*, a follow-up musical for the Stone family.

By 1927 Kern had become the most prosperous and highly-regarded composer on Broadway. He had enormous wealth and a mansion in Bronxville, New York, where he lived with his wife, the former Eva Leale, an English girl from Walton on the Thames, whom he had married on October 10, 1910, and their daughter, Betty, who had been born in 1918. He owned two automobiles, one of them a Rolls-Royce, a speedboat, and a houseboat on which he would travel to Florida. His major luxury, however, was his collection of rare books, the largest such collection owned by a private individual. It included first editions of Tennyson, Shelley, Shakespeare, and Samuel Johnson, copies autographed by Kipling, and so on. When he purchased the collection it cost him about $750,000. In 1928, perhaps having a premonition of the depression to come, he auctioned it off for $2,200,000, at the time the largest sum ever paid for such a collection. Kern also collected gold, stamps, coins, silver goblets, virtually anything of value. Yet with his enormous wealth he was one of the cheapest men on Broadway. He rarely if ever left a tip at a restaurant and tried whenever possible to force his less-pecunious friends into paying for meals.

Kern enjoyed jokes and games, but only if he was the winner, and he was the inventor of "Guggenheim," a word-association game that became the rage in the 1920's. He was also a jokester who liked to play tricks on other people. His greatest pleasure apparently came from showing up his friends if they made a mistake in a game or a puzzle. At the same time, he was never able to admit that he too occasionally made mistakes. Indeed, he was a very difficult man, and he got more difficult as he got older.

Perhaps most confusing about Kern was his method of working. Although he was very organized when it came to some things, such as betting on horse races or collecting, his work habits were quite slovenly. He slept when he felt like it and composed in the middle of the night, more often than not calling his collaborator at three in the morning to discuss something he was working on. He never had to leave his piano because he had a desk built in for writing down his music.

When Kern wrote a song, the music always came first. Once he decided that he liked a tune, there was no way for the lyricist to get him to change a single note. The words had to fit the music exactly as Kern had written it. Often, when composing for a movie or a musical, he would write far more songs than necessary, so that at rehearsal he could choose the ones he liked the best. The rejected songs, of course, as in the case of "Bill," were kept for future projects.

In 1927, Kern finally realized his dream of writing a truly American musical with songs and story so integrated that they would be inseparable. The setting was the South—not Dixie and Mammy, but the real South. Earlier in the year, Kern had read Edna Ferber's novel *Show Boat*. The story was rich in the kind of Americana Kern so appreciated, and though it was rather unusual by the standards of the day, he immediately saw its potential as the basis for a musical. The characters included a riverboat gambler named Gaylord Ravenal and Magnolia Hawks, the daughter of the showboat's owner. Also, there was a subplot about the marriage of a black girl named Julie, the star of the showboat, to a half-white man. Kern realized that there was no place for dancing girls and choruses except in the show-within-a-show sequences on the riverboat. The main difficulty was in convincing Edna Ferber that her novel was suitable for a musical production. Then Kern got Oscar Hammerstein II to write the text and lyrics. Finally, Kern asked Florenz Ziegfeld to produce the musical. There was a certain amount of risk in doing so, for Ziegfeld was as strong-willed as Kern, but Kern knew that Ziegfeld was more interested in a class production that would make money than in artistic matters.

Today we view *Show Boat* as melodramatic and even gauche; in its day, however, it was seen as realistically historical. Kern attempted to write music that would evoke the 1890's, going so far as to use Charles K. Harris's masterpiece, "After the Ball," to lend more credibility.[20] Hammerstein and Kern met or spoke every day to keep abreast of what each was doing. They decided that all aspects of the show must fit together without any obvious seams. For example, Hammerstein told Kern that he wanted a song reflecting the influence of the Mississippi River on the black laborers—"a song of resignation with a protest implied, sung by a character who is a rugged and untutored philosopher." Kern understood what was needed and wrote the classic "Ol' Man River," a song steeped in Negro spiritual music.

Show Boat's other masterpieces include "Why Do I Love You," "Bill" (words by P. G. Wodehouse), "You Are Love," "Can't Help Lovin' Dat Man," and "Make Believe." Kern never wrote better, and thanks to his inspiring influence, neither did Hammerstein. His lyrics, so closely tied to the show that they forced the audience to keep the story in mind, were an important contribution to the history of the Broadway musical.

Many aspects of *Show Boat* were direct ties back to the operetta. It could have been no other way. Prior to *Show Boat*, Hammerstein had written two operettas with Sigmund Romberg, *Rose Marie* and *The Desert Song*, and Kern had been greatly influenced by the operetta while in Europe. Furthermore, *Show Boat* was a period piece, and it was set in an era when the operetta was in flower. Finally, with Ziegfeld as producer, it was a foregone conclusion that the constumes and sets would have had to be grand indeed. Given all these facts, it is no surprise that *Show Boat* was, in effect, an American operetta, the ultimate expression of the very genre Kern had long dreamed of creating.

It is interesting to note the various ways in which Kern was influenced by other composers of the day. The opening song had a clear similarity to the songs of Victor Herbert; others were reminiscent of Romberg and Friml; finally, "Can't Help Lovin' Dat Man" sounded much like the works of a new composer on Broadway, George Gershwin.

As all the critics agreed, *Show Boat* had a masterful score. Labeled an "American Masterpiece" and "a triumph," it ran for two years and earned more than $50,000 per week gross. The national tour lasted for a year, and three film versions of the show were made. Even the concert hall enjoyed its music, for Kern arranged a symphonic version at the request of Arthur Rodzinski and the Cleveland Orchestra. The 1946 revival on Broadway ran over one year and earned $2 million.

Kern never advanced technically beyond *Show Boat*. It was his most innovative score. Although he had discovered the need to tailor the songs to fit the story, he never was totally convinced. His next show, *Sweet Adeline*, written in 1929, was a return to the old-fashioned musical of the pre–*Show Boat* era. This is not to say that he did not continue to write magnificent songs for his shows; he did. In 1931 he wrote the score to the musical *The Cat and the Fiddle*. Described as a "musical love story," the show dealt with the love affair of a European opera composer and an American girl who is "crazy about" jazz. The songs included "The Night Was Made for Love," "Poor Pierrot," and the best-selling "She Didn't Say Yes." It ran for about a year.

Music in the Air, written in 1932, was called a "musical adventure." Set in a Bavarian village, with a cast that included the schoolteacher, the actor, the prima donna, etc., it had all the aspects of an operetta, but somehow Kern's believable characters and plot kept it from being totally operetta. Brooks Atkinson wrote in his review, "At last, musical drama has been emancipated."[21] The songs in this show were largely of the German beer hall variety, but it included two classics, "I've Told Every Little Star" and "The Song Is You."

Although Kern wrote several more musicals, he had only one other success. In 1933 the musical *Roberta* opened with a cast that included Bob Hope, Sydney Greenstreet, and George Murphy. A musical comedy–fashion show rather than a musical play, it included several well-known songs. The most famous, and one reason why the show continued to run, was "Smoke Gets in Your Eyes." It consistently stopped the show when sung in the second act and has since become a classic. Other songs from the score were "The Touch of Your Hands" and "Yesterdays."

After *Roberta*, Kern and Hammerstein turned to Donn Byrne's book *Messer Marco Polo*, a story about the adventurer's love for Golden Bells, a Chinese girl, as the source for their next show. When the two men met to discuss the project, Hammerstein said, "Here is a story laid in China about an Italian and told by an Irishman. What kind of music are you going to write?" Kern responded, "It'll be good Jewish music,"[22] one of the few references he ever made to being Jewish. The assimilation his parents desired certainly was achieved.

Kern's last musical, sadly, was his greatest disaster. Entitled *Very Warm for May*, it did not run more than two months. The reviews were dismal, and the show would have been totally forgotten had it not included one of Kern's most beautiful songs, "All the Things You Are." It became one of his six most successful songs, selling several million copies of sheet music and records. With that song and show Kern's Broadway career came to an end. He had written more than ninety musicals and more than five hundred songs, of which sixty became classics.

Kern was also quite active in Hollywood, where he duplicated his success on Broadway. First of all, he adapted his own musicals for the screen: *Show Boat* and *Sally* in 1929, *Sunny* in 1930, *The Cat and the Fiddle* in 1933, and finally *Music in the Air* in 1934. After these he began writing original movie musicals. His first was *I Dream Too Much* and his last was *Centennial Summer*, which opened after his death. During his Hollywood years he wrote many classic songs, including "The Way You Look Tonight" (1936), "A Fine Romance" (1936), "Dearly Beloved" (1942), "Long Ago and Far Away" (1942), and "All Through the Day" (1946).

One of Kern's most famous songs for the screen, "The Last Time I Saw Paris," had an interesting story. In June of 1940, Oscar Hammerstein was deeply moved by the news that the Germans had captured Paris and wrote a poem describing his feelings. He asked several composers to set the words to music, finally settling on his old partner, Kern, who wrote the melody in only one day. The song was presented by Kate Smith on her radio program and became an enormous success. In 1941 it was interpolated into the otherwise totally Gershwin movie musical *Lady, Be Good*, and went on to win the Academy Award for best song.

When Kern first moved to Hollywood, he was determined to stay in California for the rest of his life and built himself an

enormous mansion in Beverly Hills. In 1945, though, he returned to New York to co-produce a revival of *Show Boat*, for
which he wrote "No One But Me," a new song that was destined
to be his last. He also agreed to write a musical comedy based on
the life of Annie Oakley for the production team of Rodgers and
Hammerstein.[23]

Kern did not live to see the revival or to complete the score for
Rodgers and Hammerstein. At noon on November 5, 1945, he
collapsed of a cerebral hemorrhage. He died two days later, with
Oscar Hammerstein at his side. Irving Berlin, who had come to
visit him, was the first person to be told of his death.

It was Hammerstein's task to deliver the eulogy at Kern's
funeral. He said, "We all know in our hearts that these few
minutes we devote to him are small drops in the ocean of our
affections. Our real tribute will be paid over many years of
remembering. . . . We will remember a jaunty, happy man
whose sixty years were crowded with success and fun and love.
Let us thank whatever God we believe in, that we shared some
part of the good, bright life Jerry led on this earth." The *New York
Herald* said it differently, "Genius is surely not too extravagant a
word for him."[24]

Jerome Kern was many things, but he was not a kind man.
Very few people knew him well or liked him. He was opinion-
ated and spared no criticism of his friends, even condemning as
"simply condescending" the songs that his former partner Oscar Hammerstein II wrote with Richard Rodgers for the classic
Oklahoma![25] Discussing Kern's relationships with his fellow
songwriters, a contemporary once remarked, "I think in those
days, certainly Jerome Kern disliked all of them and they all
disliked Kern."

There was another side, though, but it was rarely seen and
became even less evident with the passage of time. P. G. Wodehouse, for example, found Kern to be a warm and respectful
co-worker. "Nothing could have been more pleasant than my
relationship with Jerry," he recalled many years later. "Not a
cross word, as they say. But I am told that after *Show Boat* he
became a little difficult and had a good deal to say to his lyricists
about their defects. He also changed from the rollicking spirit of

the 'Princess' days into what you might call the Music Master. I never saw that side of him. To me he has always been the Jerry of *Oh, Boy!* and *Oh, Lady, Lady!* and the dozen other shows we did together."[26]

Questions of personality aside, Jerome Kern unquestionably provided the impetus for the advancements in musical theatre that followed him. We have already mentioned his influence on Gershwin and Richard Rodgers. There can be little doubt that the modern musical theatre was in large part his creation.

11

IRVING BERLIN

It would be impossible to discuss the American music industry or the American popular song without mentioning Irving Berlin. He was the twentieth-century counterpart to Stephen Foster, a comparison Berlin himself enjoyed making.[1] As one critic commented years after Berlin had made it to the top, he was a "poor Jew who won fame and fortune triumphing not through education or skill, but through his knowledge of the common heart."[2]

Legend has it that after Berlin became rich and famous, he built a "pianistic contrivance" that would take stock harmonies and modulations derived from the Massenet-Grieg method of fifty years before and fit them into the traditional thirty-two-bar tune at the touch of a lever! Although the story is apocryphal, it is true that Berlin had an uncanny knowledge of the interests and tastes of the common man. Perhaps he understood the public taste so well because he grew up as a common man.

Born in Temun, Siberia, on May 11, 1888, Irving (originally Israel) Berlin was the youngest of the eight children of Moses and Leah Baline (the original family name). His father was a shochet and chazan in the village.[3] In 1893, in search of opportunity, the family came to America. Irving Berlin was later quick to point out that although they left Russia as a result of the anti-Jewish pogroms during the reign of Czar Alexander III,[4] they were not political refugees.[5] The impetus to leave, however, was provided by a pogrom that took place when he was four years old. While the Cossacks ravaged the village, the family took refuge in the nearby woods, hiding under blankets.

133

When the Balines arrived in America with their few possessions, they moved into an apartment in a dingy basement on
Monroe Street, the Lower East Side of New York. Years later,
describing the family upon its arrival, Berlin said, "We only
spoke Yiddish and were conspicuous for our 'jew clothes.' "[6] A
few weeks later, the family rented a more commodious apartment on Cherry Street. Moses found work as a kosher butcher
supervisor, also teaching Hebrew and choir music in a small
synagogue near their home. Leah, typical of the immigrants of
the day, did not understand any language except Yiddish. She
kept a kosher home, and although the family could ill afford
one, always had a kosher cook.

Quite naturally, Irving Berlin grew up well versed in the
lifestyle and milieu of the Lower East Side.[7] Profoundly interested in singing even as a child, he was a member of the synagogue choir and went to the Yiddish theatre whenever he could
afford it.[8] His musical ear, as well as his unique ability to recall
any melody he heard, was clearly an inheritance from his father
the chazan, but whereas his father had enjoyed cantorial music,
young Irving developed a taste for the sentimental ballads of the
1890's.

The family's financial problems were compounded by the
death of Moses Baline in 1896. Four of the older children found
work in sweatshops, and young Irving helped out by selling
newspapers and delivering telegrams.[9] At fourteen, having
completed only two years of formal schooling, he ran away from
home and began to earn his living as a singing waiter in saloons
and bars—the fulfillment of an ambition dating back many
years. His mother was horrified, but as Berlin later explained, he
could not have done otherwise. "Music," he said, "was in my
blood."[10]

Berlin's singing got him jobs in various New York nightspots,
among them Callahan's in Chinatown and Chatham's on Doyer
Street.[11] For a while he worked as a song plugger for Harry Von
Tilzer, and he was also a singing waiter for "Nigger" Mike Salter,
a Russian Jew with a very swarthy complexion, in whose restaurant he worked nights from 8 P.M. until 6 A.M.[12]

In 1906 Berlin was hired as a singing waiter at Pelham's Cafe on Pell Street. In addition to entertaining the patrons while serving them, he had to write and sing parodies of current popular songs, and also had to help clean up when the cafe closed—all of this for the munificent sum of one dollar per day.

The story is told that one night Prince Louis of Battenberg and some friends were in the cafe. The prince was so impressed with the young Berlin's singing talent that he gave him a five-dollar tip, the equivalent of a week's wages. Berlin turned the tip down, and this earned him his first newspaper publicity from another future great, Herbert Bayard Swope, then a struggling young reporter.[13]

Pelham's Cafe was situated near Callahan's Cafe. A song by two of Callahan's employees "My Mariuccia Takes a Steamboat," first sung at the cafe in 1906, had later been published, bringing Callahan's a certain amount of favorable publicity. The management of Pelham's decided that they too needed a song, so they told Berlin to write one.

With music by the saloon's pianist, Nick Nicholson, Berlin composed his first song, "Marie from Sunny Italy." It was published by Joseph Stern and Company in 1907 and earned him 37 cents in royalties, but it gave him more than that because the printer inadvertently changed his name from Israel Baline to Israel Berlin. Taking the change one final step further, the budding composer adopted Irving as his first name. "Marie from Sunny Italy" reflected several aspects of Berlin's personality. First, it was a parody of the "Mariuccia" song; more importantly, it illustrated a world that Irving Berlin knew well—the world of the immigrant. In many ways, Berlin felt that he had no real home, and over the years he was to write songs of all ethnic homelands: Italy, Spain, Cuba, even Russia.[14]

A year later, in 1908, Berlin wrote his next song. By now he had left Pelham's and was working in another cafe. A vaudevillian there hired him to write a topical song for his act. Berlin wrote a poem about an Olympic runner named Dorando who had been in the news of the day. When the vaudevillian rejected it, Berlin set out to find a publisher. He approached Ted Snyder, who had just opened his own publishing house. Snyder offered him $25 if he could write the music as well, so Berlin dictated a tune to an arranger who worked for Snyder. This was the first time that Berlin composed the music for a song, and it pointed up a failing he was to bemoan for the rest of his creative life—his inability to write his music down. Lacking musical training, Berlin was always dependent on the services of a musical stenographer to get his inspirations on paper. He "heard" the songs in his head and then had to have a transcriber put them into writing. His only piano skill was playing on the black notes—key of F sharp. For this reason he later had a special piano built, designed in such a way that with a turn of a lever it would play in any key he wanted while he continued to play only the black keys.[15]

With "Dorando," Berlin and Snyder established a fruitful songwriting partnership. Berlin began as a staff lyricist for the firm and later was made a junior partner. "Sweet Italian Love Song" and "That Beautiful Rag," two of the songs he wrote with Snyder, went into the musical revue *Up and Down Broadway*, in which both men also appeared as performers.

Around the same time Berlin also wrote the hit "Sadie Salome, Go Home," with lyrics by Edgar Leslie.[16] Berlin had earlier used a Felix Mendelssohn melody for his "That Mesmerizing Mendelssohn Tune," in which he "ragtimed" Mendelssohn's "Spring Song." "Sadie Salome," the first of Berlin's Yiddish-type songs, echoed the coon songs that were so popular in those days and parodied "Bill Bailey, Won't You Please Come Home." The story concerned a Jewish girl doing things that only gentiles were supposed to do, like getting involved with a "shegetz" boyfriend.

Set in the form of an operatic aria, "Sadie Salome" helped to make Fanny Brice a star when she debuted it at a benefit. She commented later that she had never expected to do a song in Yiddish dialect and was delighted by the enthusiastic audience reaction.[17] Brice presented a similar Berlin song in the *Follies of 1910* when she sang "Goodbye Becky Cohen," permanently establishing her reputation as the primary interpreter of Yiddish songs, a status she retained for many years.

Berlin became quite adept at Yiddish-type songs. Some of his others included "Yiddle on Your Fiddle Play Some Ragtime"

(1910), a song poking fun at a Jew for playing a black man singing about love for "mine choc'late baby,"[18] "Yiddishe Eyes," "Becky Do the Bombashay" (1910),[19] and finally, "My Yiddishe Nightingale."[20] Even in these Jewishly flavored songs there was a strong black theme, for they were all conscious parodies of the popular "coon" songs. Other Berlin songs from 1910 included "Call Me Up Some Rainy Afternoon," "Stop, Stop You're Breaking My Heart," "Kiss Me, My Honey, Kiss Me," and "Next to Your Mother, Who Do You Love?" all with words or music by Ted Snyder.[21]

Pastiche songs, a mixture of various ethnic and cultural songs combined into one style, all-American in nature, were another Berlin forte. Building on the styles and songs of his predecessors, combining old and new, he merged various song types, such as ballads and Negro comedy numbers, into new songs that were peculiarly his own.[22] Berlin got his lyrics by listening to others talk and picking up current catchphrases suitable for songs. He used to sit around in a cafe near a talkative bunch of people and eavesdrop on their conversation, occasionally writing down a phrase that caught his fancy. He was so versatile that people claimed he kept a "colored boy" prisoner in his office to help him turn out song hits.[23]

By 1910 Berlin had become interested in syncopation. Feeling quite strongly that "syncopation is the soul of every American" and "ragtime is the best heart raiser and worry banisher I know,"[24] he decided to write a song based on Harry Von Tilzer's "Alexander, Don't You Love Your Baby No More," but with a syncopated beat. Not pleased with the song that resulted, which he called "Alexander and His Clarinet," Berlin put it away. A year later in 1911, when he was invited to join the Friar's Club and perform in their show, the *Frolics*, he reworked the song, now called "Alexander's Ragtime Band." For some reason, though, he did not present it at the *Frolics* and instead attempted to sell it to various pluggers. It finally became a smash when presented by Emma Carus, the star "coon" performer. Sophie Tucker, George M. Cohan's wife, Ethel Levey, and many other singers also began using "Alexander's Ragtime Band," and ultimately it became the greatest hit of the day, selling more than 1 million copies of sheet music in the first three months of publication.

Curiously, there is only a tiny dash of syncopation in "Alexander's Ragtime Band." By 1911, in fact, the term "ragtime" was applied quite loosely to any song that was up-to-date and peppy,[25] and "Alexander's Ragtime Band" was actually an excellent slow march written in pseudo-black dialect. Although the verse contained a couple of examples of syncopation, there was none at all in the chorus. The syncopated rhythms are found on the words "just the" and "ragtime" in the reference to Stephen Foster's "Swanee River." Otherwise, the song is as "straight as Sousa"[26]—about ragtime rather than actually containing ragtime.

Years later Berlin confessed that he didn't really know what ragtime was when he wrote the most famous "ragtime" song ever composed, and in 1925, in an article for the *New York Dramatic Mirror*, he admitted that "Alexander's Ragtime Band" sounded like a funeral march! Nonetheless, he said, "I have one dream. . . . I shall write an opera completely in ragtime. I have not yet fully developed my story, but it will, of course, be laid in the South. . . . The opera will be following out my idea that beautiful thoughts can best be expressed by syncopation. It alone can catch the sorrows, the pathos of humanity."[27] He never did write that opera, but he achieved something of equal importance: never before—that is, until Irving Berlin's ragtime songs—had the ballad been replaced as the most popular song style.

Berlin soon was recognized as the major songwriter of the day. In 1911 his "Everybody's Doin' It" helped make the turkey trot a dance craze. He personally introduced "That Mysterious Rag" and "The Ragtime Jockey" in the Broadway revue *The Passing Show of 1912*, and in 1913 he went to England, where he appeared as the "ragtime king" at the Hippodrome Theatre, commanding a $1,000 per week fee.[28] For that show he wrote "The International Rag."

Irving Berlin's first complete score for a Broadway musical was *Watch Your Step*, which opened in 1914. Mainly a ragtime score, it also included several songs that began the Berlin tradition of beautiful ballads. One of the ragtime pieces, "The Syncopated Walk," written for the dancing stars of the show, Irene and Vernon Castle, became an enormous hit. "Play a Simple Melody," written in a style that was to become a Berlin trademark, combined two different lyrics and two different melodies to create a very interesting musical duet.

Berlin's first ballad to achieve a moderate success was written for the black vaudevillian Bert Williams. Entitled "Woodman, Woodman, Spare That Tree," it was a modern treatment of the Henry Russell song of seventy years earlier. Introduced in the *Ziegfeld Follies of 1911*, it was one reason why Williams continued to be a *Follies* star for many years. Other Berlin songs from this period include "When the Midnight Choo Choo Leaves for Alabam" (1912) and "Do It Again."[29]

One would think that the year Berlin married would have been a time of great productivity. It was indeed, but not because his marriage brought him joy. On February 3, 1913, Berlin married Dorothy Goetz, the sister of the composer and producer E. Ray Goetz. After spending their honeymoon in Cuba, they returned to New York, where Mrs. Berlin set up a home on Riverside Drive. Two weeks later, on July 17, 1913, she died of typhoid fever.[30] Berlin was grief-stricken, and he attempted to deal with his sorrow in the best way he knew—by writing a song. "When I Lost You," his first great ballad, says, "I lost the sunshine and the flowers when I lost you." Berlin wrote other autobiographical ballads later in his career, especially when he fell in love with Ellin Mackay.

The scope of Berlin's activities widened in the years after Dorothy's death. In 1915 he wrote "The Pullman Porters on Parade," with music by Maurice Abrahams. Not very proud of this song, Berlin published it under the pseudonym Ren G. May, made up of the letters in "Germany."[31] The following year, however, saw an enormous Berlin hit with "This Is the Life," which poked fun at farmers and rubes coming to the big city. Farmer Brown comes to town, takes in the sights and says, "I love the cows and chickens, but this is the life. No more picking berries, me for cocktail cherries."[32] Convinced by Berlin's success that they had to do something to keep him with the firm, his publishers, Snyder and Waterson, became Snyder, Berlin and Waterson. This was to last for seven years, but in 1919 Berlin opened his own firm.

Although Berlin was never known for his humility, he was rarely a braggart. In 1915, though, he tried to put his contributions to music in perspective. "Now just one boast: I believe that such songs of mine as 'Alexander's Ragtime Band,' 'That Mysterious Rag,' 'Ragtime Violin,' 'I Want to Be in Dixie,' and 'Take a Little Tip from Father' started the ragtime mania in America."[33] Berlin recognized the debt he owed to those who had come before him, and knew that the public wanted new songs that sounded familiar. He wrote in *Green Book Magazine* in 1916,

There's no such thing as a new melody. There has been an outstanding offer in Vienna, holding a large prize, to anyone who can write eight bars of original music. The offer has been up for more than twenty-five years. Thousands of compositions have been submitted, but all have been traced back to some other melody. Our work is to connect old phrases in a new way so that they will sound like a new tune. Did you know that the public when it hears a new song anticipates the next passage? The writers who do not give them something they are expecting are those who are successful.[34]

Drafted into the Army during World War I, Berlin wrote his first successful show, *Yip Yip Yaphank*, to aid in raising $35,000 for a service center at Camp Upton, New York. Berlin himself was in the show, singing "Oh How I Hate to Get Up in the Morning." After a limited engagement at the camp, the show opened on Broadway on July 26, 1918, earning $135,000 profit. Berlin wrote other songs for the war effort, including "The Devil Has Bought Up Coal"[35] and "Let's All Be Americans Now," a request to immigrants that they put away remembrances of the old country and become true-blue Americans.

Berlin, too, was anxious to prove himself a good American. Embarrassed by his surname, which evoked images of the German enemy, he tried to be more American than the Americans. One of the songs he wrote for *Yip Yip Yaphank* was "God Bless America," originally intended as the finale for the second act. Deciding that the song was not needed since the soldiers in the cast had already expressed their love for their country without having to sing about it, Berlin put it away. The song was later used in another context. Berlin's Americanism was also displayed at a wartime charity rally, where he was scheduled to follow his idol, George M. Cohan, the man who had once called him "that little Jew boy." While on stage singing "Over There," his own composition, Cohan forgot the words. Berlin prompted him from the audience. How all-American can you get?

After the Great War ended, Berlin was commissioned to write the songs for the *Ziegfeld Follies of 1919*. Three of his songs from this show became tremendous hits: "Mandy," taken from *Yip Yip Yaphank*, "You'd Be Surprised," later used by Eddie Cantor, and most successful of the three, "A Pretty Girl Is Like a Melody," which from that year onward became the *Follies* theme song.

By 1919, when he broke off from Snyder and Waterson to open his own publishing house, Berlin was earning $2,000 per week as a vaudeville headliner. Berlin brought a commodity of enormous value to his publishing company, his own songs. To celebrate the company's opening, "Irving Berlin weeks" were held all over the country. Around the same time Berlin became a theatre owner. The Music Box Theatre, which he established in partnership with Sam H. Harris and Joseph Schenk, opened with a specially written Berlin musical, the *Music Box Revue*. The revue continued for three years, producing several of Berlin's most successful hit songs, among them "Say It With Music," "What'll I Do," and "Pack Up Your Sins." One merely has to look at the song sales for 1919 to see how extremely well Berlin and his new company were doing.[36]

Title	Duration of Sale	Sheet Music	Piano Rolls	Phonograph Recordings
"You'd Be Surprised"	50 weeks	783,982	145,505	888,790
"Say It With Music"	75 weeks	374,408	102,127	1,239,050
"Nobody Knows"	70 weeks	1,143,690	62,204	843,082
"All By Myself"	75 weeks	1,053,493	161,650	1,225,083

In 1924 Berlin fell in love with the daughter of a wealthy non-Jewish industrialist, Clarence Mackay, president of Postal Telegraph. During their secret courtship, while her father attempted to dissuade Ellin from seeing the Jewish songwriter, Berlin wrote five of his most moving autobiographical ballads,

"All Alone," "Always," "All By Myself," "Remember," and "What'll I Do." The couple were married in a secret ceremony in New York's City Hall on January 4, 1926. According to a newspaper story at the time, Mackay, the father-in-law-to-be, once tried to awe Berlin with an account of his family's ancient lineage, but Berlin retorted, "We trace our family back to the Exodus." The two men were finally reconciled after Mackay lost his entire fortune in the 1929 stock market crash.

By 1929, though, Berlin was deep into a dry spell. Convinced that he was through musically, he had not written a hit song for three years. To add to his sorrow, Ellin delivered a baby boy who died of a heart defect. Ellin's friends wrote her that the baby's death was a punishment from God for marrying a Jew. As if all this was not misery enough, the depression wiped out the more than $5 million Berlin had accumulated over the years, leaving him with very little except the ownership of his songs.

Fortune soon began to smile more brightly, however. In 1932, Rudy Vallee recorded two Berlin songs that Berlin had always viewed with disfavor, "Say It Isn't So" and "How Deep Is the Ocean." They both became enormous hits for RCA and the Berlin Publishing Company. Berlin also became involved in another Broadway musical, *Face the Music*, dealing with the effects of the depression. His 1933 show *As Thousands Cheer* had a similar theme. Presented in the format of a newspaper, it had individual sections on news, sports, society, and so forth. The show grossed about $1,200,000. Its most successful songs were "Easter Parade" and "We're Having a Heat Wave." "Easter Parade" had originally been called "Smile and Show Your Dimple" ("you'll find it very simple . . ."). Berlin recognized that the song was terrible and put it away. Coming back to it with a new lyric for *As Thousands Cheer*, he created a super hit that became the title song of a Fred Astaire–Judy Garland movie of 1948.

Beginning in 1935 with *Top Hat*, starring Fred Astaire and Ginger Rogers, Berlin went on to score a series of triumphs on the motion picture screen. "Dancing Cheek to Cheek," a song he wrote for *Top Hat*, brought him $250,000 in royalties. In 1938 a film compendium of Berlin songs was assembled for the movie *Alexander's Ragtime Band*, starring Alice Faye and Tyrone Power.

Soon afterward Berlin achieved one of his most brilliant and lasting successes with a revitalized version of a song that he had put aside and forgotten nearly two decades earlier. The song, of course, was "God Bless America." While on a trip to Europe, where he had a first-hand glimpse of Fascism and Nazism, Berlin became profoundly aware of how much he owed to the country of his immigration. On his return, the popular singer Kate Smith asked him to give her a song for a patriotic broadcast she was doing. Berlin recalled the melody he had originally written for *Yip Yip Yaphank*, slightly altered the lyrics, and made Smith promise that any profits from the song be donated to America's scouting movement. She agreed, and "God Bless America" became an overnight success, so much so that there were even proposals to have it replace "The Star-Spangled Banner" as the national anthem. The song was used at both national political conventions in 1940. Its fantastic popularity led to grumbling by those who thought Berlin was making a profit from his patriotism. Over the years it has earned nearly a half-million dollars for the Boy and Girl Scouts of America and the Campfire Girls.[37]

During World War II Berlin wrote several songs to boost the defense effort. He also created an all-service musical, *This Is the Army*, to raise money for the USO. Berlin wrote the show at Camp Upton, where he had been stationed during World War I while writing *Yip Yip Yaphank*. He preferred Upton, he said, because he was familiar with the surroundings, and because being there would give him first-hand knowledge of what the men of World War II were thinking.

This Is the Army opened on Broadway on July 4, 1942, with an all-serviceman cast, including Berlin himself singing "Oh How I Hate to Get Up in the Morning," taken from his World War I show. When he went out on the stage, he and the chorus of soldiers who accompanied him were dressed in World War I battle fatigues. Six members of the chorus had sung it with him the first time in 1918! When a stagehand heard Berlin's thin, quavery voice, he said, "If the composer of that song could hear the way that guy sings it, he'd turn over in his grave."[38]

The show toured all over the world, earning about $10 million for the Army Relief Fund, with $350,000 going to the British Relief Fund when it played London. Berlin received no money for this effort, but was awarded the Medal of Merit by General George C. Marshall. Another Berlin war song was "Any Bonds Today."

In 1940 Berlin wrote the most popular movie of his career, *Holiday Inn*. The film was a fantastic box-office smash, and since Berlin owned 30 percent of it, he made more than $1.5 million. *Holiday Inn*, which starred Bing Crosby, introduced Berlin's most successful song, and indeed one of the most successful songs ever written. In Bing Crosby's version alone, "White Christmas" sold over 25 million records. All told the song has been recorded in more than 300 versions, with new ones coming out each holiday season. More than 5 million copies of the sheet music have been sold, and there have been over a million instrumental arrangements. It is an irony of sorts that the most popular songs about the Christian holidays of Christmas and Easter should have been written by a Jew from Russia. Perhaps that, more than anything else, tells the story of Tin Pan Alley.

Irving Berlin was to have one more gigantic hit on Broadway immediately after the war ended. Jerome Kern had begun writing a musical about the sharpshooter Annie Oakley toward the end of his life but had died without completing it. Rodgers and Hammerstein, who owned the rights, asked Berlin to start over and write his own score. Locking himself in a hotel room, Berlin wrote five songs over that weekend. When he played them for Rodgers and Hammerstein, there was a stunned silence. Berlin misinterpreted it as disapproval, but in fact, they were amazed. All five songs were used in the show just as he had written them.[39]

The show that resulted from Berlin's efforts, *Annie Get Your Gun*, was both a masterpiece and a record-breaker. No other show in Broadway history had ever enjoyed so long a run (1,000 performances), no other show had so many hits songs, no other show sold so many records, and no other show has been revived so frequently—moreover, no other show earned Berlin as much money.[40] The songs in *Annie* included such all-time favorites as "They Say It's Wonderful," "Doin' What Comes Naturally,"

"The Girl That I Marry," and most of all, the song that became the theme song of the entertainment industry, "There's No Business Like Show Business." When *Annie* was revived in 1966, Berlin added another hit song entitled "Old Fashioned Wedding," to be sung by the star, Ethel Merman.[41]

There were other musicals after *Annie Get Your Gun*, including *Miss Liberty* in 1949, with a story about the woman who posed for the Statue of Liberty. It was a rather forgettable musical, highlighted by a few good songs, such as "Let's Take an Old Fashioned Walk" and "Give Me Your Tired, Your Poor." When the terrible reviews came out, Berlin feared that he was finished. A year later, though, he had another hit, *Call Me Madam*, based on the life of Perle Mesta, the socialite and party-giver who was appointed U.S. ambassador to Luxembourg. Berlin came up with several good songs for the star, Ethel Merman: "You're Just in Love," "It's a Lovely Day Today," "I Like Ike," and "The Hostess with the Mostess' on the Ball."

Berlin's last musical, written in 1960, was entitled *Mr. President*. The show, which told the story of a President who retires from office, was really a fictionalized tale about John F. Kennedy and his family. The reviews were dreadful. A large advance sale of tickets and a star cast kept the show going for a respectable run, but by Berlin standards, it was a flop.

After *Mr. President*, Berlin went into virtual retirement. He momentarily returned to the public eye for an eightieth-birthday celebration given him on the Ed Sullivan television show. Among the many stars and dignitaries assembled for the celebration was President Lyndon Johnson, who concluded his speech with a paraphrase of Berlin's most famous song, "God Bless Berlin." Today, well past ninety years old, Berlin still runs his publishing house. It is the most tightly controlled of all the music companies, and virtually every infringement on his copyrights is prosecuted to the fullest. The immigrant mentality does not easily fade away.

Berlin has always considered himself a Jew, and when his daughter married out of the faith, he asserted his Jewishness by requiring that a rabbi co-officiate.[42] Over the years Berlin has been honored by the National Conference of Christians and

Jews and by the YMHA as an "outstanding American of the Jewish faith." He has made enormous donations to Jewish relief organizations and the UJA, and has been a generous supporter of the State of Israel. His tribute "Israel" was written when the new state was proclaimed.

Berlin has been rather self-effacing when it comes to his talent. "It's a long way from Ellis Island," he once said. As far as his music is concerned, he has strong opinions: "Popular songs will never be missed, but Chopin and Liszt will live on. However a rose lives and dies in the very same way."[43]

A contemporary critic, summing up Berlin's place in American music, wrote: "Irving Berlin has been criticized by his competitors, maligned by his inferiors, snubbed by those who consider themselves musically superior. All of them would gladly pay a fortune for his unerring grasp of popular taste and his unique ability to satisfy it. He remains the most successful song writer of all time."[44]

Jerome Kern said it more simply. "Irving Berlin has no place in American music. He IS American music."

12

THE GERSHWINS

"True music must repeat the thought and aspirations of the people and the time. My people are Americans. My time is today. No one expected me to compose music, I just did. What I have done is what was in me; the combination of New York, where I was born, and the rising, exhilarating rhythm of it, with centuries of hereditary feeling back of me. They ask me what I am trying to do, and I can only say I am trying to express what is in me. Some people have the ability to put their feelings into words or music. There are thousands who have the same feeling and are mute. Those of us who can must speak for those who can not—but we must be honest about it."[1] George and Ira Gershwin certainly were honest about their work, they wrote from their hearts. With their aid the American musical theatre benefited; so did the opera, the concert hall, and the dance.

George Gershwin had a mission, he once said, a mission to write great music both for the theatre and for the orchestra hall, with only a very small gap in-between. That is what he did. Originally born with the name Jacob Gershovitz, he was the great-grandson of a rabbi and the grandson of a mechanic. His father, Morris, had been in the shoe manufacturing business before coming to America from St. Petersburg, Russia.[2] Morris had the right to travel because his father had been granted freedom of movement by Czar Alexander II after doing twenty-five years of military service. For the same reason he had the right to live in St. Petersburg. Morris, however, did not relish the thought of serving in the army, so when his draft day approached, he left for America.

Upon his arrival, he went to work in his maternal uncle's tailor

147

shop. On July 21, 1895, Morris and Rose Brushkin, also from Russia, were married. By that time Morris had changed the family name to Gershvin and had already worked at several of the more than seventeen jobs he would hold before 1916! Israel Gershwin, whose name became Ira, was born on December 6, 1896; Jacob, whose name would be George, was born on September 26, 1898; Arthur was born on March 14, 1900, and the last child, Frances, was born on December 6, 1906.[3]

Although the Gershwin family constantly had financial problems, they were never without a maid![4] Their religion was important to them but they did not actively practice it. Ira was the only son to be Bar Mitzvah—with a grand luncheon served for two hundred guests. At that time he was called Izzy and thought that his real name was Isadore. Only when he went for a passport did he learn that it was Israel.[5]

As a youngster, George Gershwin, whose boyhood nickname was "Cheesecake" because his father owned a bakery, was far more interested in sports than in music or religion, although his parents instilled in him a respect for Jewish tradition and the ways of the Old World. In fact, when approached by Isaac Goldberg, who was writing his biography, Gershwin stressed his religious beliefs and their influence.[6] The son of plain Russian Jews, Gershwin was always fascinated by the folk tunes of Europe and the synagogue, often incorporating both into his music.

As mentioned, baseball, not music, was Gershwin's big interest when he was a boy. As a result, when the Gershwin family purchased a piano, it was intended for Ira, who had already begun taking lessons with an aunt and generally seemed to be more musical.[7] George, on the other hand, had never taken a lesson. When the old upright was hoisted through the tenement window into the Gershwin apartment, however, he sat down and in short order, playing by ear, knocked off a popular tune of the day.[8]

Almost immediately thereafter Gershwin began training with a neighborhood piano teacher, soon progressing to a Hungarian teacher who turned out to be a dismal failure. At this point, apparently, he learned more about piano technique from going to concerts than from teachers.

Eventually, though, Gershwin received solid musical training from Charles Hambitzer, a noted pianist.[9] Hambitzer, the first great musical influence in his life, soon recognized that Gershwin was a musical prodigy. Although Gershwin was obsessed with popular music and continually badgered his teacher with his ideas about the possibilities it could have in the hands of a creative composer, Hambitzer refused to allow the young pianist to play popular songs and instead forced him to learn the musical skills required to play the masters. In later years Gershwin repeatedly expressed his gratitude for the training Hambitzer gave him.

When Hambitzer realized that he had taught Gershwin all he could, he passed him on to Edward Kilenyi, a teacher of music theory and harmony. Kilenyi respected Gershwin's search for musical knowledge and, like Hambitzer, realized that the youth was no common musician. Both Kilenyi and Hambitzer were champions of the modern music of the time, including the works of Arnold Schoenberg, and they shared their wide interests with their student.

Gershwin's first song, "Since I Found You," with words by Leonard Praskin, was a run-of-the-mill ballad of a type that could be heard everywhere in 1913. The influence of his teachers showed up more prominently in his second song, however. Called "Ragging the Traumerei," it was a ragtime version of a classical piece. When Hambitzer died, George devoted himself to the popular music he so enjoyed. Had his teacher lived longer, he might well have become a concert pianist instead of a popular composer.

Gershwin was initially excited by the music of Irving Berlin, especially "Alexander's Ragtime Band." More than Berlin, though, he found his model in the work of Jerome Kern.[10] His desire to play Kern's kind of music led him to quit school and go to the Catskill Mountains as a resort pianist. Soon after, in May 1914, he became the youngest song plugger on Tin Pan Alley, working for the Jerome H. Remick Company. Gershwin considered his salary of $15 per week enormous, especially since he was being paid to do what he wanted to do anyway. He played piano all day, traveled to nearby cities to accompany the song pluggers, and was sent at night to vaudeville houses to report on which acts were using Remick songs.

When Gershwin was sixteen, he was found one afternoon in his cubicle at Remick's practicing Bach's *Well-Tempered Clavier.* Asked if he was studying to be a great pianist, he responded, "No, I'm studying to be a great popular composer."[11] Unfortunately, his job at Remick's did not allow much room for growth. When he submitted one of his own songs to the company for publication, he was told that he had been hired as a pianist, not a composer.

In spite of this, and thanks to the direct intervention of singer Sophie Tucker, Gershwin got his first song published on May 15, 1916 by Harry Von Tilzer. The song, entitled "When You Want 'Em, You Can't Get 'Em; When You Got 'Em, You Don't Want 'Em,"[12] with words by his friend Murray Roth, earned Gershwin all of $5. Roth, it seems, was a shrewder businessman, for he was paid $15. Gershwin's fee was an advance against royalties, but there were none.

Gershwin soon found another money-making venture, though, for he became one of New York's most successful piano-roll musicians. He would travel to New Jersey and earn as much as $50 a day cutting piano rolls to be used in the player pianos of the period. He continued doing this well into the 1920's when he certainly no longer needed the money.

While at Remick's Gershwin wrote a number of other songs that would be published several years later. His next collaborator was Irving Caesar. Their first joint effort was "When the Army Disbands," copyrighted on October 21, 1916. Later that same year Remick finally agreed to publish one of Gershwin's songs, "Rialto Ripples," his first ragtime melody.

Even this early in his career, and quite frequently afterward—in fact, as much as 90 percent of the time—Gershwin would write the music for his songs before the words. Despite his exceptional talent, he was not very adept at sounding out music to fit a pre-written lyric, whether his own or a collaborator's. In addition, though he was quite musical, he was not particularly literary, a defect that plagued him throughout his Broadway career, since his shows would usually turn out to have marvelous songs set in very poor libretti.[13]

Another Gershwin melody around this time was "Making of the Girl," introduced in Sigmund Romberg's *Passing Show of 1916*. Romberg served as collaborator and Harold Atteridge set a lyric to it. The song earned Gershwin a total of $7. He didn't complain, though, because it was his first song on Broadway.

Perhaps as a result, Gershwin decided to leave Remick for greener pastures. He began by going to Irving Berlin, interviewing for the job of secretary-arranger. As a try-out piece, he brought along a Berlin song that he had arranged. Berlin later reminisced, "That arrangement is one of my proudest possessions. I'll never forget his playing. My song sounded altogether new and different." Berlin offered Gershwin the job, which paid $100 per week, but said, "I hope you don't take it. You're much too talented to be an arranger for anybody. If you worked for me you might start writing the way I do, and your own original style would be cramped. You are meant for bigger things." Gershwin took Berlin's advice and turned down the offer.[14]

Gershwin had impressed other people in addition to Berlin. After rejecting the job, he went to see Max Dreyfus of the T. B. Harms publishing house. Dreyfus gave Gershwin a most unusual job—for a salary of $35 per week, all he had to do was to compose. There were no set hours, he didn't have to be in at any time—all he had to do was produce. As a result, Dreyfus made a good friend, and enormous profits too, for Gershwin remained with him for most of his creative life.

Gershwin's first song for Dreyfus was "Some Wonderful Sort of Someone." It had several musical innovations, as compared to the songs of the day, and did not become a great hit. Gershwin's next two songs, however, "Something about Love" and "I Was So Young, You Were So Beautiful," were more successful.

As Gershwin's compositions improved, so did his scope of interest. In October of 1917, he was hired at $35 per week as rehearsal pianist at the Century Theatre for a show by his idol,

Jerome Kern, called *Miss 1917*, which would open on November 5. Gershwin kept himself from being bored at having to play the same songs over and over by changing them slightly each time. This kept the chorus on its toes and made him a favorite with them. Each evening, after playing hour upon hour of the same songs, Gershwin would stay in the theatre and improvise. Kern heard him one night and was so excited by Gershwin's playing that he rushed home to get his wife so that she too could hear it. In addition to providing him with an opportunity to meet Kern, the job enabled Gershwin to make several other valuable contacts, among them P. G. Wodehouse, Victor Herbert, and Lew Fields. He also met Vivienne Segal, who was willing to debut two songs he had written with Irving Caesar, "There's More to a Kiss than the X-X-X" and "You Just You," both published by Remick.

Max Dreyfus made it possible for Gershwin to write his first score for the Broadway stage. The show, a revue called *Half Past Eight*, opened and closed out of town. Gershwin's next show, which opened on May 16, 1919, was more successful, running a respectable one hundred performances. Entitled *La, La, Lucille*, it included a Gershwin standard, "Nobody But You."

Meanwhile, Irving Caesar and Gershwin got together to write a "hindustan," the dance that was the rage of 1919.[15] "I [Caesar] said to George that we ought to write a one step. That evening we had dinner at Dinty Moore's, discussed the song, and returned to his house. There was a poker game going on. In about fifteen minutes we turned out 'Swanee,' verse and chorus. . . . We finished it right then and there, and old man Gershwin lost not a moment in fetching a comb and tissue paper and accompanying George while I sang it over and over again at the insistence of the winning poker players."[16]

Ned Wayburn incorporated "Swanee" into a show he was doing at the Capitol Theatre. The show opened on October 24, 1919. The song was danced on a darkened stage by sixty girls, each of whom had electric lights on her shoes, but it did not make a hit.

Three months later, Al Jolson heard Gershwin play "Swanee" at a party. That same week Jolson used the song at one of his

Sunday afternoon concerts at the Winter Garden Theatre. It was very well received, and because of the favorable audience reaction, Jolson interpolated it into the show in which he was currently starring, *Sinbad*, with music by Sigmund Romberg. "Swanee" became a huge success, selling more than 2 million records and 1 million copies of sheet music in a year. It was Gershwin's first and greatest hit—he never had a bigger-selling song.

Some years later, Gershwin and Caesar took a trip to the South and saw the river they had helped make famous. They were amazed to find that it was no more than an unimposing little muddy stream. Caesar commented, "I was shocked, but I am a craftsman like a carpenter who puts in a good job whether it be carving a door for a palace or a whorehouse."[17] Gershwin and Caesar became important men on Tin Pan Alley simply on the basis of this one song.

At the peak of the "Swanee" music sales, George Gershwin went to Detroit to see George White, who was producing *The Scandals*, a revue to rival *Ziegfeld's Follies*. Gershwin wanted to write for *The Scandals*, and he was by now so prominent that White needed little convincing. Between 1920 and 1924 Gershwin produced the scores to five editions of the show, writing more than forty songs. Two of them became popular favorites, "Stairway to Paradise," from the 1922 show, and "Somebody Loves Me," from the 1924 production.[18]

Despite all this success, Gershwin was not satisfied. He recognized that he would not "grow" unless he tried some new avenues of music. First he enrolled in two courses at Columbia University, one in nineteenth-century romantic music and one in orchestration. Whereas in his youth he had been closer in temperament to Berlin than to his idol, Kern, now he moved from the popular style to an American classical style.[19] To augment his orchestral scoring methods, he hired different musicians to teach him their instruments. Then, in 1923, he became a student of Rubin Goldmark, an expert in harmony.

Four years earlier, Gershwin had attempted his first classical piece, a lullaby for four strings. Its essentially "blues" quality led him into the writing of his first "opera," *Blue Monday*, which had as its theme the blacks of Harlem. The opera was presented in the *Scandals of 1922,* but after the opening performance, George White removed it as being too serious and depressing for the show. It was revived several times under a new name, *135th Street.* Although never a success, it was a major milestone for Gershwin.

An important result of this operatic attempt was the notice Gershwin received in the classical music world. In 1922 he was reviewed favorably by several well-known classical musicians, including Beryl Rubinstein, a professor at the Cleveland Institute of Music. On November 1, 1923, Eva Gautier, the famous concert artist, presented a recital that included an entire section devoted to Gershwin's music, with Gershwin as her accompanist. When the concert ended, she brought him out for a solo bow, an honor unheard of in classical music.

Gershwin's piano skills were equally unheard of. He loved to "ad lib" at the piano, creating endless variations on his own songs and compositions, as well as those of others. At parties he was wont to play whatever song he happened to be working on at the time, a trait that led George S. Kaufman to write, "So many of George's new songs had been heard at parties that by the time the show opened, it seemed like a revival!" Gershwin's piano artistry was so striking that the composer Maurice Ravel once asked that he play for him as his birthday present, a request George was happy to fill. [20]

Blue Monday, as it turned out, was to have very important consequences both for Gershwin's composing career and for the American musical repertory. The conductor of the pit orchestra for the opera's one performance had been Paul Whiteman, the "king of jazz." Much impressed by Gershwin's effort, and needing a climax piece for a forthcoming concert of American music to be given at the Aeolian Hall, Whiteman asked Gershwin to write a formal work suitable for a symphony orchestra. Needless to say, Gershwin was very eager to comply with the request, since he had long shared Whiteman's hope of bringing popular music some respectability, but was unwilling to promise anything because he feared he wasn't ready.

Gershwin's hand was forced when he read in the *New York Herald Tribune* that he was "at work writing a symphony."

Within a few weeks' time he had written the *Rhapsody in Blue*, scored for two pianos. The piece was premiered on February 12, 1924. Although the rest of the concert was rather dull and repetitious, *Rhapsody in Blue* electrified the audience. They responded with a standing ovation. Two years later Gershwin provided his own orchestration to replace the original one by Ferde Grofe, and it became the standard for use by symphony orchestras.

Gershwin had made plenty of money, but now, more important, he had finally earned recognition. He had always wanted to be a serious musician and composer; with *Rhapsody in Blue* he was both, for it has become the most famous, most frequently performed, and most profitable piece of serious music ever written by an American. [21] In future years, moreover, he was to write several other great classical compositions, including *Piano Concerto in F* (1925), *Three Preludes for Piano* (1926), *An American in Paris* (1928), *Second Rhapsody* for orchestra (1931), *The Cuban Overture* (1932), *Variations on "I Got Rhythm"* for piano and orchestra (1931), and finally, *Porgy and Bess* (1935), a body of substantial work that has placed him at the top of the list of American composers, serious as well as popular. [22]

Returning to Gershwin's Broadway career, his next musical, following his 1919 shows, was *Lady, Be Good*, written in 1924. This was his first collaboration with his brother Ira, who wrote all the lyrics. They had worked together at various times in the past, but *Lady, Be Good* signaled the beginning of a permanent alliance. George and Ira wrote together for the rest of George's life.

Gershwin's earlier collaborations with Ira had been somewhat anonymous, for Ira insisted on using the pseudonym "Arthur Francis" (derived from the names of the two younger Gershwin siblings) so as not to trade on George's fame and to head off accusations of nepotism. However, starting with *Lady, Be Good*, Ira Gershwin was credited with the lyrics under his own name. He wrote with George for thirteen years, and his influence was enormous. His lyrics were innovative, fresh, clever, and most important, singable. He knew his brother so well that he was able to match George's subtle harmonies and rhythms with equally subtle and colorful lyrics. It is no wonder that he was called the William S. Gilbert of America.[23] Ira often led George in new directions, providing lyrics which moved the action of a show forward and allowed George's concept of theatre to shine through. It was a perfect relationship.

Lady, Be Good was adorned by the dancing skills of Fred and Adele Astaire, who were also to appear in several other Gershwin musicals, including *Funny Face*. Their talents were highlighted by a brilliant score that included such songs as "Lady, Be Good," "Fascinating Rhythm," "So Am I," and "The Man I Love." Although "The Man I Love" was to become the show's greatest hit, it was dropped during tryouts in Philadelphia because the producer thought it slowed down the action too much. Over the years, though, the total music sales and record pressings of "The Man I Love" have been surpassed only by "Swanee," and some critics have said that it is the finest popular song ever written.[24]

Following *Lady, Be Good*, Gershwin wrote the scores for *Primrose* and *Tell Me More*, both of which opened in London. When neither show was brought to the United States, the Gershwin brothers wrote *Oh, Kay!* This show, the vehicle for the American debut of Gertrude Lawrence, the popular English star, included two hit songs that had lyrics by Ira Gershwin, "Someone to Watch over Me" and "Clap Yo' Hands." The words for several other songs in the score, however, were written by Howard Dietz after a sudden attack of appendicitis forced Ira to drop out of the production.

The show *Girl Crazy*, in 1930, saw the debut of one theatrical institution and the conclusion of another. The 1920's had ended, and with *Girl Crazy*, so did the "twenties musicals." No more would Gershwin write silly plots like those he had used in earlier years; now his shows would speak with a certain social significance. The debut was that of Ethel Merman, who before the show had been Ethel Zimmerman, a clerk-typist. George and Ira gave her some of the best music they had ever written, including "I've Got Rhythm," "Sam and Delilah," and "Boy! What Love Has Done to Me." Also in the show were "But Not for Me" and "Embraceable You." The show ran for 272 performances and made Merman the reigning queen of American musical comedy.

Having decided that musical comedies were becoming rather stale, the Gershwin brothers wrote two political satires with songs. The first, in 1927, was *Strike Up the Band*, with a libretto by George S. Kaufman. The story dealt with a plot to bring about lower tariffs by driving America into a war with Switzerland, all paid for by a Swiss cheese manufacturer (who was willing to foot the bill only if the history books would name the war after him). Even with some clever and lovely songs, the show was deemed too caustic for Broadway and closed out of town.

After the Gershwins and Kaufman rewrote *Strike Up the Band*, it received favorable notices and a moderate run when it reopened in 1929. The new plot had the same character as the earlier version, but now he was a chocolate-maker angry about chocolate tariffs. As the hero of the story, he gets the girl, and becomes a commander of the United States forces (in his dreams), but loses everything when the news leaks out that he has used Grade B milk in his chocolate. Other than the title song, none of the show's songs became overly popular, but the score included some delightful parodies of army marching songs, patriotic songs, and even an American version of a Gilbert and Sullivan–type patter song.

The next year, the same team came up with a theme far easier for critics and audiences to accept, the humorous nature of the American political system. As the election of 1932 was barely a year off, it was a perfect time to satirize the President, Congress, and the Supreme Court. In *Strike Up the Band* they tried satire. In *Of Thee I Sing* they accomplished it. The score included a great number of songs that became popular: most importantly, "Love Is Sweeping the Country," "Wintergreen for President," which parodied political-rally songs, and the title song, "Of Thee I Sing," which showed Ira Gershwin's wit through the use of the word "baby," reminding the audience that this was, after all, a Tin Pan Alley love song! The critical reception for *Of Thee I Sing* was extraordinary. It was praised as "a landmark in American satirical musical comedy" and was the first musical to win a Pulitzer Prize as the best play of the season.

Gershwin's greatest achievement for the stage was also his last. The opera *Porgy and Bess,* which opened in Boston on September 30, 1935, and in New York three weeks later, was derived from a novel and play entitled *Porgy* by DuBose and Dorothy Heyward, who served as co-authors of the libretto. Ironically, the project that was to result in Gershwin's outstanding masterpiece was almost canceled before it began. While he was still negotiating with Heyward, Al Jolson contacted Heyward's agent in an effort to obtain the musical rights to *Porgy* for a show in which he intended to star. Fortunately Jolson's idea fell through because neither the proposed composer, Jerome Kern, nor lyricist Oscar Hammerstein was interested.

Gershwin had long wanted to write an opera, but at first he had planned to adapt "The Dybbuk," a story by Sholom Anski. For some reason, he changed his mind and chose the Porgy story instead, perhaps because he could identify with its alienated and oppressed characters and with its parable of the inviolability of an innocent spirit in a corrupt world. Although Gershwin never endured suffering like that experienced by the blacks of his day, his Jewishness had taught him something about spiritual isolation, and he knew poverty from his Lower East Side childhood.[25]

The score Gershwin produced for *Porgy and Bess* did not contain the typical "darky" songs of Tin Pan Alley. Instead, after spending several months in South Carolina among the gullah blacks to learn their music, he tried to write genuine black songs.[26] He was also influenced by Negro spirituals, and "Sometimes I Feel Like a Motherless Child" became a source for his marvelous "Summertime."[27] Despite these unprecedented efforts to attain musical authenticity, *Porgy and Bess* was a failure at the box office and, as usual, with the critics. The opera critics found it too much like musical comedy, and the Broadway reviewers condemned it for being too operatic.

Critics or no, Gershwin was thrilled. He knew that he had finally achieved the blending of popular and classical music that he had been seeking for so long, and he also knew that *Porgy and Bess* would eventually win the appreciation it warranted. He could never have guessed, though, how much critical acclaim it was to receive in the years after his death. In the minds of many present-day critics, in fact, *Porgy and Bess* is the best opera ever composed by an American.[28]

Ira Gershwin made as great a contribution to *Porgy and Bess* as George, although it was the music that received the attention. After seeing *Porgy and Bess,* the other great lyricist of the 1920's and 1930's, Lorenz Hart, wrote the following compliment to Ira: "I loath songwriters who have small intellectual equipment and even less courage. It is a pleasure to live at a time when light amusement is at last losing its brutally cretin aspect and such delicacies as your lyrics prove that songs can be both popular and intelligent."[29]

Following *Porgy and Bess,* George and Ira Gershwin, with Ira's wife Lee, moved to California, where they wrote for the movies. In 1935 they did the score for an RKO movie called *Damsel in Distress.* The film starred Fred Astaire, and he demanded that the Gershwins write his next movie. As the dominant force in the Hollywood musicals of the day, Astaire had great influence. His intercession was important because producers feared that after *Porgy and Bess,* the Gershwins had become too "highbrow" to write songs for the common folk. In their first movie, the brothers proved that they could. George Gershwin lived to complete only two more movie scores, but the songs he wrote for *Shall We Dance* and *The Goldwyn Follies* were among his finest. They included: "A Foggy Day," "They Can't Take That Away From Me," "Let's Call the Whole Thing Off," "Love Walked Right In," and "Our Love Is Here to Stay."

During the spring of 1937, George was in terrible pain and suffered from deep depressions. For several weeks he received psychiatric treatment for what was erroneously supposed to be a psychosomatic illness. On July 9, when he collapsed and was rushed to the hospital, the real problem was isolated. He had a cystic tumor on the right temporal lobe of the brain, ultimately deriving from a blow on the head with a bat sustained during a boyhood baseball game. Upon operating, the doctors discovered that the tumor was in a part of the brain that could not be reached. If George Gershwin lived, he would be blind and disabled. Mercifully, on July 11, 1937, he died.[30]

George Gershwin's funeral took place at New York's Temple Emanu-El. In California, a memorial service was held where the eulogy, written by Oscar Hammerstein, was delivered by Edward G. Robinson.[31] Perhaps, though, the Gershwin brothers are better remembered by their music, for year after year, it is heard more and more. We are realizing now, as the Gershwin song said, that "their *music* is here to stay."

Ira Gershwin continued to write after George's death, collaborating with a long list of composers, among them Jerome Kern, Kurt Weill, Arthur Schwartz, Harold Arlen, and Harry Warren. The songs he wrote after George's death included "The Man That Got Away," "Long Ago and Far Away," and "My Ship." Though he was still able to write hits, however, he never forged a relationship with another composer that even approached the special rapport he experienced with his brother. Ira Gershwin and his wife of fifty-five years still live in California, next-door to George's former home. In 1959 he wrote a book entitled *Lyrics on Several Occasions,* a collection of his songs with his comments about them. He is currently said to be writing a definitive biography-autobiography of the Gershwin brothers. He may also have plans to publish some as-yet-unknown music that George left uncompleted at the time of his death.

13

LORENZ HART

Of all the lyricists on Tin Pan Alley, none more thoroughly appreciated and studied the works of Sir William Gilbert, England's master of comic opera, than Lorenz Milton Hart. Lorenz Hart, or Larry as virtually everyone called him, is often considered to have been Broadway's greatest lyricist. He worked primarily with one composer, Richard Rodgers, and together they revolutionized the American musical theatre.

Born in New York City on May 2, 1895, Lorenz Hart was the second son of Max and Frieda (Isenberg) Hart. His parents, both of them immigrants from Germany, where his father's family name had been Hertz, met in this country and were married on November 6, 1886. Max Hart, a "promoter" of sorts, was at various times into real estate, railroads, business, politics, and anything else at which he could make (or sometimes lose) money. His methods were oftentimes shady, and as a result he had several close scrapes with the law, but over the years he gradually became more prosperous and staid. Active as a precinct worker for the Democratic party, until the conviction of Mayor Robert Van Wyck caused him to sever his relationship with the Tammany machine, he was acquainted with many of the most influential lawyers, judges, politicians, and show people of the day, among them Polly Adler, one of New York's most infamous madams, with whom he had a business partnership.[1]

In a typical Manhattan progression, the Harts moved uptown as their financial and social status improved. From humble beginnings on the Lower East Side in an Allen Street immigrant flat, where their first son, Jimmy, died in infancy from pneumonia, they advanced to a brownstone on East 106th Street between Second and Third Avenues, where Larry was born, and ultimately to 59 West 119th Street in Harlem, which in those days was heavily populated by Jews of German extraction. Larry and his younger brother, Theodore Van Wyck Hart (named for Teddy Roosevelt and the unfortunate Tammany mayor),[2] were both Bar Mitzvah at the Mount Zion Temple just down the block, as was Milton Berlinger, later Milton Berle, who lived not far away.

In addition to his other attributes, Max Hart was a very colorful and entertaining man who loved to give big parties. Known for his generosity and his interest in the arts, he was also famous for his crude tongue and flamboyant manner. One of the Hart neighbors was Cantor Yosele Rosenblatt. Once, during a summer heat spell, when the world-famous chazan was vocalizing in the backyard shared by the Rosenblatts and the Harts, Max poured a bucket of water on his head. However outrageous Max was, Frieda Hart, was a highly proper woman. She taught Larry German, gave him an unending love for the classics in both music and literature, and encouraged his cultural pursuits. Max Hart claimed he was related to the German poet Heinrich Heine; though the family connection couldn't be proved, Heine was always Larry Hart's favorite poet.[3]

At age thirteen Hart was sent for the summer to the Weingart Institute in the Catskills, a summer camp that was popular with wealthy German-Jewish families. Among Hart's fellow campers were the Bonwit boys (of Bonwit Teller fame), Oscar Hammerstein II, two of the Selznick boys, and Herbert Sondheim (the father of Stephen Sondheim). A few years later Richard Rodgers also attended the camp,[4] which certainly deserved its reputation as a training ground for future luminaries of the entertainment world. After two summers at Weingart, Hart went to Camp Paradox in the Adirondacks, where his camp friends again included boys with theatrical connections, among them Herbert Fields, the son of vaudeville star and theatre producer Lew Fields, and Eugene Zukor, whose father was Adolph, the movie producer and founder of Paramount Pictures.

Hart spent five summers at Camp Paradox and then went to Brant Lake Camp, where his counselor was Arthur Schwartz, later the composer half of the team of Schwartz and Dietz, writing such shows as *The Band Wagon*. A few years later Hart became the camp's dramatics counselor. During the summers that followed he worked unceasingly to put on several productions each season, aided by Mickey Tomashevsky, of the famous Yiddish theatre family, who wrote the music.

In the "off-season" Hart attended Columbia College, where he soon began writing for the undergraduate *Varsity Show*. He contributed several sketches to the 1915 edition and also appeared in the cast. The show's lead actor was Oscar Hammerstein II. One of Hammerstein's classmates, Mortimer Rodgers, brought his kid brother Richard to see the show. This proved to be Rodgers's first meeting with Hammerstein, with whom he was later to have such a fruitful partnership, but ironically, he was not introduced to Hart.

Meanwhile, Hart's friends from summer camp had been telling their theatre-connected parents about his ability with lyrics and dialogue. As a result, Billy Rose, the famed impresario, began to cultivate him, coming up to the camp to visit Hart and concluding each visit with a gift of money. Rose was the composer of several great hits of the day and it was only natural that he should want some of Hart's lyrics.

Around this time Hart embarked on a career as a translator of European operettas, producing English versions of German and Viennese productions for transplantation onto the American stage. Between 1920 and 1925 he translated Jean Gilbert's *The Lady in Ermine* into English and also changed the setting from Europe to America. Although the script was excellent, the songs created by Hart and a friend were not used. Instead, the Shuberts, who owned the piece, gave it to Sigmund Romberg, who restored the European setting and wrote appropriate songs, in the process coming up with a great hit for himself.

Next Hart translated Ferenc Molnar's *Liliom*. He received $200 for his efforts, but the credit and royalties for the very successful play were given to Benjamin "Barney" Glazer.[5] It is interesting to note that this play was eventually used by Hart's future collaborator, Richard Rodgers, and Oscar Hammerstein II as the story for their hugely successful musical *Carousel*.

Hart's partnership with Rodgers began in 1918, when the Akron Club, a local sports and athletic association, decided to put on a series of amateur shows as a fund-raiser. The music for the first show was written by Rodgers, whose older brother, Mortimer, was a member of the club, while various other people wrote the lyrics and sketches. When the second show was in production, the club decided to obtain the services of a real lyricist. Phil Leavitt, another member, remembered Hart, whom he knew from Columbia, and took young Rodgers to meet him.

It was a Sunday afternoon, late in 1919. Rodgers, a seventeen-year-old, was filled with trepidation at the thought of meeting the older and more sophisticated Hart, but what he saw was even more disconcerting than he had anticipated. Hart greeted the two men in a bathrobe and formal trousers, unshaven and unkempt. For Rodgers, even then a natty dresser, this was a bad start. Fortunately, after the obligatory small talk, the subject turned to songs and theatre. In these areas Rodgers and Hart had much in common, and by the end of the afternoon they had agreed to join forces in the creation of songs. As Rodgers wrote in *Theatre Arts Monthly* later on, "In one afternoon I had acquired a career, a partner, a best friend, and a source of permanent irritation."[6]

In passing, it is interesting to take note of how Rodgers and Hart chose their team name. Usually the lyricist's name came first and the composer's second, as in Gilbert and Sullivan, Lerner and Loewe, Hammerstein and Kern, Fields and McHugh. Rodgers would not have it that way. Even when he wrote with Oscar Hammerstein, Rodgers demanded to be billed first.

The first creative efforts of the fledgling team were for the benefit of the Akron Club, but their real goal was Broadway. In this endeavor one of Larry's camp buddies proved helpful. Phil Leavitt, who had introduced them, was also good friends with Dorothy and Herb Fields, the children of actor-producer Lew Fields. As a favor to Leavitt, Herb invited Hart and Rodgers to the Fields home so that Lew could hear some of their songs. The song Hart had intended Fields to buy, "Venus," fell flat, but Fields had a good ear for talent and asked to hear some of their other songs. In response they played "Any Old Place With You." Fields immediately purchased it and interpolated it into his current Broadway show, *A Lonely Romeo.* Sung by Eve Lynn and Alan Hale, the song premiered on August 26, 1919, and soon became a popular hit.

So much for the first Rodgers and Hart Broadway song. Their first show score was not written for Broadway. Entitled *Fly With Me,* it was a Columbia College amateur show, and its libretto, by Milton Kroop, dealt with Bolshevism. Another libretto, by Hart and Rodgers, had been rejected, and it is amusing to note that Oscar Hammerstein II was one of the members of the committee that turned it down. When *Fly With Me* premiered on March 24, 1920, it had thirteen Rodgers and Hart songs, all of which were later published. A major facet of the show's appeal was the "Pony Ballet," in which the all-male cast, dressed up as women, was involved in fairly complicated choreography. Although the men had trained carefully, their large feet and frequently hairy chests made their dancing altogether humorous, and if that wasn't funny enough, their singing voices, of course, were baritones instead of sopranos. This tradition is carried on in many theatrical ventures, the most notable being Harvard's *Hasty Pudding Theatricals.*

Among the classmates who worked with Hart on *Fly With Me* were Howard Dietz, Morry Ryskind, and Herman Mankiewicz; the choreographer was Herbert Fields—needless to say, a distinguished group of future entertainment greats. Fields continued his association with Hart and Rodgers to such a degree that the three young men decided to use "Herbert Richard Lorenz" as a combined pseudonym. Their first effort, to be called *Winkle Town,* was never produced. Even Herbert's father, Lew, refused to produce it. One can only guess what other producers would have said if the threesome had asked them to put on a show that the playwright's own father had turned down.

Although Lew Fields rejected *Winkle Town,* he purchased the Rodgers and Hart songs from *Fly With Me* for his show *Poor Little Ritz Girl.* The jubilant team joined the production in Boston but had to leave for summer camp before the "doctoring" of the play commenced. In their absence Fields made enormous revisions in the script and songs before the Broadway opening, dropping the entire libretto and replacing seven of their songs with numbers by Sigmund Romberg and Alex Gerber. In short, the show that opened on Broadway was entirely different from the one that played Boston. As producer, Fields was well within his rights and as newcomers to the theatre, Rodgers and Hart had no recourse but to accept his tampering without complaint. The show opened on July 28, 1920, to mixed notices: generally favorable for the Rodgers and Hart material, generally poor for the Romberg songs.

Rodgers, Hart, and Herb Fields took the failure of *Winkle Town* and *Poor Little Ritz Girl* in stride and began planning a new production to be entitled *The Jazz King*. After a fitful start, they purchased the rights to the Mark Twain masterpiece, *A Connecticut Yankee in King Arthur's Court,* but when little came of that idea either, they put it aside and decided to rework *The Jazz King*. It took them more than three years to finish the script.

This was a very difficult period for Hart as well as for his collaborator. Between 1922 and 1925 they both looked into different avenues for earning an income. Hart decided to become a producer and sought to put on a play entitled *The First Fifty Years* by his Columbia friend Henry Myers, who later would go on to write movie scripts and theatrical revues. Myers submitted the play to the actress Margaret Wycherly, who decided to make a few changes. The result bore little or no resemblance to the original, and plans for her involvement were scuttled. When Hart's father agreed to provide seed money, and several other investors were found, a director and cast were hired and the play went into production. It received favorable notices in previews but closed soon after its New York opening.

Following this Hart decided to stage another Henry Myers play, *The Blond Beast*. The play is of historical importance because of the way it was auditioned for potential backers. The neophyte producers, figuring that potential backers could more easily recognize the play's value by seeing it performed instead of just reading the script, mounted a full production with only one performance and invited all the Broadway producers and big shots. Again events interfered, for as the curtain rose, word of an impending actors' strike went through the audience of producers and backers and totally distracted them. The backers' audition was a flop, but Actors' Equity came into being.

With yet another failure to his credit, Hart returned to Herbert Fields and Richard Rodgers to attempt to find backers for *The Jazz King*, retitled *The Melody Man*. This time they managed to sell Lew Fields on the show, mainly by convincing him that he was perfect for the lead role, a Tin Pan Alley composer who is trying to win acceptance as a songwriter. The show, which ran fifty-six performances on Broadway, included two Rodgers and Hart songs that had been written as parodies of the worst Tin Pan Alley could offer. "I'd Like to Poison Ivy" is an example of how well they succeeded in writing really terrible songs! The play itself was also judged to be truly terrible. Said George Jean Nathan, "the plot is not only enough to ruin the play, it is enough—and I feel I may say it without fear of contradiction—to ruin even *Hamlet*."[7]

Hart's extended spell of bad luck finally ended in the year 1925. A group of bit-part players and young actors had been meeting together to write sketches, songs, and lyrics for a revue they wanted to present in order to raise money for tapestries to adorn the Theatre Guild's new theatre. A friend invited Richard Rodgers to participate. The suggestion was received in a very tepid manner, but when Rodgers and Hart heard some more about the show the young people were planning, they realized that it was just the break they wanted. More than simply an opportunity to have their work presented on Broadway, it was a chance to be associated with the prestigious Theatre Guild, and they could not pass up such a wonderful prospect. Within a very short time, about two weeks, they put together six new songs and took a seventh, "Manhattan," from their old musical failure *Winkle Town*.

On May 17, 1925, the show opened; called *The Garrick Gaieties*, after the theatre in which it was produced, it was scheduled to run two performances, a matinee and an evening. The critical and public approval was so great, however, that the Theatre

Guild decided to add four more performances, all of which were immediately sold out. On June 8 the Guild scheduled a regular Broadway run, which finally ended more than two hundred performances later. As a result of this success, Hart was earning the first regular paycheck he had ever received, about $50 per week. Rodgers also received $50 plus $83 more for acting as conductor. Perhaps more importantly, the two songwriters made a very valuable contact, Max Dreyfus of the Harms Music Company, who agreed to publish their songs. He continued to do so for the almost twenty years that Rodgers and Hart were together.

Toward the end of 1925 another Rodgers and Hart musical opened, a historical epic about the American Revolution entitled *Dearest Enemy*. The musical dealt with Mrs. Robert Murray's attempt to keep British officers at her house in New York so that George Washington could retreat from the city. The sophistication of the music and lyrics impressed critics and audiences alike.

The year 1926 saw two more Rodgers and Hart musical successes. The first was *Peggy Ann*, about a small-town girl dreaming of living in the big city. Various aspects of this show were unique: the story had a rather surrealistic feel to it, with dream sequences and reality mixed together; there was no grand chorus opening, as was the fashion in shows at the time; and the ending was a very dramatic dance number rather than the more usual huge production number.

Later in the year came another hit show, *A Connecticut Yankee*. Hart had acquired the rights to Twain's book years earlier, but the original permission had lapsed, and because he and Rodgers were now so successful, they were forced to spend considerable money to obtain the rights again. The show's plot was quite ingenious and clever. The hero gets hit on the head by a champagne bottle and awakes thinking he is in Camelot. Throughout the rest of the show he tries to impose his morals and twentieth-century attitudes upon the people of merrie olde England.

The most famous song in *A Connecticut Yankee*, "My Heart Stood Still," had originally been written for a Rodgers and Hart revue called *One Dam Thing After Another*, staged some years earlier in England. The song had an interesting origin. Apparently the two songwriters had been in a Paris taxicab viewing the sights with two women when another taxicab nearly slammed into them. One of the girls said, "My heart stood still." Hart remarked calmly, "That would make a terrific song title." In order to use the song in *A Connecticut Yankee*, Rodgers and Hart had to buy it from the producer of the English revue for $5,000. Like *Connecticut Yankee* itself, the song became an instant smash success in America.

Between *A Connecticut Yankee* in 1926–27 and 1931, Hart wrote the lyrics for seven musical productions staged in New York and London. None of these shows was enormously successful, but each of them had a standout song by which it is remembered today. *Present Arms* in 1928 featured "You Took Advantage of Me," sung by a future movie director named Busby Berkeley and Joyce Barbour. *Chee Chee*, a rather peculiar play about the seduction of a beautiful girl by the son of the Grand Eunuch, and dominated by the theme of castration, introduced the song "Moon of My Delight." *Spring Is Here*, which ran on Broadway for only 104 performances, included one of Hart's most memorable lyrics, "With a Song in My Heart." From the score of *Heads Up!*, which also ran only about 140 performances, we still remember "A Ship Without a Sail."

The next year, 1930, Hart and Rodgers provided the songs for *Simple Simon*, a show written by and starring Ed Wynn. A rather contrived mixture of fairy tales and mythology, *Simple Simon* was about the dream of one "Simon Eyyes" (the grandson of Harmon Eyyes!). The show's other star, Ruth Etting, introduced the song that proved to be the outstanding Rodgers and Hart number from this score, one of the most dramatic and, for the time, risqué songs ever performed on Broadway. Entitled "Ten Cents a Dance," it told the story of a dance hall "hostess" in depression times.

Hart's last Broadway show for the next few years was *America's Sweetheart*, intended as a parody of Hollywood and the crazy lifestyle of the movie colony. Hart found the material easy to write because he and Rodgers had just spent a short time in Hollywood writing the songs for a movie entitled *The Hot Heiress*

(1931). The film, like their trip, had been a disaster, so the lyrics for *America's Sweetheart* came easily. The songs, in fact, were the only acceptable part of this rather poor musical.

Oddly enough, the negative experience of *The Hot Heiress* did not prevent Hart and Rodgers from returning to Hollywood for the next four years. Although in general the songs they produced for films are not up to the level of those they did for the stage, several were outstanding. For the film *Love Me Tonight* (1932), starring Maurice Chevalier and Jeanette McDonald, they wrote "Lover" and "Mimi," which became Chevalier's theme song. Other movies that used Rodgers and Hart songs were *Hallelujah, I'm a Bum* (1933), which starred Al Jolson, George M. Cohan's *The Phantom President* (1932), and *Manhattan Melodrama* (1934). Hollywood, however was not the answer for Rodgers and Hart. They recognized that Broadway was the place for them to be.

The theatre they had left, however, was not the one to which they returned, for the works of Gershwin, Jerome Kern, George S. Kaufman, and their friend Morrie Ryskind had changed things. Operetta and musical comedy were no longer the rage; the book and the plot were important now, and they would have to write musical plays. In view of this, it is ironic that Hart's first effort upon returning to New York was songwriter-producer Billy Rose's *Jumbo*, really a glorified circus-burlesque-vaudeville show. Hart and Rodgers recognized, however, that they had to begin by once again proving their value to the New York producers, so they accepted the assignment. In fact they wrote some magnificent songs for *Jumbo*, including "The Most Beautiful Girl in the World" and "My Romance."

After concluding this show, Hart went into his last and greatest period of creativity. He and Rodgers wrote nine musicals, of which seven deserve recognition. Each one provided some new twist and development to the history of the musical; each one had marvelous songs.

The first of the seven musicals of this period, *On Your Toes*, opened on April 11, 1936, and played for 315 performances. Starring Ray Bolger, David Morris, Monty Woolley, and Luella Gear, it had been intended as a vehicle for Fred Astaire and

Ginger Rogers, but their roles were played instead by Bolger and Doris Carson. The show included a unique ballet sequence that is considered one of the finest pieces of music Rodgers ever wrote. During the ballet the show's entire plot is resolved, making it the first musical to end in such a serious manner. The most famous song from the score was "There's a Small Hotel," originally written for *Jumbo* but not used in that production.

Babes in Arms, which opened on April 14, 1937, and ran for 289 performances, suffered from a rather banal script but included several fresh variations. First, the cast was almost entirely made up of teenagers. Second, the score included five of the most wonderful songs ever written by the team of Rodgers and Hart: "The Lady Is a Tramp," "Johnny One Note," "My Funny Valentine," "Where or When," and "I Wish I Were in Love Again."

Only five months later came the premiere of the next Rodgers and Hart effort, *I'd Rather Be Right*. It received more publicity than any of their other shows, for its star, George M. Cohan, had come out of retirement expressly for the purpose of poking fun at President Franklin D. Roosevelt, a goal made eminently possible by the George S. Kaufman and Moss Hart libretto which was filled with strident and rather satirical comments on current events and politics, including a string of endorsements for a third term for Roosevelt.

With their next show, Rodgers and Hart achieved one of Hart's fondest dreams. He had wanted to write a Shakespearean musical ever since childhood. In *The Boys from Syracuse*, based on Shakespeare's *The Comedy of Errors*, he finally did so, and at the same time wrote a lead role that was perfect for his younger brother, Teddy. Choreographed by George Balanchine and with settings by Jo Mielziner, the son of a former Hebrew Union College professor, *The Boys from Syracuse* was an enormous success, and three of its songs have become popular standards: "This Can't Be Love," "Sing for Your Supper," and "Falling in Love with Love."

The Boys from Syracuse opened in 1938, a banner year for Rodgers and Hart. Just a few months later they wrote another musical hit, *I Married an Angel*. In addition they were featured in a *New Yorker* profile. Their most signal honor, though, and one they found especially pleasing, was a cover story in *Time* magazine which dubbed them "the U.S. Gilbert and Sullivan."

All these successes notwithstanding, Hart was well on his way to being an alcoholic. By the onset of the 1940's, his frequent drinking bouts were making him extremely difficult to work with and in addition led him to squander money aimlessly and to spend much of his time with a crowd of free-wheeling reprobates. While his relationship with Rodgers deteriorated as a result, Hart was still capable of writing two of his best shows.

The first was *Pal Joey*, starring Gene Kelly and Vivienne Segal, with whom, some say, Hart was in love. The libretto, based on a novel by John O'Hara, told the story of a small-time nightclub hoofer who made his living as a gigolo to the wealthy women of Chicago. The songs, especially "Bewitched, Bothered and Bewildered," "Zip," and "I Could Write a Book," were among the cleverest Hart had ever written, but even so the reviews were less than laudatory, mainly due to the feeling that a satisfactory musical could not be focused on such a low, despicable character. *Pal Joey*, however, was a brilliant work and a fine show, and its merits, sadly underrated in 1940, have been acknowledged by its frequent revivals on Broadway, most recently in the middle 1970's.

Around the end of 1940, the relationship between Rodgers and Hart was becoming irreparably strained. In the months that followed, Hart's drinking increased, his depression deepened, the crowd he traveled with became more and more low class, and before long he began showing definite signs of physical deterioration caused by excessive drinking and carousing. The Hart family was very worried, and Rodgers suggested that Hart be committed to a psychiatric clinic, but there was little they could do, for Hart did not want to help himself.

Hart's last show with Rodgers was *By Jupiter*, which premiered in New York on June 2, 1942. Hart was hospitalized while writing the songs, and after his release it was very difficult to get him to settle down to work, so Rodgers was forced to contribute some of the lyrics by himself. While the resulting score was not very strong, and none of the songs became hits, *By Jupiter* enjoyed one of the longest runs of any Rodgers and Hart show, 427 performances, mainly because of its first-rate cast, which included Ray Bolger, Constance Moore, Benay Venuta, and as a replacement, Nanette Fabray.

The relationship between Rodgers and Hart had always been very difficult, but by the time of *By Jupiter* it had reached the crisis stage. When Rodgers and the Theatre Guild asked Hart to musicalize a play entitled *Green Grow the Lilacs*, Hart said he would rather go to Mexico and suggested that Rodgers find another lyricist. Rodgers did; the lyricist was Oscar Hammerstein II, and the show they wrote was *Oklahoma!* At the opening night performance, Hart immediately recognized that it was a masterpiece, and afterward, at the opening night party at Sardi's, he told Rodgers, "This thing of yours will run longer than *Blossom Time*" (one of Sigmund Romberg's most successful operettas).

His achievement with Hammerstein notwithstanding, Rodgers hoped to keep the partnership with Hart going and reckoned that a modest project would provide the necessary stimulus. He proposed a revival of *A Connecticut Yankee* with several new songs. Hart kept his interest up for a while, writing one of his finest lyrics for "To Keep My Love Alive," but on opening night in Philadelphia he went off on a drinking binge. When the show opened in New York, Hart was not allowed in the theatre because Rodgers was afraid of what he might do. After the performance he was nowhere to be found. Two days later he was located in a hospital suffering from pneumonia. He died a few days later, on November 22, 1943, and was laid to rest in a small Jewish cemetery on Long Island beside his mother, with whom he had lived until her death in April 1943, and his father, who had died eighteen years earlier. [8]

With any songwriting team, it is inevitably asked whether the music or the lyrics came first. In the case of some teams, it may have been half and half, but for Rodgers and Hart the music always preceded the lyrics. Hart's genius lay in his special ability to set words to music. He provided an insight into his method of setting a lyric when he described how he had written the song "Here in My Arms." "I take the most distinctive melodic phrase in the tune and work on that. What I choose is not necessarily

the theme or the first line, but the phrase which stands out."
Then, he continued, he chose the longest or most important
musical notes on which to place his dominant lyric, the rhyming
or standout lyric for the song.

While this method might not have worked with every collaborator, it most certainly was effective in Hart's joint projects with
Richard Rodgers. The team produced many of Broadway's most
outstanding shows and songs, and it was Rodgers, in his pref-
ace to the *Rodgers and Hart Songbook*, who wrote what may well
be the best summation of Lorenz Hart's contribution as a lyricist:
"his lyrics knew that love was not especially devised for boy and
girl idiots of fourteen."[9] If Lorenz Hart had a personal credo
dealing with music, it was, "Don't have a formula, and don't
repeat it." Had he known that he would be remembered for the
intelligence and wit of his lyrics, he would have been happy.

14

RICHARD RODGERS AND OSCAR HAMMERSTEIN II

Richard Rodgers and Oscar Hammerstein, the most famous, successful, and beloved team in American musical history, have come to be regarded as the essence of what makes Broadway great. Rodgers and Hammerstein wrote more hit shows than any other composer or composing team; their productions regularly had runs that broke all existing box-office records; and no one, before or since, trod more new ground or made more lasting contributions to the development of the musical theatre.

Naturally the team of Rodgers and Hammerstein did not spring full-blown out of nowhere. Both men had brilliant creative careers in the musical theatre before they joined forces on *Oklahoma!* in 1942, and as a necessary basis for understanding their amazingly fruitful collaboration, we must begin by telling something of their lives and achievements in the period before they began working together. Since Hammerstein was several years older than Rodgers, it is logical to begin with him.

Oscar Greeley Clendenning Hammerstein, born on July 12, 1895, was the eldest son of William and Alice Hammerstein and the grandson of Oscar Hammerstein I. His grandfather-namesake, born in Stettin, Germany, was one of America's foremost theatre-builders and opera impresarios,[1] and also wrote several operettas, including *When You Said Yes, Bridgetta*, and *Leap Year in Midnight*, all published by Charles K. Harris.[2] Hammerstein's first theatre, the Harlem Opera House, has long since become world-famous as the Apollo. His masterpiece, built on Longacre Square, now Times Square, between 42nd and 44th Streets, was the Olympia—actually three theatres in one (designed for simultaneous performances of burlesque, opera, and operetta), with a total seating capacity of 6,000 and a roof-garden restaurant that proved to be its most popular feature.

Another of his theatres was the famed Victoria. Under the shrewd management of son William, the father of Oscar II, it became one of New York's prime vaudeville houses in the early decades of the twentieth century,[3] playing Weber and Fields, Fanny Brice, Al Jolson, Harry Houdini, Buster Keaton, and all the other top stars of the era. William Hammerstein disliked the entertainment business and wanted to keep his sons out of it, but he knew how to draw the paying customers in. He once booked a contest to make "Sober Sue" laugh. Most of the top comedians of the day tried and failed, and along with the comedians came lots of publicity and enormous audiences. No one knew, of course, that Sue's facial muscles were paralyzed and she couldn't smile even if she wanted to.[4]

William Hammerstein did not share his father's love for show business, viewing it merely as a means of earning a living, but like his father he was a cold, undemonstrative parent and husband, and not much of a family man. The love and affection young Oscar needed, however, was amply provided by his mother, Alice. She was a Presbyterian of Scottish stock.[5] Since William did not bring much Jewish background to the marriage, the children were baptized Episcopalian and later practiced no religion.

Oscar Hammerstein II, whose nickname as a boy was "Ockie," did not meet his paternal grandfather until he was eight, but he had a close childhood relationship with his maternal grandparents, who occupied an apartment in the Hammerstein house at 87th Street and Central Park West. Each morning, before being taken for his walk, he would join Grandpa Nimmo for a breakfast consisting of a milkshake laced with whiskey. Oscar became interested in the theatre after acting in an elementary school play and urged his father to take him to see the show at the Victoria. William refused at first but eventually gave in, and it was on that occasion, at a Saturday matinee, that the future theatrical genius finally met his famous namesake.

Alice Hammerstein died in 1910 at the very young age of thirty-five. She had been the brightest spot in Oscar's family life and her loss was immeasurable. That summer he and his brother were sent to camp at the Weingart Institute, where he made what were to be lifelong friendships with several fellow campers, among them David and Myron Selznick, Lorenz Hart, and Leighton Brill, who would serve as his assistant for more than twenty years. Together with these friends, Hammerstein wrote shows, edited the camp newspaper, and played various sports. While he was at camp his father got married again, to a sister-in-law whose nickname was "Mousie."

In 1912 Oscar matriculated at Columbia College, where he majored in English. Columbia proved a very exciting place for him. His classmates included such stimulating young men as Bennett Cerf, Richard Simon, and M. Lincoln Schuster of publishing fame, Herb Fields, Lorenz Hart, Herman Mankiewicz, Mortimer Rodgers (Richard's brother), and Milton Berle, and he soon was quite active in fraternities and student shows, becoming very popular in the process. At the end of his freshman year, however, he acceded when his father made him promise not go into theatre and instead to study law.

That summer, while Oscar was at the Weingart camp, his father suddenly died. Upon returning home he was stunned to find the newspapers treating his father as if he had been a national hero of some kind. He had not realized before that his father was such a major figure—"the Barnum of vaudeville," as one of the many tributes put it. Messages of condolence kept pouring in, and more than 1,000 mourners attended the funeral at Temple Israel in Harlem. After the funeral a bugler on Broadway sounded taps—William Hammerstein's death marked the end of an era.

Soon afterward, and in spite of his promise not to become involved in theatre, Oscar joined the Columbia University Players, becoming an active participant, both as a writer and a performer, in the group's annual *Varsity Show*. In 1916 he and Herman Mankiewicz, who later wrote the screenplay for *Citizen*

Kane, wrote the entire show. After one of its performances Hammerstein was introduced to his future partner, Richard Rodgers, then a fourteen-year-old, who had been brought to the show by his older brother, Mortimer.

Keeping at least part of the promise made to his father, Hammerstein entered the Columbia Law School. At the same time, though, he continued to write for the *Varsity Show,* collaborating on two songs with Rodgers in 1919. While in law school Hammerstein worked part-time for a law firm as a process server, earning $5 per week. Although he also had an income of $50 per week from stocks his father had left him, he asked for a raise, and when his request was rejected, he approached his uncle, Arthur Hammerstein, for a job.

Arthur Hammerstein, who had put on Victor Herbert's *Naughty Marietta* and Rudolf Friml's *The Firefly,* two of the longest-running operettas in theatrical history, was an important Broadway producer. Aware of the promise his dead brother had extracted from his nephew, Arthur refused at first, but Oscar persisted and Arthur finally gave in, hiring him as an assistant stage manager at $20 per week. When Arthur subsequently decided to give him a permanent rather than a "run-of-the-play" contract, Oscar became engaged and then married to Myra Finn, a cousin of Dr. William Rodgers, Richard's father. Soon after, his uncle promoted him from assistant stage manager to manager.

Following the advice of one of his Columbia professors, Hammerstein now began to write in earnest. His first lyric effort was for a song interpolated into one of his uncle's shows. Although primitive when judged by the standard of his later work, it was a beginning. Hammerstein's first theatrical effort was a play entitled *The Light.* Like the song, it was a failure. A four-act play without music—and, judging by the reviews, without much merit—it died in New Haven.

The failure of *The Light* did not discourage Hammerstein. Many years later he told how he sat down on a park bench outside the theatre after the show closed and immediately began planning his next production. Originally entitled *Joan from*

Arkansaw, it was produced by Arthur Hammerstein and had music by Herbert Stothart. While the show was still on the road before the New York opening, Arthur demanded that Oscar rewrite the script and work in a part for a comedian he had hired to "save" it. After much complaining Oscar did what he was told. Retitled *Always You,* the show opened on January 5, 1920. It received good reviews but was a box-office failure. Oscar's lyrics, according to one critic, were "more clever than the average musical."

While *Always You* was being prepared for a road tour, Hammerstein found out that his uncle was planning a new musical called *Tickle Me,* again with music by Stothart. He persuaded his uncle to let him write the lyrics and libretto, but Arthur, who had to look after his business interests as well as his family ties, imposed the condition that he collaborate with Otto Harbach, a veteran lyricist and librettist. The deal was sweetened by Harbach's willingness to share billing and royalties, and Hammerstein readily agreed.

Although *Tickle Me,* which opened at the Selwyn Theatre on August 17, 1920, was not a hit, Hammerstein's brief partnership with Harbach proved to be of vital importance in his professional development, and in later years he was to describe it as one of the two great blessings of his life (the other was his having been born into the Hammerstein family). Harbach taught Hammerstein the "nuts and bolts" of the lyricist's craft, starting with the basic techniques of songwriting, and imbued him with a fundamental principle that became his guiding rule: a play must be a cohesive unity made up of component parts that work together—the plot must be interesting, and the characters, dialogue, songs, jokes, etc., must all make sense in the overall context. This was an important lesson, and Hammerstein followed it for the rest of his life.

During the next decade Hammerstein worked with the greatest composers on Broadway: in addition to Stothart, Jerome Kern, George Gershwin, Vincent Youmans, Sigmund Romberg, and Rudolf Friml. In 1923 Hammerstein, Harbach, Stothart, and a very young Vincent Youmans wrote *Wildflower,* which became a giant hit, playing Broadway for more than 400 performances. Both the title song, "Wildflower," and "Bambalina" became popular favorites.

Hammerstein's next hit was *Rose-Marie*, with music by Stothart and Rudolf Friml. A rather unusual facet of this show was its plot, for it included a murder. Instead of the customary huge chorus number at the show's conclusion, only two people were left on stage. Even the show's program was unique in that it did not include the names of the songs and instead had an explanatory note stating that they were so integral to the plot that they could not be listed individually. Nonetheless, two of the songs were outstanding hits: "Rose-Marie" and "Indian Love Call." The show ran for sixteen months, making it the longest-running musical of its day, and as a result Hammerstein finally became financially secure.

Following *Rose-Marie* Hammerstein was paired with the incomparable Jerome Kern, who had already been active on Broadway for more than twenty years, first as a rehearsal pianist and then as a composer. Together they wrote *Sunny*, which opened on September 23, 1925, and ran for more than a year and a half. It is remembered mainly for the song "Who."

Hammerstein's next musical, *Song of the Flame*, is primarily of historical importance, for it gave him his only opportunity to work with George Gershwin, who was called in when the intended composer, Rudolf Friml, dropped out because of contract difficulties. The last of the great composers Hammerstein worked with during this period was Sigmund Romberg. Their first collaboration, *The Desert Song*, opened on November 30, 1926, and ran for more than 470 performances. Over the next fifteen years they wrote four more shows together, *The New Moon*, *East Wind*, *May Wine*, and *Sunny River*. Among their most popular hit songs were "When I Grow Too Old to Dream," "Lover, Come Back to Me," "Stouthearted Men," and "One Kiss."

Meanwhile, in 1926, around the time Hammerstein was working on *The Desert Song*, Jerome Kern called him to propose a new musical based on the novel *Show Boat* by Edna Ferber. The result of their collaboration, lavishly staged by Florenz Ziegfeld as the first production in his new theatre, proved to be a milestone in the history of musicals and the fruition of Kern's long-time dream of writing an authentic American operetta.

Show Boat, which opened on December 27, 1927, before a glittering first-night audience, was a masterpiece. It had all the attributes that make up a hit: the sets and costumes were magnificent, the songs were brilliant, the script and story were fascinating and precise; moreover, and perhaps most impor-tant, all the songs fit smoothly into the story, the dialogue rang true, and the plot was so well integrated that the play could have stood by itself without the songs, which even today is the test of a good libretto. When the curtain came down after the first performance, there was a long silence, and then the theatre was shaken by thunderous applause. Ziegfeld knew he had a hit, the critics knew they had a hit, and the members of the audience knew they had witnessed an event of historical importance. Arthur Hammerstein, Oscar's uncle, is said to have commented that he had just seen the perfect show and that his breaking of his word to his brother William had been vindicated.

Show Boat ran for 572 performances on Broadway and has been revived many times since. Several of its marvelous songs, including "Ole Man River," "Bill," "Can't Help Lovin Dat Man," and "Make Believe," have become perennially popular stan-dards, and the members of the cast, many of them relative unknowns when the show opened, went on to become big stars. Amazingly enough, though, it was to be fifteen years before Hammerstein had another great show.

Throughout his career Hammerstein had wanted to elevate the Broadway musical into something more natural and believ-able than the stilted, unreal shows of the 1920's, set in faraway places with unlikely characters in impossible situations. Like Gershwin he wanted to change things, but he lacked the intel-lectuality and irony that tempered Gershwin's work. [6] He wrote well with Romberg and Friml because he shared their strong feeling for romanticism and schmaltz, but as the world and its musical tastes began changing, he was not able to adjust to the new trends. In short, he was not a leader or a pace-setter, but a consummate craftsman who fine-tuned the styles of the day and depended on someone else to set the trends.

As a result, Hammerstein went through an extremely bad period during the late 1920's and the 1930's. None of his musicals ran for more than seven weeks, and his film contract was bought out by the studio for $100,000 just to get rid of him. Seemingly nothing went right; his family finances suffered, and he felt unwanted, unnecessary, and depressed. All this finally changed, however, in 1942, when Hammerstein entered into a creative partnership with Richard Rodgers. Given the opportunity to work with a composer who had fresh ideas, he was soon able to regain his former prominence.

Richard Rodgers, the second son of William Abraham and Mamie Rodgers, was born at his family's summer home on Long Island on July 28, 1902. His father born in Holden, Missouri, into a family that originally hailed from Alsace-Lorraine, was a graduate of City College and the Bellevue Hospital Medical School. His mother, of Polish immigrant stock, was the daughter of Rachel (Lewine) and Jacob Levy, a wealthy textile manufacturer.

Rodgers grew up at 3 West 120th Street, a large house owned and partially occupied by his Levy grandparents, with his father's medical office on the ground floor. He began studying the piano as a child, with an aunt as his first teacher. Although he hated practicing and refused to do the exercises required of any good piano technician, he had a remarkably good ear and could pick out melodies with ease after hearing them only once. By the age of seven or eight he was already composing his own songs. Soon after he was introduced to the musical theatre, and in the years that followed he was taken to see most of the popular operettas of the day.

By all accounts Rodgers had a happy childhood unmarked by anything extraordinary. He spent his summers at camp, first the Weingart Institute in Highmount, New York, later Camp Wigwam in Harrison, Maine, and at both places made friendships that would later serve him well throughout his professional life. Although his parents were not especially concerned about his religious training, his grandfather was, and in consequence he became both a Bar Mitzvah and a confirmand at Temple Israel on Lenox Avenue at 120th Street.

After completing elementary school Rodgers was enrolled at Townsend Harris Hall, an elite preparatory program for City College, but he had little interest in academic work and soon dropped out. Instead he attended De Witt Clinton High School, where his music teacher encouraged him to attend Saturday afternoon opera performances and helped him to develop an appreciation for serious music. It was popular music and the hope of being a composer that captivated Rodgers, however, and in the year 1917, when he was fifteen years old, his older brother, Mortimer, provided the opening he needed.

Mortimer belonged to a local athletic club that was putting on a series of amateur musical revues to raise money, and he arranged for Richard to write some of the songs. There were seven songs by Rodgers in the club's first show, which raised $3,000, and twenty in the second, which justifiably led the young composer to feel that he was well on his way, even though his bold attempt to get the songs published by Max Dreyfus of the Harms Music Company did not meet with success.

Soon after, on a Sunday afternoon in 1918, Philip Leavitt, a friend of Mortimer's, introduced Rodgers to Lorenz Hart, an up-and-coming lyricist with extensive camp and college show experience. Though their personalities and lifestyles were quite different, the two young men hit it off at once and agreed to become musical collaborators, much to the horror of Mortimer and his friend Bennet Cerf, later the head of Random House, who both considered Hart an irresponsible and undependable no-account.

Despite their efforts to make him change his mind, Rodgers stuck up for his new partner, and rightfully so, for in the next three weeks they wrote fifteen songs together. At this time, just after World War I, popular music was pretty standard fare, and except for the work of Kern and Bolton in their "Princess" shows, it showed little technical creativity or excitement. Rodgers and Hart's new approach to popular music was reflected even in their first published song, "Any Old Place with

You," which Lew Fields interpolated into one of his shows, *A Lonely Romeo*. In addition to creative lyrics, the song had several interesting technical innovations, including a reversal of the normal sixteen-bar verse, thirty-two-bar chorus, as well as some lively chord progressions which gave it a special sprightliness.

The next effort by Rodgers and Hart, a 1920 Columbia College amateur show entitled *Fly With Me*, received very good reviews. One critic wrote, "We had not heard of Richard Rodgers before. We have a suspicion we shall hear of him again." He could not have been more right, because producer Lew Fields bought the score of *Fly With Me* for his new musical, *Poor Little Ritz Girl*. After the Boston tryout the play doctors got to work, however, and by the time they finished, the play retained only seven Rodgers and Hart songs; its other eight songs were written by Sigmund Romberg. Regardless, the show received very favorable reviews, and Rodgers was thrilled to have made his Broadway debut.

Rodgers and Hart now tried their hand at a straight play without music, but to no avail, and by 1921 Rodgers was very discouraged. He quit the Columbia course he was taking and transferred to the Institute of Musical Art, later renamed the Julliard School of Music, where he received training in several facets of classical music. In 1922 he took a leave of absence from the Institute to travel with *Snapshots of 1922*, a Lew Fields musical, and to write songs for several lyricists.

Encouraged by his success in these endeavors, Rodgers quit the Institute altogether to try professional music life again. Coupled with Hart and Herbert Fields, he wrote a parody of Tin Pan Alley called *The Melody Man*. Produced by and starring Lew Fields, the show got mixed reviews and folded after fifty-six performances. Rodgers was terribly depressed, but no more so than his father, who was torn between pride in his son's musical accomplishments and the desire for him to have a stable means of earning a living. At twenty-two, Richard Rodgers had no money, seemingly no musical future, and no idea what to do. He was plagued by insomnia for more than a year and during this low period decided to give up music and become a salesman for children's underwear at a salary of $50 per week.

Fortunately fate intervened and Rodgers never tried selling underwear. A family friend invited him to participate in the writing of a musical for the Theatre Guild's younger performers, who were planning to put on a show to raise money for tapestries for the Guild's new theatre. Rodgers agreed on the condition that Hart write the lyrics. Now the team was finally on its way. *The Garrick Gaieties* was originally to have just a few performances, but by popular demand it ran for more than six months.

All told, Rodgers and Hart worked together for twenty years. Their joint output included almost a dozen musical classics, among them *A Connecticut Yankee* (1926), *Simple Simon* (1930), *Jumbo* (1934), *On Your Toes* (1936), *The Boys from Syracuse* (1938), *Pal Joey* (1940), and *By Jupiter* (1942), and their list of hit songs was enormous; virtually all of their shows had at least one.

Everything good has to end, however, and the Rodgers-Hart partnership was no exception. As was related in the preceding chapter, Hart was slowly drinking himself to death. He refused to show up at rehearsals or working sessions, began suffering blackouts, and in every way became more and more difficult to work with. Rodgers was deeply troubled, especially because the Theatre Guild had asked him to musicalize the play *Green Grow the Lilacs*, a major project that would require his and Hart's best efforts. Seeking both advice and a new partner, he consulted his many friends in the music business, among them Oscar Hammerstein II, who at the time was suffering through a long dry period. Hammerstein told him to continue working with Hart until it was no longer possible, promising to secretly step in, when and if necessary, to complete any lyrics Hart left unfinished.

Though Hammerstein was willing to do this without receiving credit or payment, his generous offer did not satisfy the level-headed Rodgers, who wanted a full-time partner. At a dinner arranged for the purpose by Louis Dreyfus, the son of music publisher Max Dreyfus, he approached Ira Gershwin, who had not worked much since the death of his brother George. Rodgers and Gershwin discussed the problems Rodgers was having with Hart. Apparently they did not talk openly about the possibility of Gershwin teaming up with Rodgers, but the suggestion was there loud and clear, and Gershwin turned it down.

Rodgers returned to Hammerstein, who agreed to work with him only if Hart definitely bowed out. Perhaps predictably, given his deteriorating condition, Hart refused to go along when Rodgers told him about *Green Grow the Lilacs*. Rodgers responded that he would find another lyricist if Hart did not want to do the play. Hart asked whether he had someone in mind. Rodgers replied, "Oscar Hammerstein." Realizing that their partnership was over, Hart told Rodgers that he couldn't have picked a better man and, with that, left the room. The stage was set for the emergence of Broadway's newest and brightest team.

Their first show, of course, was *Oklahoma!* Some years earlier Hammerstein had tried to persuade Jerome Kern to join him in writing a musical based on *Green Grow the Lilacs*. Kern had refused, maintaining that the play presented too many technical problems, but Hammerstein continued to believe in its potential and needed no convincing when Rodgers broached the subject. After agreeing to go ahead with the venture, the two men purchased the movie rights to the script from MGM, a small investment that ultimately earned them a fortune and became their modus operandi in the years ahead.

Setting down the ground rules for their collaboration, Rodgers and Hammerstein agreed that the lyrics would be written before the music because the dialogue and songs had to flow one from the other, with no obvious seams or loose ends. Since the story line concerned common people in the Midwest, they aimed at creating a kind of folk musical, and thus there were no chorus girls, no big production numbers, no high-powered dance sequences, and none of the usual broad comedy. The very opening scene of the show proclaimed its uniqueness, for instead of the conventional mass of gorgeously costumed dancers, *Oklahoma!* began with a woman sitting alone at a butter churn while off stage a man sang the magnificent "Oh, What a Beautiful Mornin'."

Rodgers was convinced that they could do anything they

wanted, however unconventional, so long as it was done properly and with taste, and he was right. The show they created, a totally original mix of musical comedy and serious drama, revolutionized the theatre and has ever since been regarded as a classic. Its many hit songs, among them "People Will Say We're in Love," "Surrey with the Fringe on Top," and of course the title song, "Oklahoma!", are still loved by millions.

Oddly enough, the Theatre Guild had a terrible time raising the $83,000 needed to finance the show, and when it premiered in New Haven before the New York opening, the word-of-mouth was very poor indeed, despite its having a fine cast that included Alfred Drake, Celeste Holm, Joan Roberts, and Howard da Silva. Billy Rose, for instance, is said to have commented, "No girls, no gags, no chance."

When *Oklahoma!* finally opened in New York on March 31, 1943, however, the critics and the audience went wild. There had never been anything like it before, and instantaneously a classic and a legend were born. *Oklahoma!* went on to enjoy the longest run of any Broadway play until that time—more than 2,200 performances, or over five years. While it was still on Broadway, a touring company was sent out for a year, and productions were staged throughout the world, even for American troops overseas. *Oklahoma!* was the first show in Broadway history to be recorded in its entirety as an original-cast album, selling hundreds of thousands of copies, and in 1955 it was made into an extremely popular movie.

All told, *Oklahoma!* earned more than $7 million for its backers, a fantastic success that was just the boost the Theatre Guild needed. The various investors all received about $50,000 for their initial $1,500. As for Rodgers and Hammerstein, they made about $1 million each. Maximizing their profits by expanding into new money-making ventures, they jointly founded the Williamson Publishing Company, so named because both of their fathers were named William, and began producing their own plays as well as those of other writers.

After writing the film musical *State Fair*, which won the 1944 best song Academy Award for "It Might As Well Be Spring" and also included the superlative "It's a Grand Night for Singing,"

Rodgers and Hammerstein followed their first Broadway triumph with another, *Carousel*. The show was based on the play *Liliom* by Ferenc Molnar, but the setting was changed from twentieth-century Budapest to a late-nineteenth-century New England seacoast town. From the standpoint of Broadway conventions the adaptation posed many problems, most especially the challenge of working in the story's dream sequences, the murder of the leading man, and a heavenly intervention. Rodgers and Hammerstein were up to it, however, and created a beautiful score that included some of their finest songs. The "Carousel Waltz," "You'll Never Walk Alone," "If I Loved You," and "June Is Bustin' Out All Over" have all become perennial favorites. *Carousel* opened in New York in 1945, ran 890 performances, and has been revived on Broadway several times. It too has been made into a very successful musical film.

In 1947 Rodgers and Hammerstein came up with *Allegro*. It told the story of a doctor who abandons a solid medical practice to gain money and status but eventually returns to his hometown and to curing his neighbors. The show had many unusual aspects; while the critics appreciated some of its creative innovations, such as the Greek chorus and the scant use of scenery and costumes, and recognized that the songs "A Fellow Needs a Girl" and "The Gentleman Is a Dope" were outstanding, *Allegro* proved to be rather unpopular. It ran for only 315 performances, quite a respectable run for someone else, but unquestionably a failure for the team that had written *Oklahoma!* and *Carousel*.

After *Allegro* it was natural for observers of the Broadway scene to wonder whether Rodgers and Hammerstein could still write hits, especially since both of them had run dry in the past. Their next show, *South Pacific*, laid all such questions to rest. Opening in 1949, with a stellar cast headed by the incomparable Mary Martin and Ezio Pinza, it enjoyed the greatest advance ticket sale in the history of Broadway ($1 million), ran for almost 2,000 performances, took in more than $9 million in overall ticket sales, won the Pulitzer Prize, and sold several million copies of sheet music as well as more than a million original-cast albums. Like *Carousel* and *Oklahoma!*, *South Pacific* is frequently revived, and in 1958 it too was a box-office smash as a movie.

During its original run on Broadway, tickets for *South Pacific* were so hard to get that stories about attempts to procure them, some authentic, some perhaps a bit fanciful, were widely circulated. When available, tickets sold for more than $40 a pair, a price which Hammerstein said was outrageous. Rodgers received a letter one day from a man who said that he absolutely had to have tickets to *South Pacific* as a wedding gift for his fiancée. When Rodgers responded with a query as to the date of the wedding, the groom-to-be replied, "Whenever we get the tickets!"[7]

The libretto for *South Pacific* was adapted from James Michener's best-selling *Tales of the South Pacific,* winner of the 1947 Pulitzer Prize for literature. Its songs were quite diverse in style, ranging from the cheerful "I'm Gonna Wash That Man Right Outa My Hair" (which the star had to do live on stage) to the haunting "Bali Ha'i." The show's most popular song, and one heard often today, was "Some Enchanted Evening." "Younger Than Springtime" and "Happy Talk" are also well remembered.

While *South Pacific* was primarily a love story—actually two parallel love stories—it also had a serious theme, reflecting a concern that had engaged Hammerstein since early in his career. As far back as *Show Boat* he had attempted to show blacks in a favorable light, and his commitment to full equality for racial minorities was also reflected in *Carmen Jones* (1943), his all-black updated version of the Bizet opera. *South Pacific* provided him with an admirable vehicle for delicately but nonetheless forthrightly introducing the theme of racial tolerance to Broadway. He did so both in the story line, with its subplot of a romantic liaison between a white marine and a beautiful Tonkinese girl, and its main plot complication when the heroine discovers that her planter fiancé had previously been married to a native woman, and also in the lyrics for one of the show's outstanding tunes, "Carefully Taught," with the refrain, "You have to be taught to hate."[8]

Much of *South Pacific's* special appeal derived from its exotic setting on the far-off island of Bali Ha'i and from the colorful presentation, in music and lyrics, of Bloody Mary and Liat, two Tonkinese women. In this respect the show was a testing ground, for Rodgers and Hammerstein utilized the same kind of local color, only far more extensively, in their next musical, *The King and I*, which was set in nineteenth-century Siam.

The score of *The King and I* posed some difficult problems. Rodgers knew that he couldn't write genuine Oriental songs even if he wanted to, and he was also well aware of the danger of writing songs that were too Western. His music for the show struck a very happy balance between these two extremes, Western music with subtle melodic shadings that gave a hint of Eastern flavor. The score is one of the most popular and best-known in the Rodgers and Hammerstein repertory. "Hello, Young Lovers," "Whistle a Happy Tune," "Getting to Know You," and "I Have Dreamed" are the jewels of this crowning achievement.

The King and I was the first Broadway musical to be adapted from a film. Rodgers and Hammerstein were persuaded to write it by the great English actress Gertrude Lawrence, who had seen *Anna and the King of Siam* (1946), starring Rex Harrison and Irene Dunne, and was convinced she would make a wonderful Anna. She was right, and her performance was a tour-de-force. Staged by a neophyte Jerome Robbins, with sets by Jo Mielziner and costumes designed by Irene Sharaff, *The King and I* was a breathtaking musical with an authentic Oriental ambiance and a Western love story. It opened in 1951 to highly enthusiastic reviews, ran for 1,250 performances on Broadway, and subsequently enjoyed great popularity as a movie musical.

Soon after this Rodgers made his debut in the new medium of television, composing the music for the award-winning NBC documentary series "Victory at Sea," which was aired for the first time during the 1952–53 season. Also in 1953, with *Me and Juliet*, Rodgers and Hammerstein once again demonstrated, as they did with *Allegro*, that they were mere fallible mortals. The play was a musical comedy about the backstage life of a Broadway hit, but no one in the cast ever found out what being in a hit was really like, because *Me and Juliet* was dreadful. It ran only 353 performances—a disaster for the likes of Rodgers and Hammerstein. Their next show suffered a similar fate. Entitled *Pipe Dream*, and based on John Steinbeck's story "Sweet Thursday," its plot development focused on the bums and misfits living on Cannery Row in Monterey, California. Playgoers stayed away in droves, and this effort, too, closed very quickly.

Soon after, while working on their next show, both members of the team fell seriously ill, Rodgers with cancer of the jaw, and Hammerstein with a serious stomach disorder. Both men required surgery, but as soon as their health was restored they returned to work at their usual pace. Their new show, *Flower Drum Song*, which opened in 1958, was set in San Francisco's Chinatown and introduced audiences to the traditional Chinese marriage broker, the cultural gap between new immigrants and second-generation Chinese-Americans, and the theme of assimilation. The score had several beautiful songs, most notably "I Enjoy Being a Girl," "A Hundred Million Miracles," and "Grant Avenue." *Flower Drum Song*, unlike its two predecessors, was a hit; it ran for more than 600 performances and in 1962 was made into a successful movie.

As their next project Rodgers and Hammerstein wrote the delightful musical *Cinderella* as a TV special for the impending video debut of the immensely popular Julie Andrews. With Andrews in the title role, *Cinderella* was first televised in 1957 and was seen by an audience of 80 million people. Eight years later it was shown again with a totally new cast and enjoyed the same popularity it did the first time around. Two of the show's songs were especially good, "In My Own Little Corner" and "Do I Love You."

By one of those ironies that make history so interesting, the last show written by these two great creative forces in the American musical theatre was highly reminiscent of the very genre they had both striven to supersede some thirty-five years earlier. *The Sound of Music*, set in Austria around the time of the German takeover and telling the story of one anti-Nazi family's participation in the resistance and eventual escape to America, was as close to an operetta as anything the team had ever written.

The critics were divided in their appraisals of *The Sound of Music*, but playgoers weren't. They flocked to see it, and the show, which ran 1,440 performances on Broadway and another

1,000 on tour, proved to be the most financially rewarding work that Rodgers and Hammerstein ever wrote. Its film version, released in 1965, was the most profitable movie musical until that time, and if that wasn't enough, the original-cast album and the film soundtrack album together sold more than 10 million copies.

Very soon after *The Sound of Music* opened on Broadway, Oscar Hammerstein began suffering stomach pains again. This time his condition was diagnosed as terminal cancer. When he learned the grim news, he had only one request—that he be allowed to die at home; and so he did, on August 23, 1960. His passing was memorialized in New York and London by the turning out of lights in the theatre districts. It seemed an appropriate tribute; indeed, the same honor had been rendered to his grandfather, Oscar Hammerstein I, many years before.

Oscar Hammerstein II played a preeminent role in the development of the American musical theatre. He was motivated throughout his entire career to make the musical play more important, and he sought to accomplish this by using more natural settings and by writing songs and libretti that brought a new sense of reality and meaningfulness to the Broadway stage. Hammerstein was passionately interested in people and their relationships to each other. He hated bigotry and racism; he wanted each of us to love our neighbors regardless of color, creed, or religion. Oscar Hammerstein II brought a warmth and humanity to the theatre from which it has benefited ever since.

Hammerstein's death left Rodgers disconsolate, but despite his grief he continued to work on his own. In 1962 he wrote the music and lyrics for the show *No Strings*, the story of a Paris love affair between a beautiful black model and a white novelist. As the show's title suggests, there were no stringed instruments in the orchestra; in addition, Rodgers stationed the musicians right on the stage and sometimes had them wander through the action to provide commentary. Though the critical reactions were mixed, *No Strings* ran for a respectable 580 performances.

Realizing that he needed a partner, Rodgers tried to collaborate with Alan Jay Lerner, but the two men could not work together and soon broke up. Lerner completed the show they had begun, *On a Clear Day You Can See Forever*, with Burton Lane, while Rodgers now tried teaming up with Stephen Sondheim, a former protégé of Hammerstein's, who had written the lyrics for *West Side Story* and *Gypsy* and both words and music for *A Funny Thing Happened on the Way to the Forum*. Their joint effort, *Do I Hear a Waltz*, based on an Arthur Laurents play, *The Time of the Cuckoo*, was not very good, and in addition their personal relationship was strained, so this partnership, too, soon came to an end.

In the years that followed Rodgers attempted three other musicals on his own: *Rex*, a story about King Henry VIII; *Two By Two*, the story of Noah and the Ark; and his last, *I Remember Mama*, based on a play he had produced long before. All three were failures, but at least they made it possible for him to boast that he had been represented on Broadway for a period of sixty years—a very formidable achievement.

Richard Rodgers was a complex man, amazingly well disciplined and organized, and throughout his career, contrary to what one might expect of an "artist," he revealed himself to be a shrewd businessman with a firm grasp on matters of profit and finance. During his partnership with Lorenz Hart, Rodgers wrote music that was bright and brittle, "smart" music in a style that typified the pace and tenor of the period. With Hammerstein his melodies were more mellow, reminiscent of the past, of love, of days gone by, yet displaying a freshness that was new and exciting.

Rodgers died just one day short of seeing the year 1980. His funeral, attended by his many friends and the luminaries of the entertainment world, was held at New York's Temple Emanu-El. With his passing, a magnificent chapter in the history of the American musical theatre was closed.

The Great Songs

NEW VOCAL COMPOSITIONS OF

HENRY & GEO. HENRY RUSSELL.

Cheer boys Cheer	Composed by H.Russell.	2s	We are brothers, a Masonic song	Composed by Geo.H.Russell.	2s
Pull away cheerily.	Do.		On we came to the sound of the Drum	Do	
Far, Far upon the Sea.	Do.		A Farmers Wife I'll be	Do	
To the West, to the West.	Do.		There's fortune on before us boys	Do	
Canadian Sleigh song	Do.		The Sealers	Do	4

BOSTON.
Published by OLIVER DITSON & CO. 277 Washington St.

C.C.CLAPP & CO.   S.T.GORDON   BECK & LAWTON   TRUAX & BALDWIN
Boston   N. York   Philada.   Troy

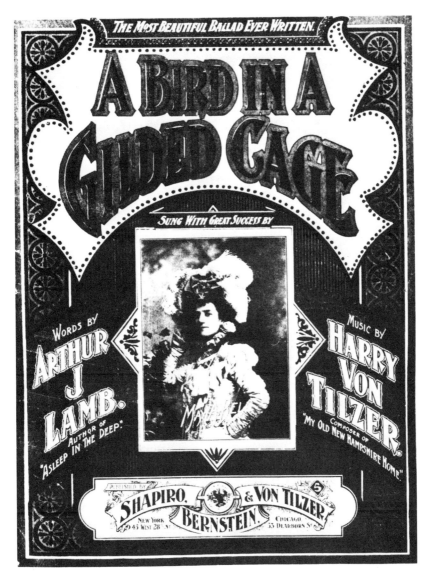

Courtesy of Harris Gilbert Family

I FOUND A FOUR LEAF CLOVER

FOURTH ANNUAL PRODUCTION

George White's Scandals

LYRICS BY
B. G. DeSYLVA
MUSIC BY
GEORGE GERSHWIN
BOOK BY
ANDY RICE
AND
GEORGE WHITE
ENTIRE PRODUCTION STAGED BY
GEORGE WHITE

Scenes by
The Law Studios
from Sketches by
John Wenger

VOCAL

ARGENTINE
CINDERELATIVES
I Found A Four Leap Clover
She Hangs Out In Our Alley
Where Is The Man Of My Dreams
I'll Build A Stairway To Paradise

HARMS
NEW YORK

MOUNTAIN GREENERY

The Theatre Guild presents
The Theatre Guild Studio in

The GARRICK GAIETIES 1926

LYRICS BY
LORENZ HART
MUSIC BY
RICHARD RODGERS

STAGED BY
PHILIP LOEB
DANCE NUMBERS
STAGED BY
HERBERT FIELDS

Little Souvenir
Keys To Heaven
Mountain Greenery
What's The Use Of Talking
Sleepy Head

HARMS
NEW YORK

MADE IN U.S.A.

EMBRACEABLE YOU

Conclusion

It can safely be said that without the Jewish contribution, popular music in America would be very different. From their earliest arrival in any number on these shores, Jews have played an essential role in the development of the popular song.

Songs are more than entertainment; they tell of the history, the lifestyle, the mores, and the interests of those about whom they are written, for whom they are written, and by whom they are sung. In the beginning of popular music in America, sentimentality was the essence of the song. John Howard Payne and Henry Russell represented the Jewish contribution in the early and middle nineteenth century.

As the American Republic expanded and developed in many spheres, the professionally written and commercially distributed song became a major element of popular entertainment. It is here that the Jewish contribution really begins. When burlesque and vaudeville became popular, it was in large part Jews who wrote the songs. David Braham wrote for the first great vaudeville team, Harrigan and Hart. Weber and Fields, both Jews, continued the tradition. Vaudeville also fostered the beginnings of most of the great popular composers. Irving Berlin, Jerome Kern, Irving Caesar, and Charles K. Harris, all Jews, both wrote for vaudeville and were influenced by it. Indeed, Jewish composers, lyricists, singers, and musicians—some still remembered, some long forgotten—played a disproportionate role in every phase of creating and disseminating popular songs.

For a song to become widely known and accepted, there had to be a way of introducing it to the people, and this was the function of the music publishing industry, another field in

195

which Jews predominated. The New York "music factory" known as Tin Pan Alley was made up of a number of Jewish firms—M. Witmark and Sons, Charles K. Harris, Inc., Joseph W. Stern and Company, Shapiro and Bernstein, Von Tilzer and Company, Leo Feist, Inc., T. B. Harms, Irving Berlin, Inc. The businessmen-artists who ran these firms churned out song after song in a process that is perhaps best described as "manufacturing" rather than "composing." Amazingly, many of these songs were masterpieces of the songwriter's craft—best-selling hits that are still standard elements of the American popular repertory.

The first song to sell a million copies of sheet music, "After the Ball," was written by a Jew, Charles K. Harris. The most prolific writer on Tin Pan Alley, Harry Von Tilzer, was Jewish. So was Irving Berlin, the composer who sold the most copies of his songs, and wrote the most successful popular song in American musical history. The songs by these men and their Tin Pan Alley colleagues have become almost traditional. What would summer be without Albert Von Tilzer's "Take Me Out to the Ball Game" (he had never been to one!)? How could we face autumn and the new school year without Gus Edwards's "School Days"? What would the midwinter holiday season be without Irving Berlin's "White Christmas," or Easter without "Easter Parade"? All these are now "Americana" songs, not popular songs.

The men whose biographies are given in detail in this book each represented a specific aspect of the burgeoning American music industry. Henry Russell was the first great songwriter of Jewish birth. Charles Kassel Harris wrote the most popular song of the nineteenth century and began the music industry. Monroe Rosenfeld coined the name by which that industry was to be known around the world, Tin Pan Alley. Harry and Albert Von Tilzer typified the kind of men who wrote for Tin Pan Alley, giving us more standards than any other composers in its first fifty years. Jerome Kern changed the face of the musical theatre and helped the popular song to mature. Irving Berlin was the quintessential American-Jewish songwriter—an immigrant who quickly acclimated, he became as all-American as his song "God Bless America." George and Ira Gershwin, more than any other songwriting team, contributed to every genre of American music, popular and classical. Lorenz Hart, perhaps the greatest lyricist of his time, wrote songs that are still unsurpassed for sophistication and wit. Richard Rodgers and Oscar Hammerstein II, raising the Broadway musical to unprecedented heights of grandeur and achievement, together wrote one of the most magnificent chapters in the history of the American theatre. Their songs will be sung and played, and their shows will live on, for as long as there is a Broadway.

The Jewish composers and lyricists of today, and truly, all the composers and lyricists now working on Broadway and in other phases of the entertainment industry, owe their careers to those who preceded them. Each succeeding generation of songwriters paved the way for those who followed. The achievements of the people discussed in this book can well be said to have made possible the achievements of Alan J. Lerner and Frederick Loewe, Leonard Bernstein, Stephen Sondheim, Stephen Schwartz, John Kander and Fred Ebb, Jerry Herman, Marvin Hamlisch, and the many other composers and songwriters whose works we so enjoy. Indeed, whether we are singers or listeners, we all owe a tremendous debt to the Jews on Tin Pan Alley.

Notes

CHAPTER 1
1. Rufus Learsi, *The Jews in America*, p. 81.
2. *Universal Jewish Encyclopedia*, Vol. 8, p. 493.
3. *Catalogue of Americana, Judaica and Hebraica* (Brooklyn: Aldine Book Co., n.d.).
4. I am deeply indebted to Dr. Jacob Rader Marcus of the Hebrew Union College and the American Jewish Archives for telling me about Jonas B. Phillips. My own research for this book had indicated that Henry Russell was America's first Jewish songwriter. Considering the traditional Jewish interest in music and poetry, it will probably be only a matter of time before an even earlier American Jewish composer or lyricist is discovered.
5. Charles Hamm, *Yesterdays*, p. 167
6. Henry Frederick Reddall, *Songs That Never Die*, p. 149.
7. Hamm, p. 169.
8. David Ewen, *All the Years of American Popular Music*, p. 53.
9. David Ewen, *Songs of America*, p. 14.
10. Ewen, *All the Years*, p. 55.
11. Julius Mattfeld, *Variety Music Cavalcade*, p. 58.
12. Sigmund Spaeth, *A History of Popular Music in America*, p. 88.
13. Ewen, *All the Years*, p. 37.
14. In *Utopia Ltd.*, 1893.
15. Ewen, *Songs of America*, p. 13.

CHAPTER 2
1. David Ewen, *Songs of America*, p. 110.
2. *Jewish Encyclopedia*, Vol.12, p. 371.
3. Sigmund Spaeth, *A History of Popular Music in America*, p. 174; and David Ewen, *All the Years of American Popular Music*, p. 84.
4. Statement of the producer to the press.
5. Spaeth, p. 181.
6. Abel Green and Joe Laurie, Jr., *Show Biz from Vaude to Video*, p. 168.
7. Jack Burton, *The Blue Book of Tin Pan Alley*, Vol. 1, p. 126.
8. Ronald Sanders, "The American Popular Song," p. 198.
9. Isaac Goldberg, *Tin Pan Alley*, p. 124.
10. Ewen, *All the Years*, p. 103.
11. David Ewen, *The Life and Death of Tin Pan Alley*, pp. 12–13.
12. Ian Whitcomb, *After the Ball*, p. 44.
13. Spaeth, p. 239.
14. Ewen, *All the Years*, p. 105.
15. Burton, *Blue Book of Tin Pan Alley*, p. 74.
16. Whitcomb, p. 44.
17. Spaeth, p. 271.

18. Goldberg, p. 128.
19. Whitcomb, p. 44.
20. Spaeth, p. 272.
21. Goldberg, p. 131.
22. Ewen, *Life and Death of Tin Pan Alley*, p. 65.
23. Ewen, *All the Years*, p. 109.
24. Goldberg, p. 138.
25. Whitcomb, p. 7.
26. Spaeth,p. 252.
27. Goldberg, p. 197.
28. Charles K. Harris, *After the Ball*, p. 219.

CHAPTER 3
1. Ian Whitcomb, *After the Ball*, pp. 18–19.
2. Ibid., p. 19.
3. Isaac Goldberg, *Tin Pan Alley*, pp. 11–12.
4. Theodore Dreiser, "Whence the Song," pp. 244–245, 249.
5. Chaim Bermant, *The Jews*, p. 83; and Goldberg, p. 1.
6. Charles K. Harris, *After the Ball*, pp. 360–361.
7. Ibid., p. 234.
8. David Ewen. *All the Years of American Popular Music*, p. 125.
9. Whitcomb, p. 42.
10. Ewen, *All the Years*, p. 154.
11. Sigmund Spaeth, *A History of Popular Music in America*, p. 313.
12. Abel Green and Joe Laurie, Jr., *Show Biz from Vaude to Video*, p. 98.
13. Whitcomb, p. 48.
14. Spaeth, p. 315.
15. Ian Whitcomb, *Tin Pan Alley*, p. 11.
16. Whitcomb, *After the Ball*, p. 43.
17. Ewen, *Tin Pan Alley*, p. 146.
18. Goldberg, p. 120.
19. David Ewen, *Popular American Composers*, p. 56.
20. Jack Burton, *Blue Book of Tin Pan Alley*, Vol. 1, p. 223.
21. Daniel I. McNamara, ed., *A.S.C.A.P. Biographical Dictionary*, pp.180–181.
22. Spaeth, p. 368.

CHAPTER 4
1. Abel Green and Joe Laurie, Jr., *Show Biz from Vaude to Video*, p. 9.
2. Philip French, "Show Business Entrepreneur," p. 182.
3. David Ewen, *Great Men of American Popular Songs*, p. 50.
4. Green and Laurie, p. 38.
5. Ibid., p. 85.
6. Irving Howe, *World of Our Fathers*, p. 165.
7. Ibid., p. 557.
8. David Ewen, *The Life and Death of Tin Pan Alley*, p. 126.
9. Charles Hamm, *Yesterdays*, p. 375.
10. Alec Wilder, *American Popular Song*, p. 191.
11. Ibid.
12. Samuel Marx and Jan Clayton, *Rodgers and Hart*, p. 101.
13. Randolph Carter, *The World of Flo Ziegfeld*, p. 10.
14. Ian Whitcomb, *Tin Pan Alley*, p. 14.
15. French, p. 182.

16. Jerry Stagg, *The Brothers Shubert*, p. 5.
17. Carle H. Scheele, "American Entertainment: An Immigrant Domain," p. 443.
18. Ewen, *Tin Pan Alley*, p. 116.
19. Jack Burton, *The Blue Book of Tin Pan Alley*, Vol. 2, p. 166; and Whitcomb, *Tin Pan Alley*, p. 249.
20. Whitcomb, *Tin Pan Alley*, p. 17.
21. Isaac Goldberg, *Tin Pan Alley*, p. 46.
22. Abraham Shulman, *The New Country*, p. 168.
23. Sigmund Spaeth, *A History of Popular Music in America*, p. 370.
24. Green and Laurie, p. 80.
25. Whitcomb, *Tin Pan Alley*, p. 156.
26. Whitcomb, *After the Ball*, p. 57.
27. Ibid., p. 62.
28. Ibid., p. 68.
29. Chaim Bermant, *The Jews*, p. 90.
30. Goldberg, p. 256.
31. Whitcomb, *After the Ball*, p. 71.

CHAPTER 5
1. Sigmund Spaeth, *A History of Popular Music in America*, p. 415.
2. David Ewen, *All the Years of American Popular Music*, p. 259.
3. David Ewen, *The Life and Death of Tin Pan Alley*, p. 295.
4. Ian Whitcomb, *After the Ball*, p. 47.
5. Spaeth, p. 432.
6. Samuel Marx and Jan Clayton, *Rodgers and Hart*, p. 197.
7. Whitcomb, *After the Ball*, p. 52.
8. Ewen, *Tin Pan Alley*, p. 315.
9. Ewen, *All the Years*, p. 275.
10. Daniel McNamara, *A.S.C.A.P. Biographical Dictionary*, p. 166.
11. Whitcomb, *Tin Pan Alley*, p. 248.
12. Ewen, *All the Years*, p. 401.
13. Max Wilk, *They're Playing Our Song*, p. 49.
14. Ewen, *Tin Pan Alley*, p. 524.
15. Ronald Sanders, "The American Popular Song," p. 212.
16. Ewen, *All the Years*, p. 413.
17. Spaeth, p. 477.
18. Whitcomb, *After the Ball*, p. 135.
19. Spaeth, p. 512.
20. Sammy Cahn, *I Should Care*, p. 36.

CHAPTER 6
1. Charles Hamm, *Yesterdays*, p. 178.
2. Henry Russell, *Cheer, Boys, Cheer*, p. 23
3. Ibid., p. 61.
4. David Ewen, *All the Years of American Popular Music*, p. 52.
5. Hamm, p. 178.
6. Sigmund Spaeth, *A History of Popular Music in America*, p. 79.
7. David Ewen, *Great Men of American Popular Song*, p. 11.
8. Hamm, p. 179.
9. Ewen, *Great Men*, p. 13.
10. David Ewen, *Popular American Composers*, p. 149.
11. Hamm, p. 180.

12. David Ewen, *Songs of America*, p. 15.
13. Spaeth, p. 80.
14. Ewen, *Great Men*, p. 13.
15. Provided by Dr. Jacob Rader Marcus, *Kiev Festschrift*, No. 56, p. 187.
16. Hamm, p. 183.
17. Ibid., p. 183.
18. *Jewish Encyclopedia*, Vol. 10, p. 517.
19. *Encyclopaedia Judaica*, Vol. 14, cols. 432–433.
20. *Jewish Encyclopedia*, Vol. 10, p. 518.

CHAPTER 7
1. David Ewen, *The Life and Death of Tin Pan Alley*, p. 48.
2. Sigmund Spaeth, *A History of Popular Music in America*, p. 230.
3. Jack Burton, *Blue Book of Tin Pan Alley*, Vol. 1, p. 63.
4. Ewen, *Tin Pan Alley*, p. 7.
5. Ian Whitcomb, *After the Ball*, p. 44.
6. Ian Whitcomb, *Tin Pan Alley*, p. 8.
7. Isaac Goldberg, *Tin Pan Alley*, p. 135.
8. David Ewen, *All the Years of American Popular Music*, p. 113.
9. David Ewen, *Great Men of American Popular Song*, p. 125.
10. Spaeth, p. 231.
11. Ewen, *Tin Pan Alley*, p. 51.
12. Burton, *Blue Book of Tin Pan Alley*, p. 63.
13. Ewen, *Great Men*, p. 125.
14. Goldberg, p. 135.
15. Burton, *Blue Book of Tin Pan Alley*, p. 163.
16. Goldberg, p. 168.
17. Spaeth, p. 232.
18. Ewen, *All the Years*, p. 114.
19. Tony Palmer, *All You Need Is Love*, p. 22.
20. Charles Hamm, *Yesterdays*, p. 327.
21. Joseph Csida and June Bundy Csida, *American Entertainment*, p. 386.

CHAPTER 8
1. Charles K. Harris, *After the Ball*, p. 1.
2. Ibid., p. 9.
3. Isaac Goldberg, *Tin Pan Alley*, p. 225.
4. Harris, p. 15.
5. Charles Hamm, *Yesterdays*, p. 297.
6. Sigmund Spaeth, *A History of Popular Music in America*, p. 259.
7. Harris, p. 48.
8. Goldberg, p. 91.
9. Harris, p. 52.
10. Ibid., p. 41.
11. Ibid., p. 57.
12. Ibid., p. 5.
13. Ian Whitcomb, *After the Ball*, p. 4.
14. Spaeth, p. 260.
15. Gerald Bordman, *American Musical Theatre*, p. 127.
16. Ethan Mordden, *Better Foot Forward*, p. 19.
17. Hamm, p. 299.
18. David Ewen, *American Musical Theatre*, p. 538.
19. David Ewen, *All the Years*, p. 107.

20. Harris, p. 98.
21. Warren Forma, *They Were Ragtime*, p. 26.
22. Goldberg, p. 94.
23. Harris, p. 81.
24. Ewen, *American Musical Theatre*, p. 475.
25. Mordden, p. 108.
26. Spaeth, p. 261.
27. Tony Palmer, *All You Need Is Love*, p. 99.
28. Harris, pp. 145–146.
29. Whitcomb, *After the Ball*, p. 3.
30. Ibid., p. 41.
31. Harris, p. 198.
32. Spaeth, p. 321.
33. Harris, p. 206.
34. Ibid., p. 327.
35. Ibid., p. 326.
36. Hamm, p. 300.
37. Special thanks to Dr. Jacob Rader Marcus and the American Jewish Archives for the lyrics and sheet music for this song.
38. Harris, p. 279.
39. Goldberg, p. 109.
40. Spaeth, p. 261.
41. Ibid., p. 262.

CHAPTER 9
1. Tony Palmer, *All You Need Is Love*, p. 103.
2. Ian Whitcomb, *After the Ball*, p. 45.
3. Charles Hamm, *Yesterdays*, p. 308.
4. Isaac Goldberg, *Tin Pan Alley*, p. 109.
5. David Ewen, *The Life and Death of Tin Pan Alley*, p. 138.
6. David Ewen, *Great Men of American Popular Song*, p. 54.
7. David Ewen, *All the Years of American Popular Music*, p. 155.
8. Sigmund Spaeth, *A History of Popular Music in America*, p. 293.
9. Ewen, *Great Men*, p. 58.
10. Spaeth, p. 303.
11. Ewen, *All the Years*, p. 157.
12. Hamm, p. 309.
13. Ewen, *Tin Pan Alley*, p. 139.
14. Ewen, *All the Years*, p. 157.
15. Spaeth, p. 304.
16. Goldberg, p. 134.
17. Ewen, *Great Men*, p. 62.
18. Spaeth, p. 308.
19. Hamm, p. 310.
20. Goldberg, p. 173.
21. Ewen, *Tin Pan Alley*, p. 143.
22. Goldberg, p. 109.
23. Ewen, *All the Years*, p. 159.

CHAPTER 10
1. Ian Whitcomb, *After the Ball*, p. 134.
2. Sigmund Spaeth, *A History of Popular Music in America*, p. 258.
3. Max Wilk, *They're Playing Our Song*, p. 12.

4. David Ewen, *Great Men of American Popular Song*, p. 124.
5. Martin Gottfried, *Broadway Musicals*, p. 162.
6. Artur Holde, *Jews in Music*, p. 249.
7. Ewen, *Tin Pan Alley*, p. 152.
8. Wilk, p. 15.
9. Ewen, *Tin Pan Alley*, p. 132.
10. Gottfried, p. 162.
11. Whitcomb, *Tin Pan Alley*, p. 13.
12. Isaac Goldberg, *Tin Pan Alley*, p. 258.
13. Whitcomb, *After the Ball*, p. 183.
14. Ronald Sanders, "The American Popular Song," p. 203.
15. Ewen, *Great Men*, p. 129.
16. Whitcomb, *Tin Pan Alley*, p. 18.
17. Sanders, pp. 206, 208.
18. Carl H. Scheele, "American Entertainment: An Immigrant Domain," p. 416.
19. Ewen, *Great Men*, p. 133.
20. Whitcomb, *After the Ball*, p. 134.
21. Gottfried, p. 173, and Ewen, *Great Men*, p. 137.
22. Hugh Fordin, *Oscar Hammerstein: Getting to Know Him*, p. 126.
23. *Annie Get Your Gun* was Berlin's most successful venture. Some theatre devotees say that he only accepted the assignment from Rodgers and Hammerstein on the condition that he could use and claim as his own the songs Kern had already written in his uncompleted score.
24. Ewen, *Great Men*, p. 141.
25. Jan Clayton and Samuel Marx, *Rodgers and Hart*, pp. 237 and 259.
26. Wilk, p. 17.

CHAPTER 11
1. Ronald Sanders, "The American Popular Song," p. 199.
2. Wilfred Mellers, *Music in a New Found Land*, p. 384.
3. Ewen, *Tin Pan Alley*, p. 148.
4. Ian Whitcomb, *After the Ball*, p. 49.
5. Michael Freedland, *Irving Berlin*, p. 14.
6. Ibid., p. 15.
7. Judith Eisenstein, *Heritage of Music*, p. 269.
8. Hutchins Hapgood, *The Spirit of the Ghetto*, p. 96.
9. Aron M. Rothmuller, *The Music of the Jews*, p. 250.
10. Freedland, p. 17.
11. Ewen, *Great Men*, p. 104.
12. Spaeth, p. 456.
13. Ewen, *Great Men*, p. 105.
14. Whitcomb, p. 50.
15. Isaac Goldberg, *Tin Pan Alley*, p. 225, and Artur Holde, *Jews in Music*, p. 250.
16. Carl H. Scheele, "American Entertainment," p. 438.
17. Ewen, *Tin Pan Alley*, p. 99.
18. Sanders, p. 202.
19. Abel Green and Joe Laurie, Jr., *Show Biz from Vaude to Video*, p. 102.
20. Freedland, p. 37.
21. Spaeth, pp. 368 and 375.
22. Goldberg, p. 239.
23. Whitcomb, *After the Ball*, p. 45.
24. Ibid., p. 17.

25. Ibid., p. 29.
26. Goldberg, p. 240.
27. Warren Forma, *They Were Ragtime*, p. 196.
28. Green and Laurie, p. 2.
29. Spaeth, p. 377.
30. Ewen, *Tin Pan Alley*, p. 167.
31. Spaeth, p. 383.
32. Whitcomb, *After the Ball*, p. 53.
33. Goldberg, p. 239.
34. Ibid., p. 220.
35. Green and Laurie, p. 127.
36. Goldberg, p. 218.
37. Green and Laurie, p. 456.
38. Ewen, *Great Men*, p. 113.
39. Gottfried, p. 244.
40. Ewen, *Great Men*, p. 112.
41. Fordin, pp. 243–244.
42. Freedland, p. 178.
43. Whitcomb, *After the Ball*, p. 51.
44. Spaeth, p. 465.

CHAPTER 12
1. Edward Jablonski and Lawrence Stewart, *The Gershwin Years*, p. 7.
2. Ibid., p. 29.
3. Daniel McNamara, *A.S.C.A.P. Biographical Dictionary*, p. 178.
4. Jablonski and Stewart, p. 31.
5. Ibid.
6. Ronald Sanders, "The American Popular Song," p. 199.
7. David Ewen, *Great Men of American Popular Song*, p. 171.
8. Robert Kimball and Alfred Simon, *The Gershwins*, p. 7.
9. Sanders, p. 199.
10. David Ewen, *The Life and Death of Tin Pan Alley*, p. 227.
11. Ewen, *Great Men*, p. 171.
12. Sigmund Spaeth, *A History of Popular Music in America*, p. 506.
13. Isaac Goldberg, *Tin Pan Alley*, p. 230.
14. Ewen, *Great Men*, p. 172.
15. Ian Whitcomb, *Tin Pan Alley*, p. 102.
16. Jablonski and Stewart, p. 173.
17. Whitcomb, *Tin Pan Alley*, p. 102.
18. Charles Schwartz, *Gershwin: His Life and Music*, p. 59.
19. Sanders, p. 208.
20. Whitcomb, *After the Ball*, p. 136.
21. Ewen, *Great Men*, p. 175.
22. Spaeth, p. 510.
23. Sir William S. Gilbert was the lyricist of the English comic-opera team of Gilbert and Sullivan.
24. Wilfred Mellers, *Music in a New Found Land*, p. 388.
25. Ibid., p. 392.
26. Whitcomb, *After the Ball*, p. 134-135.
27. Spaeth, p. 177.
28. Ewen, *Great Men*, p. 183.
29. Whitcomb, *After the Ball*, p. 136.

30. Jack Burton, *Blue Book of Tin Pan Alley*, Vol. 2, p. 292.
31. Hugh Fordin, *The World of Entertainment*, p. 151.

CHAPTER 13
1. Samuel Marx and Jan Clayton, *Rodgers and Hart*, p. 15.
2. Ibid., p. 14; Dorothy Hart, *Thou Swell, Thou Witty*, p. 13.
3. Ronald Sanders, "The American Popular Song," p. 209.
4. Hart, p. 17.
5. Ian Whitcomb, *Tin Pan Alley*, p. 249.
6. Marx and Clayton, p. 39.
7. Ibid., p. 65.
8. Hart, p. 171.
9. *Rodgers and Hart Songbook*, 1951.

CHAPTER 14
1. Ronald Sanders, "The American Popular Song," p. 212.
2. Charles K. Harris, *After the Ball*, p. 256.
3. Frederick Nolan, *The Sound of Their Music*, p. 33.
4. Hugh Fordin, *The World of Entertainment*, p. 23.
5. Ibid., p. 16.
6. Sanders, p. 212.
7. Abel Green and Joe Laurie, Jr., *Show Biz from Vaude to Video*, p. 13.
8. Wilfred Mellers, *Music in a New Found Land*, p. 387.

Bibliography

JEWISH MUSIC

Eisenstein, Judith. *Heritage of Music: Music of the Jewish People.* New York: Union of American Hebrew Congregations, 1972.

French, Philip. "Show Business Entrepreneur." In *Next Year in Jerusalem*, ed. Douglas Villiers. New York: Viking Press, 1976.

Holde, Artur. *Jews in Music.* New York: Bloch, 1974.

Idelsohn, A. Z. *Jewish Music and Its Historical Development.* New York: Holt, Rinehart & Winston, 1929.

Nulman, Macy. *Concise Encyclopedia of Jewish Music.* New York: McGraw-Hill, 1975.

Rothmuller, Aron Marko. *The Music of the Jews.* South Brunswick, N.J.: Thomas Yoseloff, 1967.

Sanders, Ronald. "The American Popular Song." In *Next Year in Jerusalem*, ed. Douglas Villiers. New York: Viking Press, 1976.

Werner, Eric. "The Jewish Contribution to Music." In *The Jews: Their History, Culture, and Religion*, ed. Louis Finkelstein. New York: Harper & Row, 1949.

JEWISH AND AMERICAN HISTORY

Bermant, Chaim. *The Jews.* New York: New York Times Publishing Co., 1977.

Feldstein, Stanley. *The Land That I Show You.* Garden City, N.Y.: Anchor Press, 1978.

Forma, Warren. *They Were Ragtime.* New York: Grosset & Dunlap, 1976.

Hapgood, Hutchins. *The Spirit of the Ghetto.* New York: Funk & Wagnalls, 1902.

Howe, Irving. *World of Our Fathers.* New York: Harcourt, Brace & Jovanovich, 1976.

Jones, Maldwyn A. *Destination America.* New York: Holt, Rinehart & Winston, 1976.

Learsi, Rufus. *The Jews in America: A History.* New York: Ktav, 1972.

Scheele, Carl H. "American Entertainment: An Immigrant Domain." In *A Nation of Nations*, ed. Peter C. Marzio. New York: Harper & Row, 1976.

Shulman, Abraham. *The New Country*. New York: Scribner's, 1976.

COMPOSER AND LYRICIST BIOGRAPHIES

Armitage, Merle. *George Gershwin: Man and Legend*. New York: Duell, Sloan & Pearce, 1958.

Bordman, Gerald. *Jerome Kern: His Life and Music*. New York: Oxford, 1980.

Carter, Randolph. *The World of Flo Ziegfeld*. New York: Praeger, 1974.

Ewen, David. *A Journey to Greatness: The Life and Music of George Gershwin*. New York: Holt, 1956.

————. *Richard Rodgers*. New York: Holt, 1957.

————. *Popular American Composers*. New York, H. W. Wilson, 1962.

————. *Popular American Composers: Supplement One*. New York: H. W. Wilson, 1972.

————. *Great Men of American Popular Song*. Englewood Cliffs, N.J.: Prentice-Hall, 1970.

Freedland, Michael. *Irving Berlin*. New York: Stein & Day, 1974.

Fordin, Hugh. *Getting to Know Him: Oscar Hammerstein*. New York: Random House, 1977.

Hammerstein, Oscar, II. Introduction to *Jerome Kern Songbook*, ed. Jerome Kern. New York: Simon & Schuster, 1955.

Hart, Dorothy. *Thou Swell, Thou Witty*. New York: Harper & Row, 1976.

Jablonski, Edward. *Harold Arlen: Happy With the Blues*. Garden City, N.Y.: Doubleday, 1961.

————, and Lawrence D. Stewart. *The Gershwin Years*. Garden City, N.Y.: Doubleday, 1973.

Kimball, Robert, and Alfred Simon. *The Gershwins*. New York: Atheneum, 1973.

McNamara, Daniel, ed., *A.S.C.A.P. Biographical Dictionary*. New York: Crowell, 1952.

Marx, Samuel, and Jan Clayton. *Rodgers and Hart*. New York: Putnam, 1976.

Moody, Richard. *Ned Harrigan: From Corlear's Hook to Herald Square*. Chicago: Nelson-Hall, 1980.

Nolan, Frederick. *The Sound of Their Music*. New York: Walker, 1978.

Overmyer, Grace. *America's First Hamlet*. New York: New York University Press, 1957.

Sanders, Ronald. *The Days Grow Short: The Life and Music of Kurt Weill*. New York: Holt, Rinehart & Winston, 1980.

Schwartz, Charles. *Gershwin: His Life and Music*. Indianapolis: Bobbs-Merrill, 1973.

Stagg, Jerry. *The Brothers Shubert*. New York: Random House, 1968.

Taylor, Deems. *Some Enchanted Evening: The Story of Rodgers and Hammerstein*. New York: Harper & Brothers, 1953.

Taylor, Theodore. *Jule: The Story of Composer Jule Styne.* New York: Random House, 1979.
Wilk, Max. *They're Playing Our Song.* New York: Atheneum, 1973.

AUTOBIOGRAPHIES
Cahn, Sammy. *I Should Care.* New York: Arbor House, 1974.
Dietz, Howard. *Dancing in the Dark.* New York: Quadrangle Press, 1974.
Duke, Vernon. *Passport to Paris.* Boston: Little, Brown, 1955.
Gershwin, Ira. *Lyrics on Several Occasions.* New York: Knopf, 1959.
Hammerstein, Oscar, II. *Lyrics by Oscar Hammerstein.* New York: Simon & Schuster, 1949.
Harris, Charles K. *After the Ball.* New York: Frank-Maurice, 1926.
Rodgers, Richard. *Musical Stages.* New York: Random House, 1975.

AMERICAN MUSIC
Burton, Jack. *Blue Book of Tin Pan Alley, Book One.* Watkins Glen, N.Y.: Century House, 1962.
————. *Blue Book of Tin Pan Alley, Book Two.* Watkins Glen, N.Y.: Century House, 1975.
Chase, Gilbert. *America's Music.* New York: McGraw-Hill, 1955.
Dreiser, Theodore. "Whence the Song." In *The Color of a Great City.* New York: Boni & Liveright, 1923.
Ewen, David. *Songs of America.* Chicago: Ziff-David, 1947.
————. *The Life and Death of Tin Pan Alley.* New York: Funk & Wagnalls, 1964.
————. *All the Years of American Popular Music.* Englewood Cliffs, N.J.: Prentice-Hall, 1977.
Goldberg, Isaac. *Tin Pan Alley.* New York: John Day, 1930.
Hamm, Charles. *Yesterdays.* New York: Norton, 1979.
Lewine, Richard, and Alfred Simon. *Songs of the American Theater.* New York: Dodd, Mead, 1973.
Mattfeld, Julius. *Variety Musical Cavalcade.* New York: Prentice-Hall, 1952.
Mayer, Hazel. *The Gold in Tin Pan Alley.* Philadelphia: Lippincott, 1958.
Mellers, Wilfred. *Music in a New Found Land.* New York: Hillstone, 1964.
Palmer, Tony. *All You Need Is Love.* New York: Grossman, 1976.
Reddall, Henry Frederick. *Songs That Never Die.* Philadelphia: J. H. Moore, 1894.
Spaeth, Sigmund. *The Facts of Life in Popular Song.* New York: McGraw-Hill, 1934.
————. *A History of Popular Music in America.* New York: Random House, 1948.

Whitcomb, Ian. *After the Ball*. New York: Simon & Schuster, 1972.
———. *Tin Pan Alley*. New York: Paddington Press, 1975.
Wilder, Alec. *American Popular Song: The Great Innovators (1900–1950)*. London: Oxford University Press, 1972.

AMERICAN MUSICAL THEATRE
Atkinson, Brooks. *Broadway*. New York: Macmillan, 1970.
Baral, Robert. *Revue*. New York: Fleet Press, 1962.
Bordman, Gerald. *American Musical Theatre*. New York: Oxford University Press, 1978.
Burton, Jack. *Blue Book of Broadway Musicals*. Watkins Glen, N.Y.: Century House, 1969.
Churchill, Allen. *The Theatrical 20's*. New York: McGraw-Hill, 1975.
Csida, Joseph, and Jane Bundy Csida. *American Entertainment*. New York: Watson-Guptill, 1978.
Engel, Lehman. *The American Musical Theatre: A Consideration*. New York, C.B.S., 1967.
———. *The American Musical Theatre*. New York: Collier Books, 1975.
Ewen, David. *Story of American Musical Theatre*. Philadelphia: Chilton, 1961.
———. *Complete Book of American Musical Theatre*. New York: Holt, Rinehart, & Winston, 1970.
Fordin, Hugh. *The World of Entertainment*. Garden City, N.Y.: Doubleday, 1975.
Gottfried, Martin. *Broadway Musicals*. New York: Harry Abrams, 1979.
Green, Abel, and Joe Laurie, Jr. *Show Biz from Vaude to Video*. New York: Holt, 1951.
Green, Stanley. *Ring Bells! Sing Songs! Broadway Musicals of the 1930's*. New Rochelle, N.Y.: Arlington House, 1971.
———. *The World of Musical Comedy*. South Brunswick, N.J.: A. S. Barnes, 1974.
———. *Encyclopaedia of the Musical Theatre*. New York: Dodd, Mead, 1976.
———. *Rodgers and Hammerstein: Fact Book*. New York: Lynn Farnol Group, 1980.
Laurie, Joe, Jr. *Vaudeville*. New York: Holt, 1953.
Mordden, Ethan. *Better Foot Forward*. New York: Grossman, 1976.
Morehouse, Ward. *Matinee Tomorrow*. New York: Whittlesey House, 1949.
Morris, Lloyd. *Curtain Time*. New York: Random House, 1953.
Sobel, Bernard. *A Pictorial History of Vaudeville*. New York: Citadel Press, 1961.
Taubman, Howard. *The Making of the American Theatre*. New York: Coward-McCann, 1967.

Index of Songs

211

Index of Names and Subjects